Ted Lambert

Ted Lambert

The Man Behind the Paintings

Edited, with an introduction and epilogue, by Lew Freedman

University of Alaska Press
Fairbanks

University of Alaska Press
P.O. Box 756240
Fairbanks, AK 99775-6240

Library of Congress Cataloging-in-Publication Data

Lambert, Ted (Theodore Roosevelt), 1905–ca. 1960.
Ted Lambert : the man behind the paintings / by Ted Lambert ;
edited by Lew Freedman.
p. cm.
Includes index.
ISBN 978-1-60223-165-8 (pbk. : alk. paper)
ISBN 978-1-60223-166-5 (electronic book)
1. Lambert, Ted (Theodore Roosevelt), 1905–ca. 1960.
2. Painters—United States—Biography.
3. Alaska—Biography.
4. Alaska—Description and travel. I. Freedman, Lew. II. Title.
ND237.L264A2 2012
759.13—dc23
2011032940

Interior design by Andrew Mendez
Cover design by Dennis Roberts
Cover art: *The Freighter* by Ted Lambert.
This publication was printed on acid-free paper that meets the
minimum requirements for ANSI / NISO Z39.48–1992 (R2002)
(Permanence of Paper for Printed Library Materials).

Printed on recycled paper in the United States

This publication was funded in part by the
Terris and Katrina Moore Endowment.

Contents

Plates following page 88

Preface

As an Alaskan who grew more and more fascinated by Alaska paintings but also had a limited budget, I began collecting original paintings, prints, and posters in the 1980s.

The more I became enamored of the scenes of this beautiful state, the more I sought to learn about the artists who painted them. I gained an appreciation for the painters who were regarded as the best of the best and became curious about their lives.

One of the artists whose works most impressed me whenever I spotted one in a museum was Theodore R. Lambert. He seemed to have a passion for painting dog-teams, wilderness cabins, and mountains, all subjects that appealed to me. On a 1993 visit to the Alaska Heritage Museum housed in the then National Bank of Alaska (now a Wells Fargo bank), I requested the Lambert file to read about his life.

The file turned out to be as slender as a slice of cheese. It contained perhaps two old magazine stories about the painter. The singular fact that leapt out at me was that Lambert had vanished in 1960 and never been heard from again. The conclusion was that he had died, but there was no proof of it—only supposition.

A few months later, I invested vacation time from my job as sports editor of the *Anchorage Daily News* to try to determine what happened to this famous Alaskan. I hoped to solve the riddle of his disappearance from his cabin on Bristol Bay. Admittedly, as melodramatic as it sounds, a small part of me hoped to find Lambert himself, alive in a Pioneer Home, or elsewhere, living under an assumed name.

The trail led me to experts on Lambert's art, aging contemporary artists who had known him in the years before he became more or less a recluse at Bristol Bay, old friends from the days when he lived in Fairbanks, and the neighbor family that lived through the trees a short walk from his cabin, with whom he dined the last night he was seen alive.

I discovered a trove of Lambert's belongings in storage in the University of Alaska Fairbanks' historical archive and I hunkered down in the research rooms to meticulously scour every piece of paper, learn what I could about the man's life, and hopefully pick up any clues to his disappearance.

The most revealing and surprising document that I found was an eighteen hundred page handwritten memoir that barely discussed Lambert's interest in art but told his story of coming to Alaska as a young man, his impressions of the country, his hard work as a miner, and how he became a dog-mushing enthusiast.

Although the manuscript sometimes veered off into bizarre directions regarding Lambert's personal politics and prejudices, the book was filled with lively prose, keen observations, and flavorful Alaskan stories. In his own words, though never claiming to be much of a writer, Lambert told a good story. There was much more to the man, from his tumultuous personal life, to his growing success and fame as a painter, and above all the mysterious disappearance, but this captured a period in the famous Alaskan's life when he was young and just falling in love with the territory.

I always believed that cutting through Lambert's tangents and allowing his unique yet universal Alaska experiences to shine through would make pleasurable reading for the masses in an edited, trimmed-down diary.

It took many years after my first reading of the manuscript to reach a point where I had the time to revisit it. In the meantime, the diary reposed in the Fairbanks archives, with few people aware of its existence and fewer with the initiative or time to read it. Pat, Lambert's daughter, similarly had harbored the desire to see a version of her father's diary made more accessible to a public unlikely to wade through a handwritten book cloistered in a university library, so she is very enthusiastic about seeing his words and thoughts come to life for others.

Ted Lambert did not own a doctoral degree. Nor was he a formal researcher. He did not attempt to analyze what was going on around him in Alaska in any type of scholarly way. What he had was a talent for observation, a wry outlook, and a capability of telling the story of a period of years in his own life that would educate others who never saw what he saw.

For more than fifty years, Lambert's manuscript languished, virtually unexamined in Fairbanks. The story he tells is set between eighty and ninety years ago. It is about a bygone era of Alaska that did not revolve around the Klondike Gold Rush, World War II, or an oil boom. Lambert's beginnings in Alaska mark a time when a young man from the Lower 48 just wanted to explore a new place and make something out of himself.

That is a common thread throughout all of the epochs of Alaska history since the 1890s. Lambert's words offer insight and education to all of those who have come wide-eyed to the North with great aspirations.

He began recording his thoughts after he left Illinois and arrived in Montana. Lambert is introduced in the first chapter in the first person. Here he begins writing about Alaska. The last chapter, at the conclusion of Lambert's greatest adventure, is where he chose to end his diary. After that he moved on to become a famous Alaska painter.

—Lew Freedman

Introduction

When Ted Lambert was fifteen years old, he won a drawing award. Drawing was what he enjoyed doing most in the strict household in Illinois where his dictator-like father ruled. It did not seem likely to become an important life skill for him, but later is what eventually made Lambert's name and reputation in Alaska.

However, in his late teens Lambert was more restless boy than determined art student. The youthful Lambert dreamed of Alaska's wide-open country and of living a wilderness existence. He was too late for the Gold Rush, but sought the self-sufficient lifestyle. He grew up in Zion, Illinois, only forty miles north of Chicago, but wanted to escape from the Midwest's largest city, its skyscrapers, and the other trappings of civilization.

Ted Lambert left home on his own, with limited resources and high hopes, working his way west first by relying on his own manual labor. When he finally saved what he believed would be enough cash, he embarked for Alaska via steamship. He sailed the Inside Passage for what he viewed as an opportunity for adventure and the start of a new life.

Much later in life, Lambert penned a massive diary about his exploits in the North as a young man. The gargantuan 250,000-word book that he named "Tide North" amounted to 1,848 handwritten pages. The title apparently referred to the direction on the compass his life was pulled in. It is not clear when Lambert completed this opus, but during the 1950s it languished in his log cabin at Bristol Bay, where he lived alone for roughly ten years with few neighbors. It was found among his possessions when he vanished in 1960.

Although some friends knew he was working on the tome, it was never clear if Lambert ever attempted to get it published. Pat, Lambert's only daughter, endeavored to type the complete manuscript years ago, but that was when mimeograph machines still churned out their copies in purple.

Lambert did not write in detail about his early life in Illinois. He did not write about his later life in Alaska when he was painting, when he came under the tutelage of Eustace Ziegler, another of Alaska's famous painters, nor did he write of his personal life when he married and had a daughter. All of that came later. His early experiences in Alaska were challenging and satisfying to him and, almost from an outside-looking-in vantage point, he watched himself evolve from a Cheechako to a Sourdough.

Lambert actually began reporting his journey as he hitchhiked west, paused in Montana and struck up an enduring friendship, and then stalled in Seattle as he tried to make enough money to fund the last leg of the journey and for survival when he stepped onto Alaska's shore.

This edited version of Lambert's manuscript begins with the young man about to realize his dream of departing the Lower 48 for Alaska, but it is worthwhile to note that his original diary discussed events of importance shaping him and allowing him to reach his promised land.

Lambert fled his prim and proper Illinois home to explore life on his own terms. Lanky and strong, Lambert had the build for the physical labor required for most jobs in Alaska. The Gold Rush had settled the territory, but the frenzy was long over. A man could hunt and fish in the outdoor paradise. He could unload freight. He could mine the Gold Rush leftovers for a big company. He could tote bales off of barges. He could dig ditches and lay foundations.

Lambert, filled with youthful spirit, believed he could find some job to support himself. But as ill-informed about what awaited him as most Americans have been since Alaska became a possession of the United States in 1867 and a state in 1959, Lambert just assumed his broad back and winning attitude would carry the day.

Ted was born Theodore Roosevelt Lambert on November 23, 1905. His family home was in Zion, Illinois, nestled against the shore of Lake Michigan. His father, George, was religious and a strict disciplinarian. The parental rules chafed at the boy who dreamed of open spaces and people who lived far removed from electricity and streetcars and who didn't wear suits with ties.

To Lambert, Alaska sounded like a place where a man's status was purchased not with his savings account but by the deeds he accomplished. Not yet twenty years old, he left home, headed North with Alaska on his mind. Ideals in place but short on cash, Lambert stopped to work in Montana.

It was not an easy journey that summer of 1925, Lambert wrote, noting ". . . passing cars raised clouds of dust. But in spite of the heat, dust and sweat, the air was much cleaner and cooler than the sticky, smoke-laden atmosphere of the industrial Midwest I had just left behind. The breeze from the mountains smelled sweetly of sagebrush and occasionally deer, elk, and antelope strolled through the yard." Clearly, Lambert was intoxicated by open spaces. He was indeed fleeing what he considered to be a stultifying place, but he was also going to something.

This was Lambert's second attempt at escape from the Midwest. He had dropped out of high school at fourteen and had ended up broke in California. After trodding through Southwestern states, he had returned to Illinois.

"The year spent there had at times been a rough education and I had learned what it was to be jobless and hungry," Lambert wrote. "But returning to the Midwestern community had been like returning to a vacuum. There was some element that I was searching for, but I did not know what it was, nor its relationship to my unaccountable restlessness. I knew only that the stuffy conservatism of the Midwestern atmosphere was oppressive and in encountering the West I had found less of it."

His first sojourn to the wider world led to Lambert's fixation on Alaska. However, he could not make the distance to Alaska in one gulp. Soon, Lambert was down to his last ten dollars in Gardiner, Montana, on the outskirts of Yellowstone National Park. He spent months doing jobs that enabled him to save enough money to resume his quest. He shoveled concrete, worked on a smokestack gang, and at the end of summer took on odd jobs. In the process, Lambert met another young man, George "Bud" Guiler, whom he at first dismissed as "an eastern dude." But the duo became close friends and, in time, partners in financial dealings and adventures.

The young men sweated by day and spoke of their dreams by night. Alaska, they agreed, was the place to be. As soon as he could afford to do so, Lambert quit his job in Montana and made his way to the docks in Seattle, prepared to sail to Alaska.

Lambert's diary came into the possession of the University of Alaska Fairbanks library archives in 1960 where for more than fifty years it reposed, read by few. Until now, it was never published.

What follows is the first widespread public viewing of artist Ted Lambert's thoughts and experiences as a young man, the journeys, travails, and adventures that contributed to his later powerful canvas views of Alaska. The edited diary begins with Lambert on the boat carrying him from Seattle's Pier Two on a weekly steamship run northward.

It should be noted that Lambert used mining terminology that may not be as widely known to the average reader (and that he was learning on the job) and makes reference to early twentieth-century contraptions that are no longer in use or often discussed. Some definitions: "Tin Lizzie" was a slang description for the Ford Model T; a "jitney" was a form of minibus; the Volstead Act established Prohibition; "snoose" is snuff tobacco; "bannock" is a kind of bread commonly carried on long-distance trips because it didn't spoil; and a "gee pole" was tied to a dog sled for steering. "Shushanna," called Chisana today, is located between the Wrangell and Nutzotin Mountains. This was the site of Alaska's last major gold rush when it began in 1913. Many of the miners Lambert worked with in the 1920s had experienced that stampede.

Lambert headed North "with a steerage ticket in my pocket for some strange port in Alaska called Cordova," he wrote. He was not specific about the date in his diary, but his ship docked in March of 1927 after pausing first in Ketchikan, Wrangell, Petersburg, and Juneau. Three days into the sail, the ship reached Cordova with "the hoarse blast of the steamer whistle announcing our arrival."

When the gangplank was lowered, Lambert mixed with the passengers headed ashore. Eyeing the robust construction going on downtown, Lambert immediately sensed he was in a place of industrious people.

"There was a clearer note in the air here," Lambert wrote. "These [people] were not bandying concerning possible defeat, nor was it a brief stand for easy plunder. Theirs was a clear-eyed purpose, with an avowed determination to live in the country and make their homes in it come hell or high water. These were the core and fiber of the country's future."

Lambert whiffed the tail end of America's commitment to westward expansion and manifest destiny.

"The migratory tide was now reaching its most westerly expansion on the northernmost shores of the North American continent bound by the Bering and frozen polar seas," he observed. "Alaska was not The Last Frontier in name only. It was the last great virgin wilderness to pass under the tide of exploitation. The conquest and settlement of Alaska marks the end of the epochal periods of the great migrations." Lambert, frisky and with a great appetite for adventure, was part of this migration.

Some people do all of their research in classrooms and libraries. Ted Lambert was about to absorb extensive self-taught lessons in real life. Years later he imparted every bit of what he learned for others' gain.

As a figure of towering talent in the field of Alaska art, Lambert adds to the important body of knowledge about his influences and what vivid scenes he experienced that formed the backdrop of his paintings and his way of thinking.

During the heyday of his artistic endeavors in the 1930s and 1940s, Lambert was sometimes hailed as a people's artist. If writers, painters, and others who create communications that tell stories to the public are asked to "write about what they know" or "paint what they know," Lambert's knowledge was obvious to average Alaskans. They immediately recognized that he knew what he was painting about. They understood that here was an artist who lived as they had lived. The cabin in the painting he created might well have been one that he lived in. The dog team in another painting might well have been one he steered.

Alaska journalist Kay Kennedy, a contemporary of Lambert's and a friend, wrote that "Ted's paintings have guts."

That was not the type of art critique likely to be found in a newspaper in New York or Paris, but Alaska was a different animal. It was a sprawling, rough place with its own appeal and soul, and Lambert captured it on canvas. It was a comment apropos for a man weaned in the more rugged days of the territory who learned how to adapt his painting skill to his environment.

Kesler Woodward, a current Alaska painter and a former professor at the University of Alaska Fairbanks, has studied the state's big-name artists from the past and notes that Lambert was "inspired by" Eustace Ziegler. The two not only took their famous painting-boating adventure through northern areas of Alaska, but Lambert was tutored by Ziegler at the older man's studio in Seattle.

The men painted many of the same subjects, and certainly many more of the same type of subjects. Both painters were popular. Ziegler was more famous, but he was also far more productive and repeated subjects much more often. With Lambert somehow it seemed he attacked a subject with his brush and memory and then was prepared to let it rest for a while. There is just a touch more wildness in Lambert's work than Ziegler's.

Indeed, Lambert's attraction was that he was authentic. He was just as true with his word choices as with his oil paints. For decades, Alaskans thought that Lambert's only contribution to explaining their lifestyle had gone on canvas. It turns out that he could convey the same emotions with words, by way of his diary, and those words only enhance his legacy.

The manuscript that Lambert labored over in his own hand makes a fresh and significant contribution to Alaska's knowledge and understanding of the man and what he painted, and it adds to the understanding of this long-ago period in Alaska's history.

1

Welcome to Cordova

Dodging through the crowd thronging the gangway, I made my way to the end of the wharf where it joined the land. Letting my packsack and bedroll down, I paused to take a glance at the place which through chance rather than purposeful design I had chosen for my Alaska destination.

It was the time of year when it is neither winter nor spring, but something unmentionable in between. Patches of thawing snow lay amidst puddles of dirty water and mud and water were everywhere, gurgling and gushing from the timbered hillsides, which were still buried in winter-long snow. A dank mist overhung the countryside, and across the bay wreaths of fog trailed down to the water's edge. A thin drizzle, part rain, part snow, fell. There was a sodden listlessness pervading the chill March air that struck to the bone.

The town was situated on rising ground near a half mile from the wharf and was connected by a rutted road which made a long ascent up the hill. Below the road, roughly adjacent to the beach line, was a railroad. A few fishing boats were tied to pilings or sat forlornly on the mud flats. Their slovenly appearance showed they were inactive. They looked more like derelicts than seaworthy craft. A lone man in a rowboat splashed around some old pilings and raised a few crab traps.

The somnolent atmosphere was ominous and depressing. There was something about this place that warned me to go easy considering the few coins amounting to $3.65 in my pocket.

Streets were nearly deserted and large groups of men lounged in pool halls. I passed a couple of hotels of modest proportions, but I had my sight peeled for some battered derelict that forsook all pretensions at comfort and offered bare board for bare pay. I noticed down a side street a ramshackle frame building with peeling paint and a small weathered sign over the door stating ROOMS.

A musty odor pervaded the place—like stale incense tinged with boiled cabbage—and I thought some of the lodgers must be trying to conceal that they were cooking in their rooms.

My small room contained a single bed with quilts, an old chair, a washstand with a crockery basin and pitcher of water, and a battered dresser with a cracked mirror nailed to the wall above it. I stayed only long enough to tidy up my appearance and then went in search of work.

A HELP WANTED sign was unknown. The best that I received from potential employers was, "Well, maybe." The damp dusk settling over the town was in accord with my mood. It was evident I was limited to seasonal employment and such jobs didn't open up until May. I had arrived in the country more than a month too early.

My last meal had been taken aboard ship that morning. Now I sat down and devoured a can of cold baked beans with a couple of slices of baloney sausage wrapped between pieces of bread.

When I lay down, my thoughts chased one another around like fish trapped in a weir. My dead-end condition was beyond my experience. My head hurt from thinking of the problem of finding work. My first day in Alaska ended when I fell asleep with my clothes on.

The next morning I departed without breakfast, once again in pursuit of a job. By early afternoon I had tried everything short of joining a lodge or marrying a merchant's daughter. I had the disconcerting feeling that by now everybody in town knew I was broke, a vagrant and a public nuisance, and I expected to see headlines in the local newspaper demanding my arrest and expulsion.

Back in my room I opened another can of beans and ate the remains of the baloney sausage. People looked at you as though you were cracked when you asked for a job at this time of year. I had read that Cordova was located in one of the wealthiest parts of Alaska, where copper, gold, timber, oil, coal, salmon, halibut, herring, clams and crabs were on the scene. Yet here was a town of about 1,500 population whose only means of existence was as a port for shipping our raw materials, a town living hand-to-mouth with everybody hanging onto the other fellow's coattails, going around in circles and everybody waiting for the seasonal work to begin.

Why live in the country at all if you had to hole up six, eight, ten months of every year just to get in a few months' work? The landlady knocked on the door and told me I had to release the room for one of her regulars. I nodded, parted with a dollar-and-a-half, and threw my belongings into the packsack. I could not chance the price of another day's lodging anyway.

I crossed to a pool hall and a brusque, businesslike gent wearing a green eyeshade was behind the cigar counter. He understood my problem while I was yet talking and he sketched a rough map with an X on the chart. I was near the railroad yard facing a false-fronted one-story building. It featured a sign reading

BUNKS, FOUR BITS. ROOMS, ONE BUCK. Now that was straight talk a man could understand.

A curly-headed, swarthy French Canadian greeted me and signed me up for a bunk. Then with a toothy grin he said, "Where ya been all the time? The boat was in yesterday morning."

I told the Frenchman about my hotel, and his brow furrowed in puzzlement. Suddenly, his face flashed open with a shout of astonished laughter. "Hell, kid!" he cried, "that ain't no rooming house. That's a whorehouse, the crummiest one in town!"

His rooming house was called Copper River Rooms. There were about a dozen single rooms with a long hallway leading to a larger room the operator called "the bullpen." It was here that the double-deck wooden bunks were lined up along three walls. The facilities were comfortable for a bunkhouse and as neat as a Dutch housewife's kitchen.

I continued my dogged search for work. On the wharf I encountered the dock boss and despite pulling out all of the stops he said, "No chance, no chance at all, boy. I've got twenty fellows standing by right now if one of the boys misses a turn. If there was an opening on the gang, half the town would be down here."

Talking with the fishermen was even worse. They told me they were all living on credit. Those poor fellows were in much worse shape than I. Darkness was setting in when I returned to the lodging house with two bits worth of cheese and hardtack and another can of baked beans. I felt beaten and my feet ached from constant walking. I had just a couple of silver dollars left, enough that might carry me through four days.

In Montana, my steamfitter boss had assured us nobody ever starved in Alaska as long as they were willing to work. I had never actually seen a man drop dead on the street from starvation, but I felt there was a good chance I might be present when such a thing occurred.

The following morning I set out to get a job as a dishwasher. Not even this strategy worked. "No chance, kid," I was told. "We've got more dishwashers now than we have customers." I returned to the lodging house and lay down on my bunk. This must be the way a condemned man feels just before the warden comes and leads him to the rope, I thought.

While sweeping the room, the Frenchman greeted me with a cheery good morning. He talked about the weather and repeated that a fellow could always get by in the country. He tipped me off that sometimes the placer mining companies picked up a few men at that time of year and that one of them was at the Windsor Hotel. Within minutes, I was on my way to the Windsor, considered the town's finest hotel.

I was pointed to Charles Kraemer across the lobby as a man who was running a camp. The mining man was engrossed in letter writing. He had strong, intelligent features and his face was deeply tanned from wind and weather. Obviously, he didn't spend much time living in hotels. Kraemer ran a casual survey over me, beginning at the feet and following through to the head. I explained I had just arrived from the States and was looking for work.

Kraemer's dark eyes rested on me thoughtfully. Then he spent a few minutes studying several pages in a notebook. "Yes," he said finally. "I can use you. We pay five dollars a day and board, with a fifty-cents-a-day bonus if you stay the full season." Before I could summon my stunned wits into words of acceptance, he asked my name. He jotted it down, snapped the notebook shut, and put it in his pocket. "Show up in Chitina in ten days," he said, "and I'll put you on." Then he turned back to his letter writing.

An ecstatic feeling drummed inside me when I left the hotel. I felt like running, leaping over fences, turning handsprings, and shouting in a mighty voice for all the world to hear: "I've got a job! I've found a job in Alaska!" I had secured a foothold in the country. I was not going to be beaten. In ten days I would be going to work. Why, a man could go that long without eating anything at all if he had to!

The lodge owner must have seen my elation shining like an aura around my head, for the moment I entered the building he gave me a perfunctory nod and asked, "How did you make out?"

I quickly spit out what had occurred. The Frenchman bobbed his head, happy for me, and asked, "Where is the mine?" I told him I didn't know exactly, but it must be somewhere around there. "Where is Chitina?"

The Frenchman strolled to the front window with a thoughtful frown on his face. He stared into the bright spring sunshine and then yelled towards the rooms, "Hey, Ole! Where is Chitina?" A small, sad-eyed Scandinavian sidled into view down the hall. He shambled with a crablike gait toward the lobby, his gnomish features rapt in thought. "Chititoo? Chititoo? Aye don't know." Suddenly, his face brightened. "Yah, aye remember now. Yah, I hear some of the boys talking about it." Then he turned back to his room.

The Frenchman sent a boy to find another man who might know. I sat at the card table and dealt a hand of solitaire. A half hour passed before a husky, square-built Swede entered. He wore frayed, faded duck work clothing, much patched with canvas. The tops of his rubber hip boots were rolled down and flapping loose-ly around his knees. He might have passed for one of the pirates in *Treasure Island*.

"You got job Chititu, huh?" he asked me. He let drive a forceful brown jet straight into the bull's-eye of a spittoon. "Yu vant to know vere Chititu iss," he said. "It iss McCarthy, maybe twenty, thirty mile. Dar iss a road out dot vey. Maybe you get ride."

The Frenchman interpreted. McCarthy was near Kennecott, the Kennecott Mine at the end of the rail line. I had not imagined that in reaching Chitina there were distances involved that were more than a few hours' hike or a day or two walking from Cordova. "How far is Kennecott from here?" I asked.

"Well, let's see," the Frenchman said. "It would be around two hundred miles, something like that." He yelled again for Ole for confirmation, who said it was 196 miles, "maybe mile one way or other."

Then add the distance to McCarthy. Once again I retreated to my bunk to ponder the circumstances. My job was not less than 215 miles distant! The appalling discovery sent a shivering sensation over me as though I had fallen into icy water without touching bottom. How was a man to travel over two hundred miles of wilderness when he had only enough money to eat a few mouthfuls of hardtack and beans for three more days?

I asked the Frenchman how much rail fare would be to McCarthy and he guessed twenty-five dollars—at least. That was the straw that drowned the man! I was right back where I had started from that morning. I had been planning and saving for over a year, had traveled over three thousand miles, all to the end that I might beg vainly for a job as a dishwasher! Now this. A flood of hot anger welled up in me.

I marched out of the lodging house, not knowing where I was going. But I ended up in the grocery store counting out my last silver dollars, minus fifty cents, for a paper sack of trail grub. I walked away with beans, rice, sugar, tea, hardtack, and a small piece of bacon. All of the portions were small. The remaining fifty cents was to pay for a last night in my bunk.

Back at the lodging house I informed the proprietor of my determination to walk to the mine. He was surprised. "What the hell, kid? You aren't broke, are you?" I lied. "Not exactly, but I can't afford to ride the cushions."

He began thinking out loud, considering and rejecting options. I could not ride the rails because I would freeze to death. It was pointless to ask the brakemen because they were under orders not to allow passengers.

My pack was packed. It weighed thirty-five or forty pounds, not so very heavy. The Frenchman told me to stay another night, on the house, and offered to put me up as long as I liked. Shaking my head, I passed the fifty-cent piece over. He didn't reach for it.

A curious welt bobbed up in my throat for an instant. I swallowed hard to put it down. I doggedly held out the four-bit piece. The Frenchman, his eyes all the while on mine, reached one hand out of his pocket and took it slowly, a hesitant movement.

The transaction complete, the Frenchman began lecturing me on precautions. "Now look," he said, "you got everything you need? How's your socks and insoles? You know you'll be hitting cold weather long before you get to McCarthy. You won't get back in this area far before it will be zero and colder. I see you are carrying light blankets. They're not much good if you have to make an open camp.

"There are track walker shacks all along the line, every fifteen or twenty miles or so. They're pretty good fellows, those track walkers. If it's cold and you're stuck, make it to one of their places. I've stopped with them several times myself when I was out sheep hunting. One of the fellows has a shack at Mile 18. Or maybe it's 19. You can likely make his place tonight before it gets too dark. When you get there, tell him I told you to see him."

When he finished speaking, I nodded and reached for the pack. I did not express my thanks in a formal way. We had looked straight into one another's eyes and in an instant had plumbed the depths of a wordless understanding. In that moment we knew that it was not two lone individuals playing their roles single-handed, but man and man standing together as they had stood together since time out of mind.

We walked out of the lodging house into the warm spring sunshine. Hunching the packsack around, I wrestled my arms into the harness and shook the pack comfortably down on my shoulders. I turned for a parting farewell and my hand met the Frenchman's sinewy grip. He nodded his head cheerily and said, "Take it easy, kid. Don't bust yourself. Lots of time. You'll make 'er all right. Good luck!"

2

Hiking the Iron Trail

The railroad ties seemed destined to lead forever to an ever-receding horizon. The steel rails, always holding out promise of joining in the distance, were as far apart as they had been eight days before when I left Cordova. A quarter of a mile ahead I could see a wooden bridge supported on pilings where the railroad crossed a mile-wide expanse of river flats frozen and covered with hard-packed snow. A late afternoon sun was shining on the flats and the reflected heat waves made the settlement beyond the river look unreal, as though seen in a mirage. But I knew it was not a mirage, for even a mile away from McCarthy one could hear the howling and barking of scores of sled dogs.

The village I was approaching was a rough frontier town which commanded the trails leading across the Wrangell Mountain Range. Bright light from the low sun was slanting ruddily on a row of false-fronted buildings facing the river, and thin clouds of smoke from the town's stovepipes were rising straight into the motionless air to mingle in a pinkish smoke haze overhanging the town. The place, even at a distance, had the rough, informal appearance of a western cow camp that somehow had turned up in northern surroundings.

Buildings were scattered over a considerable area, but the site was dwarfed by the magnitude of its surroundings. Rugged hills and mountains beset the town everywhere except on the westerly side, the side looking down the Chitina Valley, and the direction from which the railroad entered from the coast. Northward, the Kennecott Valley, which joined the Chitina Valley, was rimmed in high peaks and locked with a great ice field. Although there were subsidiary channels on the middle reaches of the ice field where the ice flowed down from cirques, the main body of ice headed far back towards Mount Regal and Mount Blackburn. This ice field was Kennecott Glacier. The broad front of its terminal moraine ended just a half mile short of McCarthy.

Tracks from the railroad passed directly in front of the moraine. After leaving the depot at the far end of the bridge, the railroad made a sharp bend to continue up the valley. It had to climb a steep grade and the passage soon narrowed with the glacier on one side and with a high, mountainous ridge on the other. The ridge, called the Kennecott Range, was over a mile high and about ten miles long. It was bored through and through with tunnels and slopes where hundreds of men were at work extracting copper ore from one of the richest ore bodies in the world. The mill and the company town of Kennecott were situated at the base of the ridge. It was there, at Mile 197, that the rails I followed ended.

The Wrangell Range is lavish in stately scenery, but the imposing landscape made little impression on me. My mind was too intent on pushing my sore feet along the railroad ties. Besides, the condition of being flat broke and a stranger in a strange land was haunting me as never before. This would have been of small consequence if it had been physically possible for me to continue to Chitina. As it was, I was barely able to make it to McCarthy.

Every step my butchered feet threatened to leave me lying on the tracks for crow bait. I had realized even before leaving Cordova that I was undertaking a perilous journey and that I was ill equipped to walk two hundred miles in the poor footgear I was wearing. But in that matter, there had been no choice. Before leaving the coast I had changed from light leather boots that were entirely unsuitable for cold weather to a new pair of shoepacs with rubber bottoms and leather tops that I had purchased in Montana.

The new pacs were broken in as I walked the ties, but it was my feet that did most of the changing. At Mile 18, while stopping with a track walker, I had soaked the pacs overnight and put them on wet. It made little difference. Before I had walked fifty miles my ankles and heel tendons were chafed raw and bleeding. One of the track walkers had given me a couple of rolls of bandage and I had been using that to tape the abrasions every morning before setting out. In addition, I had been wrapping strips of gunnysacking over my socks, using as much as the shoepacs would allow while still getting my swollen feet into them.

Twice along the way track walkers had urged me to stay over for a few days, long enough, at least, to give my bruised feet a chance to heal. If I did so, I might be able to toughen my feet gradually. The invitations had been appreciated, but were turned down. The time set for my arrival for work did not allow for a layover. Consequently, my feet had been getting worse. The previous two mornings they had been so badly swollen that to squeeze them into the shoepacs it was necessary to take off the burlap wrapping entirely. That had completed the ruination of my feet.

Now limping the last painful mile into McCarthy, my mind fixed on somewhere I could crawl into for a rest—I imagined a basement or the back room of a store—for a couple of days. My feet needed time to mend. Missing a few meals did not bother me so long as my job remained open. It was not till later, after I had suffered to reach my destination in a timely way, that I learned that arrival a few days later would have been acceptable to Kraemer.

The famed Iron Trail had lived up to its reputation. Since I had lacked the price to offset the mileage, it had taken a toll in flesh. Due as much to inexperience as to circumstances, I had made the trip too lightly clothed for the rigorous weather which I encountered. The mild, humid coastal climate of Cordova had been left behind on the second day of the walk. Beyond, the grip of northern winter was hardly broken and the temperatures, though moderating during the daytime, dropped sharply to points ranging from ten to thirty below zero at night. Bitter winds swept the Copper River Valley, freezing winds, which on some days offset the warming effects of the spring sun. My clothing consisted of two woolen shirts, a sleeveless sheepskin jerkin, a light mackinaw, a small woolen cap, and two woolen mitts.

My nose and ears had been frostbitten so repeatedly that they were pink, peeling, and watery as a soggy potato. My lips were swollen and cracked from wind and blazing sun and two dark brown streaks furrowed the sides of my cheeks and jaw where a thirty-below breeze one early morning had bitten to the bone.

Except for one night's open camping and two nights in an old deserted shack, I had stayed overnight with track walkers. These men whose business it was to patrol their respective beats, guarding against snow slides, freezing overflow, heaving ties, loosening rails, and all of the other hazards of railroading in a rugged region were princely fellows.

It was due to their unstinting hospitality that I had begun each day well ballasted with a good breakfast. They showed no curiosity over the fact that I was traveling afoot. They seemed to consider it on par with the life of the North. "A man don't have much chance to talk to anybody but himself on this job," complained one grizzled old chap, whose shack was in the vicinity of the Bremner River.

He reached over to the windowsill and with the mysterious air of a confirmed prospector, handed me a sizeable piece of quartz that was richly shot through with gold. "I just lay that down on the track when I want the train to stop," he said. "That gets 'em. They start asking lots of damn fool questions then!"

I had walked over 191 miles of track when McCarthy showed itself in the distance. Approaching the railroad bridge, I came upon a bobsled trail which led towards town. The route offered easier footing and I followed the trail across the frozen flats. After crossing the river, the trail mounted the sloping bench, then turned and entered the upper end of a long street fronting the town.

The rough frontier character of McCarthy was discernible at once to a stranger and contrasted strongly with the stagnant atmosphere of the tidewater port I had left behind. One felt instinctively that life had not been snuffed out in this place. There was plenty of noise, for the area along the riverbank was filled with scattered groups of dog kennels and the clamorous barking of what I guessed to be two hundred dogs announced my arrival.

Log cabins, houses, barns, and structures of various kinds were scattered on neighboring streets, while others dotted the outlying trail crisscrossing the village. Limping down the board sidewalk, my eyes were scanning the various trade signs, although I was not clear what I was looking for. Halfway down the block a couple of weathered old rounders stepped aside, staring me full in the face with frank amazement. It seemed plain that these hardy folk were not used to seeing strangers in town. Especially not the kind of darned fool who showed up in trail-battered condition from walking two hundred miles to get there. The frontier element held no romantic illusions about such matters. To show up in such a condition was a mark of ineptitude and a man with good sense kept such untidy affairs off his record.

I continued on and stopped in front of a two-story structure painted yellow ochre. Over the door hung a yellow sign reading GOLDEN HOTEL. My stomach gave a slight flutter. It was a good omen. Was not gold the talisman that had led men to defy the inexorable character of the northern wilderness? The sudden change from stabbing sunlight on snow to the comparatively dim interior blinded me for an instant and I set the packsack down. A hearty voice on my left boomed, "Just in from Outside, kid?"

I turned to see a sturdy old fellow with ruddy features and rumpled gray hair standing behind an old-fashioned bar that appeared to be a relic of the gaslight era. It was built of solid oak, ran half the length of the long room, and resembled a pier on battleship row more than an accoutrement of house furnishing. A brass footrail ran the length of the bar and several brass spittoons were spaced at handy intervals on the floor.

The man appeared to be the bartender, although he wore an old, worn shirt and sweater. I acknowledged his greeting with somewhat of a bewildered nod, surprised to see liquor being sold right out in the open with not even a blind on the front window. Possibly, I thought, they didn't have Prohibition in Alaska, since it was a territory, not a state.

My legs were shaky and I feared they would not hold me up. There was a swimming sensation in my head and only with great concentration could I keep the bartender in focus. He was absently polishing the bar, but then reached down and produced two small glasses that he set on the bar. "Come on over, kid," he said. "Have a drink."

Until this point my experience with hard liquor had been greatly neglected. The community where I had been reared, like most religious communities, held that liquor was a primary tool of the devil and had anticipated Prohibition by a score of years. I was ill prepared for the baptism awaiting me in McCarthy.

Not knowing any better, and with no instruction or guidance from the bartender—I wished I had been better versed in my Emily Post—I stepped up to the bar and filled the glass. The bartender looked at me with mild astonishment and what I interpreted to be admiring approval. He filled his glass to a level hardly above one finger. "Well, here's good luck," he said, and tossed off the drink.

I, too, tossed off the drink, as much as I could swallow in one gulp. The raw liquor hit my throat like the blast of a blowtorch and I strangled. Choking to death, I grabbed the bar and held on while the room disappeared in an explosion of coughing. Lights twinkled before my eyes like the winning score on a pinball machine. The room reappeared, made a couple of uncertain gyrations, then stood still and shuddered.

While I slowly regained consciousness I realized there were others in the room. Four or five wooly-looking characters appeared from someplace and elbowed for places at the end of the bar. A long row of astonished eyes were riveted on me in the gravest wonderment. The bartender, still wearing his owlish look, slid the bottle down the bar and set out a handful of glasses before my unbidden audience.

I recovered my health sufficiently that I was feeling my disgrace keenly. During my earlier youth, behind my school geography book, I read tall stories of the masterly way in which men in a man's country handled their women, their guns, and their liquor. The realization that my record was wide open to impeachment on all counts came as a shocking discovery. In an effort to salvage some shred of honor, I glared at the half-empty glass. Then, on a sudden impulse, I reached for it and gulped, once, twice, and beat the fireball down. I carried it off satisfactorily that time. Or at least I had done better since I was braced for the shock. Still, the outsized drink had transformed the room into a rosy haze and the holocaust raging in my throat and stomach felt like a prairie fire.

Now that the rites of hospitality were over, the bartender looked me over and I was certain this time it was one of approval. He picked up the glass, rinsed it, and giving the bar a few swipes with a towel, asked casually, "How you fixed, kid, broke?"

The suddenness of the question startled me, but I nodded. "Where you headed for?"

"Chitina," I said. "I've got a job there. The man who owns the mine said to show up in ten days."

"Kraemer," the bartender recognized immediately. "He's the superintendent. The camp won't be going for a few days yet. The skinner took the cook and several of the boys out yesterday to open up. You might as well lay over for a couple of days and rest up."

The bartender reached into the till and slipped a twenty-dollar bill across to me. I was astonished. "That will hold you for a couple of days," he said. "If you need more, come back and get it." A moment later he yelled to an assistant of sorts named Charlie, then pointed to my packsack and said, "Take the kid's stuff and put him in room two. He will be sticking around for a few days."

3

Recuperation

By frontier standards, my room was spacious. It was light and airy and its two front windows looked across the river flats and down the valley by the route I had traveled my two hundred miles on foot. These were plush accommodations compared to my bunks in Cordova. I had a large double bed with clean linen sheets, soft wool blankets, and quilts neatly folded at the bottom.

The room also included a large writing table, several chairs, and a clothes closet inset in one wall. But the miracle of it all was a private bathroom connected to the room, a bathroom modern in every respect and actually having hot water running out of a tap marked HOT. I really had struck gold. Not until the following fall did I discover I had been given one of the two best rooms in the hotel. All of the other rooms used a bathroom down the hall.

Suddenly, a reaction to my days of being alone on the Iron Trail for so long set in. For eight days I coped with grueling, foot-sore walking, the gnawing worry over being broke and a stranger, and the knowledge that I would have to hole up in McCarthy. It had been supremely stressful. Without fully realizing it, I had been at the end of my rope before reaching McCarthy and I had propelled myself forward as much on nerves as physical stamina. Only ten minutes earlier I had been standing in the street, exhausted, in pain, without money, and fearful of asking anyone for a favor. Now, through some strange act of intuitive reasoning, all of my needs had been anticipated and remedied.

The prodigious drink on an empty stomach, the warm room, and my weary condition combined to draw a dark curtain gently and swiftly over my consciousness. I was not aware of the moment I passed out, lying stretched out across the bed.

Sometime during the hours after midnight I began to have a sense of coming alive. I opened my eyes to pitch darkness and couldn't remember where I was. For a moment I had the horrible thought that I had fallen asleep in the snow by the railroad tracks. Cautiously, I rubbed my fingers together. They had feeling, so I knew they were not frozen. I stared at the sky searching for stars. There was only blackness overhead, though, and without knowing where I was, I dared not move much for fear of falling off a cliff and down a mountainside. Where had I last been when I could remember something? I remembered only ten thousand times ten thousand railroad ties extending in an endless ladder to the horizon.

The throbbing pain in my feet finally straightened me out. I cursed as I recalled it all, cursed my negligence that now, after having reached a place where I could give my feet some rest and care, I had completely forgotten to take off my shoepacs. Rousing myself from the bed I fished along the wall for the light switch. A soft light came on in the room—the hotel light plant was shut down at midnight and the room light switched to batteries. I went to work removing my foot gear.

"No brains," I informed myself. "Not a lick of sense. Lucky if I don't have to cut the shoepacs to pieces to get my damned feet out." My feet really were a mess. They were a swollen, inflamed, flagellated pulp. Looking at them somberly, I wondered when things would get squared off so I could get back to living an orderly, normal existence.

That's when I recalled that I was the lucky possessor of a private bathroom. What luxury! All my life I had wanted a big, white porcelain bathtub to float around in. The family washtub was good, but it got a little bit crowded on Saturday nights. A porcelain bathtub! I footed it tenderly across the room. The hot water filled the tub. I pulled off my clothes, slid into the tub, and lay back with a contented sigh to let the liquid wash away my nervous tension.

Quite some time passed. I was waterlogged, glowing with warmth, and overpoweringly sleepy. A moment after rubbing down with the towel I was asleep between the sheets. When I next awakened, the sun was bright. Except for my interlude in the bathtub, I slept for eighteen hours.

I spent three days in McCarthy and never once stepped outside the hotel. My room was comfortable and the hotel reading rack was stocked with fine books. I could choose from among the works of James Oliver Curwood, Rex Beach, and Jack London. There was a small restaurant next door that connected to the hotel's lobby. I marched a trail between the two establishments.

The rest of the time I lay in bed, allowing my feet to mend. This gave me time to read up on life in the North. My research convinced me that I was losing out on Alaska's romantic pageantry because I had not arrived in the proper locale or at the right time of year for the whims of adventure to present itself.

The restaurant was run by a big, friendly fellow named Louie the Greek, who, having heard of my unorthodox arrival in town, said, "You don't have to do things like that, kid." I think he meant that someone would have helped me get from

Cordova to McCarthy. "I was like that, a punk just like you when I first come," he said. "Didn't believe anything, didn't trust nobody. I was used to living Outside, living like a wolf, see? You don't have to live like that up here."

I told him my walking the two hundred miles was the only way I could see to go from Cordova to McCarthy in time to start my job.

"You're talking about the job all of the time," Louie said. "I'm talking about living. You don't want to hold down a job up here if you don't want to. That's why this country is different from Outside. We give a man a chance. We give him a break. Christ, that don't cost nothin'!"

As Louie talked he pulled a gallon of firewater out from under the counter and splashed a couple of drinks into watch tumblers. Taking a cue from other customers the day before, I spiked my coffee. Then I wrapped my legs around the stool to keep from falling on the floor while I drank it.

"You don't know this country," Louie said. "If you're broke, got no money, why ask somebody. They'll stake you. Hell, nobody goes hungry in this country."

After a few days' rest I felt strong enough to start another two-hundred-mile trek—as long as it was not over railroad ties. Three days' layover had nearly remade my feet. The swelling had gone down and the abrasions on tendons and ankles were healing nicely. Still, before I began walking to Chitina, I took the precaution of bandaging my feet well.

The trail out of McCarthy led over a wooden bridge and then ascended a steep grade to reach the rim of gentle rolling plateau country. Portions of the country along the trail had been burned over and wood cutters had removed most of the timber for the town's fuel needs. What remained was a scattering of spruce and birch.

The morning was calm and crisply cold. It was a beautiful morning in early spring as the seasonal changes begin coming to the North. There was not a cloud in the blue sky overhead and the snow-covered hills and mountains shimmered under dazzling light. An iridescent light played upon the leafless bushes which were covered with hoarfrost. Sparkling particles of frost blew through the quiet air. Snow still lay deep on the uplands, and there was a racy tang in the atmosphere which served as a warning and a promise that the days of cold winter were numbered.

Sled dogs were the primary users of my trail. The dog-sled track was narrow, hard-packed, and smooth from winter-long runs. Parallel to the dog-sled track was a horse-drawn bobsled track. I noted the care the teamster had taken to keep his horses exactly astride the narrow trail.

McCarthy's big sled-dog focus fascinated me from the moment I first heard their baleful howling on my approach to town. I watched the teams from my hotel window, long, orderly processions of dogs pulling freight sleds. I also saw lighter teams dashing through the streets and around corners as though in pursuit of one another. I recalled that as a boy in knee pants I spent endless hours trying to train the big family dog to pull a sled. My method had been to try to inveigle the dog to pull in harness by leading her nose around with a piece of buttered bread. The results were disappointing. The dog always got the bread, but I never got the ride.

Now as I walked I saw a dog team approach on the trail, bearing down rapidly. I stepped off the trail and a long train of dogs was streaming past in a mad lope headed to town. The snow-goggled driver riding the runners had lifted his arm in a casual salute while sweeping past in a swirl of snow. I was thrilled. I watched the team until it passed from sight. As I walked, I wondered what it was like to control such a temperamental hurricane and do it all with a single word: "Mush!" There must be some trick to it, to get them all started together and pulling in the same direction. I knew that the lead dog did some of the steering, but without reins, how did one stop such a team should they take a notion to run away like some horses I had driven?

My travel went at a leisurely pace. By late morning I crossed the apex of Sourdough Hill, which formed the divide between the Kennecott and Nazina valleys. The crest of the hill was only slightly higher than the surrounding locality, but the country was open and offered a sweeping view of mountain ranges near and far. Tall peaks raked the horizon in every direction. In the middle ground lay the spruce-carpeted Chitina Valley, with its winding river flowing westward to lose itself in the blue-green haze of distance.

Here was wilderness no end, for one could see mountains and valleys for distances of fifty, sixty, and even a hundred miles, and there was scarcely a mark of human habitation in it. I was beginning to gain some conception of the immensity of the country when I realized my two-hundred-mile trek from the coast had penetrated such a small portion of Alaska as to make the distance hardly worth mentioning.

Several miles beyond the crest of Sourdough Hill the trail dropped steeply into the Nazina Valley and soon after I was crossing the frozen river on a long bridge supported on pilings. The trail beyond the bridge crossed wide flats, and then turned upstream to follow hard along the riverbank.

Near the mouth of Young Creek I paused to gaze wonderingly on an old log structure—it was called Sourdough Cabin—which had served packers and dog drivers. Tattered remains of mountain sheep hides along with remnants of canvas and old horse blankets clung to the outer walls and the chinks were caulked. The austere landmark reminded me of news pictures of dugouts in Flanders that had come under artillery fire.

I continued along the wooded flat, and after a couple of miles the trail turned into the clearing of a roadhouse yard. The Nazina Roadhouse was situated at the confluence of Chititu Creek and the Nazina River.

In the North the term "roadhouse" did not bear the same connotation that it did in the States. The northern roadhouse was strictly a utilitarian affair and seldom, if ever, during earlier years was it associated with the recreational facilities of its counterpart Outside. Usually, by the time a traveler reached a northern roadhouse he was too tired to care what kind it was, so long as he got something in his belly and a place to bed down.

The roadhouses in the smaller settlements served as focal points of community life. All settlements had roadhouses, and others were strategically spaced at intervals along the main trails. Some combined a post office and a trading post, too. The roadhouse man or woman was usually looked upon as something of a public institution. He or she knew everyone's affairs, family history, character rating, financial standing, health, hobbies, romantic follies, and the whereabouts of everyone and his dog at any given time.

As for the stranger who wanted details concerning the next hundred miles of trail, or needed a couple more dogs, or was trying to find someone he hadn't heard from in ten years, whatever the circumstances, the roadhouse man was given first call. If he couldn't help you, he would steer you to someone who could. I formed these impressions later, for the Nazina Roadhouse was my first roadhouse.

It stood two stories high, made of logs, and there was a row of dog kennels. A pile of miscellaneous junk was heaped between some outbuildings. There were parts of old double-ender sleds, bobsleds, wagons, and other scrap. The dog drivers and teamsters who frequented the trails were always smashing something or pulling some of their rigging apart. They did a makeover with the junk and seemed twice as strong afterwards.

Jim Murie, the roadhouse owner, appeared as I was shouldering out of my pack. He was a stalwart, solidly built individual with a square set to his shoulders and rugged regular features. We introduced ourselves and he invited me inside for lunch. Murie reached for a gallon jug, pulled the cork, and poured sizeable drinks into water tumblers. "Water?" he asked with a guileless look in my direction. Murie took his firewater straight. This policy of pulling the cork, I was learning, was part of the informal hospitality that was a dominant feature of the country.

Alaska's sparse population was driving a hundred spearheads into a half-million square miles of wilderness, much of it without roads or established trails. It was towards the end of an era when one man, or a handful of men, scattered around in the hills were the means by which large areas were opened up to mineral production and settlement. Before wealth could be accumulated for compounding greater wealth, the wilderness had to be won. At the time, the scattering of men at work probing out-of-the-way wilderness places was one of the principle reasons Alaska, according to various figures and published reports, was producing from twelve to fifteen times as much wealth per capita as the averages for the United States.

Already, although this natural bond between Alaskans was as yet incomprehensible to me, I was part of the invisible tie which bound man to man and settlement to settlement throughout the northern reaches. Here was teamwork of the highest efficient kind that picked a sore-footed lad off the street, staked him, and sent him on the way to add his weight, however small, to the united thrust that was going on all along the entire frontier. The teamwork was of an indomitable kind which, so long as man and man were standing together, recognized no hazards, nor bounds nor barriers insofar as physical obstacles were concerned.

The job could not have been done where petty strife and friction were involved, where distrust and dissensions were fostered, where group fought group, and where each was seeking to gain some personal advantage at cost to the other fellow. When I left the roadhouse I was no longer feeling an extra stranger to the country.

The trail up Chititu Creek was no more than a bobsled track which a teamster had left in passing, and it wound about through undergrowth and timber and keeping to easier ground. About four miles from the roadhouse the rough trail ended abruptly in encircling hills and a mile beyond the gap I came upon the site of past placer mining operations where the topsoil and gravel had been removed, exposing bedrock.

A mile of tailings piles and rock dumps were passed. Then, less than a half mile beyond the first cut, I could see a group of white tents ranged against the spruce-green hillside. That was Chititu Camp—the end of my long walk from the coast.

4

The Mine

I showed up in camp just as supper was being finished. Several men appeared from the doorway of a large tent where a triangle gong was hanging. They paused on the tent stoop to pass an appraising eye over me before moving on to other tents which served as bunking quarters.

One man, who turned out to be the foreman, stood waiting. He nodded with an amiable grin and seemed to know who I was. "The boss said you'd be showing up about now," he said. "My name's Bob Johnson."

We shook hands. Then, before I even had time to slip the pack from my shoulders, I was given my first order. "You'd better hit the cook house now, before the cook clears off the table," Johnson said. "You can fix up your bunk afterwards."

The history of mining on Chitina Creek followed much the same pattern as did most northern placer camps. Chitina passed through successive stages of discovery, small-scale mining by hand methods, consolidation of individual holdings, capitalization from Outside sources, and mechanized mining on a large scale.

Gold was struck on Chitina Creek by two men in the spring of 1902. By July of that year a small stampede was under way which drew several hundred gold seekers. The richest and the most easily mined ground was worked by pick and shovel. Thereafter the creek holdings went through several consolidations for more economical methods of mining.

Although its operational costs were relatively high due to the excessive amount of large boulders that had to be removed, more than twenty years later the creek was still producing under the same superintendent, Kraemer, which must have been something of a record. Charles Kraemer understood men as well as mining. Born in Peoria, Illinois, in 1874, Kraemer came to Alaska in 1898 as a prospector in the Copper Valley and discovered other gold sites in the

Chistochina mining district with some partners. He became manager of the Chitina mine in 1925.

Smaller camps were credited with serving wholesome, palatable food. The policy paid off. The owners had no difficulty getting experienced men who worked hard and willingly and returned to the same camp season after season. Such a camp almost ran itself with no lost motion and no hard words. The corporations mining in richer areas reverted to the nineteenth-century practice of cutting wages and food costs to a substandard level while on the other hand using every sweatshop device known for increasing working hours and production to the utmost. Such a labor policy had no relationship whatever to sanity, humaneness, or intelligence, much less was it efficient and economical.

Every dog handler knows he can't get the work out of a dog unless it is well fed and given reasonably good care, a simple and obvious fact which was never learned by the corporations in their dealings with men. There were camps where the niggardly ration of food of unpalatable quality raised open revolt and violence. In other camps, tainted swill often drenched with a strong horseradish sauce to conceal the nauseating taste and smell resulted in food poisoning.

The mining on Chitina Creek and its tributary, Rex Gulch, was carried on from two separate camps situated about three miles apart and designated simply as the Lower and Upper Camps. The hydraulic plants used in both camps were similar in size. The working complement of each camp, when seasonal mining was in full swing, was eighteen to twenty men, including the cook and his helper. The period of active mining extended from the latter part of May to the end of September.

During that season work went on around the clock, the men in each camp divided into two opposite ten-hour shifts, with alternating shift changes every two weeks. I was assigned to the Lower Camp. The camp consisted of about ten wall tents, the largest being the cook house and mess. Each sleeping tent was large enough to accommodate four men comfortably, yet leave ample room in one corner for a wood heater with a rack over the stove for drying wet clothing and footwear.

It is customary for many smaller mining camps, and even larger concerns, to use tents for bunking quarters and mess. Northerners have long been used to such accommodations. Yet the same type of quarters used for temporary housing raised howls of protest and much melodramatic sympathy in Stateside newspapers for government-sponsored colonists arriving in the Matanuska Valley in 1935. It appears impossible for the press to do any responsible reporting on Alaska affairs.

At Chitina, during the first weeks of early spring when night temperatures were dropping to zero and often much lower, the stoves kept the tents comfortable enough until nearly morning. That is, unless some kind soul roused himself to stoke the fire during the night. But that seldom happened. The placer miner is proverbially immune to insomnia. He commonly complains of having to prop his eyes open after only eight or nine hours of sleep.

The Lower Camp also featured a warehouse where mining equipment and camp supplies were stored. A quarter-mile upstream from the tents the warehouse housed canvas gloves, work clothing, rubber hip boots, and slickers. But it also served as a commissary with such goods on the shelves as chewing tobacco snoose, without which a placer camp could not expect to operate a single day. All supplies were charged out virtually at cost and deducted from an individual's paycheck at season's end.

The well-equipped mining camp was self-sufficient and included a blacksmith shop, a log barn, and a sawmill which furnished rough spruce lumber for general mine use. There was also a combined office and home for the superintendent.

Little more than a mile upstream from the Lower Camp was a canyonlike constriction in the narrow valley where a dam extended across the creek with a floodgate and penstock, or sluice, built into the dam. A steel pipeline about three feet in diameter led downstream. Through a pipeline system high water pressure built up from the steep downgrade of the creek, a fall of 180 feet to the mile, the hydraulic operations were carried on.

In northern placer mining there is a good deal of preparatory work, dead work, as it is called, before the water runs and actual mining can begin. When I arrived in April, the camp had just been dug out of the snowdrifts and put into habitable condition, and the dead work was just beginning. There were only six other men in camp at the time.

The small bull gang went to work and within a few days was beefed up by several more men. The hydraulic equipment, which had been dismantled and stacked the previous fall, was also dug out of the snow, overhauled, and readied for use. The penstock and the main pipeline were overhauled.

The more tasks completed, the more jobs seemed to pile up. It was rugged, healthy work, ten hours a day every day. According to the boys, "You worked like a horse, ate like a pig, and slept like a bear." New arrivals drifted into camp almost daily. Within two weeks each camp had at least a dozen men handling the dead work. The bull gangs were feeling their oats and chanted as they worked, "Yo, heave ho, and let's have 'er again, boys."

The postal book I carried told me I still had two hundred dollars in Gardiner, Montana, which I had been unable to retrieve as I moved northward. My immediate needs were now being met in the camp, but I still needed money. My friend Bud was working in Idaho and still wanted to join me in Alaska. Kraemer said if Bud could get to camp in time for the real mining work, he could have a job. I wanted to transfer my money in Montana to Bud to allow him to come north, but the rules indicated it had to be sent directly to me and only then could I finance Bud's trip north.

Mail service between Chitina and McCarthy was irregular. There was a summer freighter who carried mail in and out via horses and buckboard along with supplies, but he came only every one to three weeks. If Bud were to use my postal savings it might well take two months to complete the transaction. That was much too late. Still, when the mail went out I sent two letters, one to get the money sent to me in McCarthy and one to Bud. I told him of the job, but because of the restrictions on access to my money, I dumped the whole matter of financing into Bud's lap and recommended him to the gods.

April was nearing its end with many days of cloudless blue skies overhead. The now-burning sun was devouring streaks of snow remaining on the flats, softening the deep snow on the timbered hillsides to a sugary pulp, and starting rivulets of water coursing down the gulches. The creek was still sheeted with ice where overflow had frozen and built up successive layers of ice during the winter. But even these bastions of deep winter were disappearing under the insistent onslaught of the sun. The days were lengthening rapidly. Night temperatures hardly dropped below freezing. The rising sun quickly undid the night's frost. The springtime sound of gushing water was everywhere. There was slush and slop and mud everyplace.

Most of the summer crew arrived during the last two weeks of April. Singly and in pairs and threes they came sloshing into camp carrying bedrolls and packsacks, a straggling file that reminded me of homing geese winging their way overhead toward arctic nesting grounds.

Just before the last snow disappeared, the skinner made a trip into town for a load of camp freight. When he returned three days later the horses and bobsled were splashed with mud and dripping with water. The skinner swore loudly that it was time to shift to the wagon. That officially ended winter and inaugurated the summer season.

Nearly all of the men arriving at Chitina were old hands, some veterans of a half-dozen seasons or so. They picked up the work without any direction from foremen. "That's my ax you got there, young fellow," remarked an elderly Swede who arrived from Cordova ten days after I had gone to work. He pointed to a cross mark burned on the handle. "See," he said, "that's my mark. I used that ax last season." I went off grumbling to myself about squareheads who take their tools to bed with them and whetted up another double-bit for myself, one without any marks on the handle. After all, we had hired out for placer miners, not loggers.

The majority of the men were in their middle years. Possibly a third were in their late fifties or early sixties. One old chap who tended the dam was in his seventies. All were physically tough, hard workers who had spent most of their lives out of doors. They were active men who made no concession to advancing years. Aside from myself there was hardly a man in camp who was not an experienced hand at placer mining. Most of the hands were part-time prospectors, or had spent years following prospecting and sluice-box mining.

The hard-hitting pace these placer miners set was beyond the average for similar rough work that I had experienced on similar jobs in the States. I soon found that my youthful brawn was a poor match against experience, even when working with the oldsters. The steady, unrelenting work pace scarcely let up even when moving about the field from job to job. Despite the backbreaking work, these placer miners seemed to do things easily. There was no undue rush, but every movement was made to count.

These were Sourdough workmen and I was to meet their kind in other placer mining camps in the North. They knew all of the ins and outs of their work and took particular pride in being self-reliant and doing a good job. It was very much an Alaskan trait. Whenever difficulties of any kind showed up, they preferred taking the initiative rather than standing around waiting on orders or being given detailed instructions.

Such qualities in workmen American industrialists pretend to value, but corporations in the North did not hold that viewpoint. They regarded northern resident labor as a nuisance. They held that resident labor was too independent, for the Sourdough workmen were the kind of men who are led, but can never be driven.

5

Low Man on the Totem Pole

Since I was the youngest worker in Lower Camp by at least ten years and was a Cheechako—a newcomer to the North as well—I came in for some special attention which the camp fondly regarded as the traditional initiation for candidates aspiring to Sourdough honors. My susceptibility to practical jokes was taken for granted, and no matter what singular story or eccentric chore was turned my way, it had the solemn approbation of the entire camp.

If I committed some error in the course of the work it brought a swelling chorus of grunts and growls. On the other hand, if I failed to exhibit stupidity in some ambiguous situation that too was greeted with growls and grunts and I would be threatened with having my ears knocked down.

On every possible occasion my mistakes were pointed out to me, always with the grave admonition that I must do better. Occasionally, during evenings, I listened to various eyewitness accounts of the curious fauna of the North, the sidehill gougers, the three-legged gazompees, and whifflepoofs with eyes in the back of their heads.

In the same sober vein I was treated to more useful knowledge. I was taken in hand and shown the fine points of sharpening an ax—whereupon every man in camp suddenly remembered he had an ax to sharpen. My role in this was to turn the grindstone one evening until my arms just about fell off. Within a short period of time I was unable to determine if anything I heard was based on fact, or if anything I did had a useful purpose.

After being befuddled, I realized I had to begin thinking independently. By the painful process of analyzing and weighing facts against each other I gradually began assembling order. The boys began to note this turn in affairs and it was accepted with a kind of guarded satisfaction. Whenever I balked at being led into some whimsical bear trap, they winked slyly at one another. "The kid may amount to something yet," one of the other miners said. "It's a shame at that age to throw 'em out for wolf bait."

I would be singled out to lend a hand in some matter where instruction was part of the procedure and I would be rapped soundly if I had to be shown twice. I learned how to set and file a crosscut saw, how to sharpen and temper tools such as picks, mattocks, and chisel bars, and how to splice rope and steel cable. I was shown how to fell a tree without its looking as though a beaver had chewed it down, how to handle an ax in thick undergrowth so as not to endanger one's self or the lives of those around. I learned how to fell a tree and fell it to any given mark, although I sometimes had to change the mark to the opposite side after the tree had fallen.

While constructing wing dams and driving long steel drift pins through timbers, I learned how to swing a maul track-layer fashion—with a sweeping, all-out arm's-length arc over the head and around. I learned how to handle powder and set off a series of dynamite shots blasting frozen ground or reducing the size of boulders.

There was all of that before I was even exposed to the bare rudiments of what goes into making an experienced placer miner.

One phase of this instruction shook my morale badly. Ever since I was a boy I had handled a pick and shovel. I felt I knew something about the use of those elementary tools. Now, it seemed I knew nothing. These longtime prospectors and sluice-box miners were experts, though they never boasted of it. Expertise with these fellows meant doing half again the amount of work of the average workman, yet through economy of skills doing it with less effort.

The expert could dig a trench in frozen ground in not much longer time than required when the ground was thawed. I grew discouraged and began to wonder what the lowest common denominator for learning was in the placer field.

The arrival of spring in the North is a recurring miracle that intrigues those impassive old Sourdoughs who for the better part of a lifetime have been watching it happen. One week there is ice and snow all around, accompanied by snow squalls and freezing weather. The raw wind nips to the bone, howls down the stovepipe, and makes it seem as if winter will hold the line until the summer solstice, June 21.

By the next week there is a subtle change in the atmosphere. One cannot see it, but one can sense it as surely as though a tropical zephyr had whispered into one's ear. The harsh weather moderates and within another week a torrid sun is pouring its heat upon the frozen earth, disarming winter with the swiftness of a starting avalanche.

The snow on the slopes and along the lower valleys vanishes in a gush of water. The rivers begin to rise and gutter. The ice rots and buckles and goes out with a rush. Overhead, where wedges of waterfowl are winging their way northward, there is much family squabbling and honking over the season's nesting arrangements. Early flocks of migrant birds arrive, lending ecstatic notes to the spring crescendo.

Another week passes and the leafless bush is burgeoning into vivid green dress despite patches of snow still clinging to the hills in the background. It is summer and you have been caught napping. You are standing around with an entranced, silly smile on your face, entirely unmindful that you are still wearing winter flannels and the old fur cap with the flaps dangling down around your ears.

Spring has its own secret message to impart to each individual, especially in Alaska, where the winter has been so harsh and long. It offers wisdom to step lightly around the young signs and promises which delight the poets as we go on about our affairs. The season's work is still piled up ahead and spring's message to the placer miner, whether it is carried on beauty or not, is, "Hurry, hurry, hurry!"

With the water rising in the creek and the frost evaporating it is almost time to begin active mining. At Chitina, as at every well-run placer camp the dead work had to be finished when the land was ready. The success of the season's mining would be measured by the productivity during the active mining period—the stretch between spring breakup and the freezing weather of early fall.

So now with the weather beginning to cooperate, it was rush, rush, rush, push this log, pull that cable, dig that hole there, and fill in that one over there. The creek flats echoed with the sounds of axes, the clatter of shovels and picks, and the ring of sledges driving steel drift pins into wing dams and bridge timbers on creek crossings. There was the slam of cant hooks into timbers, a "Go, heave-ho!" and shouts to bring up the carrying hooks. Then a "Whoa! Hold up there a minute." Bang, slam, bang, it was going on all around.

Watch out for the wheelbarrows coming up the plank. Slam, crash. There goes another wagonload of rocks into the dam. Over in the mining area, where frozen topsoil was being blasted in order to open the sluice runway, there would occasionally come the long warning cry "FI-I-I-RE!" followed by six to a dozen dynamite shots. Frozen mulch, stumps, and gravel would shoot high in the air. The rattle, rattle thump-bump of falling debris would hardly cease before picks and shovels and sledges and saws and axes were at work again.

The workaday music is pleasant to the miner's ears, but the sweetest note of all was the raucous jangle beat on the steel triangle hanging by the mess tent door. Hard work in the open air whetted big appetites, and the mess is the focal point in every camp for keeping affairs on an even keel. Chitina was fortunate to have a good cook. It also had a superintendent who believed in leaving the good man alone to work out his destiny by whipping up meals that got eaten rather than being thrown in the garbage.

When we were served lemon meringue pie as a special Sunday treat we would tell from the delectable nature of the pie that it was made with lemons instead of corn starch, lemon extract, and water. All the other ordinary fare at our meals measured up to the same high standard. On Sundays the cook also rewarded us by serving either chocolate or vanilla ice cream for supper dessert. The ice cream was made from canned evaporated milk and cranked up in the freezer.

At the end of meals, there were appreciative belches of satisfaction instead of growls and threats to blow up the camp. Just like an army, it is said, a placer mining camp moves on its stomach. The smartest superintendents make sure their men are fed well. The capitalist order would probably hold its own indefinitely if cooks were running state affairs instead of politicians.

Sometime around the middle of May, one evening after supper, I was sitting on my bunk with a makeshift drawing board on my lap. The upper end of the board was propped over an upended egg crate and I was industriously working on a drawing of a dog team in action. I was pondering the problem with a slide rule and calculus when one of the men shoved his head in the doorway and shouted, "Hey, kid, there's somebody out here that wants to see you!"

I laid the drawing board aside, wondering who the person might be that would want to talk to me about anything. Aside from the men around camp, who always barged right in to make their wants known, there was nobody else in the country that had concerns as to my whereabouts. I opened the door and lo, the sight rocked me back on my heels.

6

Bud Is Back

For an unaccountable time I stood there in one spot and gaped. It was Bud! It was Bud in the flesh, but how? He was supposed to be in Idaho, practically broke, and waiting to be bailed out.

But Bud was not a lad who waited patiently for anything after his mind had been made up. As he stood in the yard eyeing me, I couldn't miss the satisfied, triumphant look on his face. He had a grin going across it from ear to ear. I didn't say anything because I couldn't. My mouth hung open and an invisible question mark was poised above my head.

On his back, Bud had a new packsack splashed with mud and he wore new work clothes, though they were soaked with mud and water. He looked as if he had fallen in the creek and bumped his head a few times before coming up to get me.

I became aware that half of the crew had gathered around. It seemed important to settle any suspicions that this meeting might end in a shooting and I settled it. "My partner from Montana," I stated in a strangled voice that was meant to register unshaken calm. "I didn't know he was coming this soon."

The brief statement seemed to account for everything. A partner is a partner, whether it is a man, a horse, or a dog.

The story behind Bud's appearance had to wait until he saw the cook. I joined him in the mess tent and sat around drinking coffee while the cook passed him warmed-over victuals. Bud speared the food as fast as it came out. In between mouthfuls he told me he had not eaten since leaving McCarthy early that morning. Since he had passed up the roadhouse I knew that whatever his fortunes had been upon leaving Idaho, he was traveling very light now. I figured he had less than a dollar in his pocket. But I couldn't account for the new pack and clothes.

When Bud had cleared the table of everything except the pickle jar and salt and pepper shakers, we retired to a pile of logs in the yard where we sat to exchange recent news. I congratulated him on his bedraggled appearance and asked if he wanted to change into dry clothes.

"Hell, no!" he replied promptly. "These were brand-new store clothes when I started out this morning and I keep them on. That road out here is sure a bitch, isn't it? I fell down crossing some of those damn creeks. I might have known you'd pick some damned place like this to live in."

Bud didn't swear like that when I first met him. I wondered what sort of companions he'd been associating with in Idaho. He soon enlightened me. I had gathered from his letters he was having difficulties, but the utter hopelessness of the situation was worse than words expressed. He had remained on the job with a cheap contracting outfit for little more than bed and board, and finally, growing disgusted, had tried changing locations. The move did him no good. There were hundreds of idle men in each locality. When my most recent long letter reached him, he decided it was time to leave Idaho and come to Alaska. He didn't have the money to get past Seattle, but the uncertainty of his venture was less distasteful to him than further stagnation.

In Seattle, Bud scouted around and poked his nose into anything that spelled Alaska. He picked up a rumor that Kennecott Copper Corporation sometimes shipped contract laborers north to work in the copper mines. Bud knew from my letters that Kennecott was near Chitina. He tracked the rumor and he treed it in an employment office. Kennecott was shipping some hands north from the States. Such labor was bound by contract to work in the mines for a stipulated period and the transportation expenses were deducted from earnings. All Bud had to do was sign a contract and he was shunted aboard a northbound steamer without having to pay the fare. The whistle gave a long toot and Bud was on his way to Alaska.

There was nothing steerage about Bud's passage either. His berth was inside the lower deck, but on the Alaska run that was no social error. Everything was regarded as first class insofar as service and conveniences were concerned. Even ranking bootleggers, who could afford the bridal suite, often preferred the inside lower deck, particularly in winter when gales swept the open gulf. As a bonus, the inside lower deck opened directly on the dining room. Such a strategic position when the dinner chimes sounded was like drawing the inside position on a racetrack. One could be finished with soup and salad and be starting on the main dish by the time the first of the upper-deck passengers began showing.

Bud enjoyed the trip immensely. It was more luxury than he was used to, for sure. He wore his best Sunday glad rags, complete with necktie, oxfords, and silk socks and carried on insidious flirtations with some of the female passengers. There was a transported look on his face as he recalled the voyage. Also, he was still trying to properly pronounce *filet mignon glace aux champignons* and make it sound like something besides Indian trade talk.

When the boat docked at Cordova, Bud had a different experience than I had. He went to the best hotel and ate at the best restaurant and charged it all to Kennecott. The following morning he went directly to the train and settled himself comfortably in the tourist coach. His journey went so smoothly he lacked the time to even count the number of railroad ties at the depot, never mind the thousands upon thousands of ties I had trod over.

From that moment on Bud traveled in comfort. He gazed at the scenery with vague interest, unaffected by the elements. For lunch he was served some more filet mignon you-pronounce-the-rest-of-it-the-way-you-want. His only complaint was that there was excessive warmth in the coach. To pass the time he mingled with other passengers and took swigs from his hip flask.

Bud was now surprised to learn that thirty miles of trail separated Chitina from Kennecott. He knew the mines were owned by different concerns, but was under the impression they were only a good shouting distance apart. He was somewhat disappointed. He thought we would at least have the chance to see one another occasionally even if we worked at different job stations. After all, what's the use of having a partner if you can't just get together and warm up an argument once in a blue moon?

In emergencies it was Bud's habit to use his head first and muscle afterwards— a practice just reverse of my standard operating procedure. He set about picking up an odd assortment of information from everyone on the train, avoiding only the conductor, brakeman, and locomotive engineer. When he thought he had gathered enough information he sifted it over. As for his contract with the copper mine, in his mind Bud had already put aside that obligation with the indifference of a utility magnate unloading watered stock.

Bud had been learning the rudiments of business from contractors and saw no reason why the same preemptory law shouldn't be played turnabout. If in the end Bud had to give himself up to the copper mine, he was determined to at least see the placer mining superintendent at Chitina first.

When the train reached McCarthy, still dressed in his finest, he set out on the thirty-mile walk through bottomless slop. His shoepacs and other rough duds were rolled up inside his blanket roll and that bundle was in the train's baggage car with the tagged destination Kennecott. He knew any attempt to withdraw that indispensable luggage short of Kennecott would raise an alarm and set all dogs to barking.

However, Bud still had a few dollars. By playing them close they could be stretched for a scanty re-outfitting. By the time the train whistle wailed its lonely greeting to McCarthy, Bud had retrieved a few personal effects from his hand valise and stowed them in his overcoat pocket.

One unique feature of the Copper River and Northwestern Railroad was that it had no hard-and-fast schedule. The train usually started out on time on the right day, according to schedule, but beyond that gesture to official authority it followed according to the acts of God depending on whatever happened to be encountered on the route. This renowned railroad ran through some redoubtable wilderness and it was a toss-up sometimes which was the best man. In the course of a commuter's perilous life, one might encounter rock slides, bridge washouts, creeping glaciers, avalanches, loosening rails, and once in a while the caboose jumping the track. In winter, sometimes the rotary snowplow got stuck. Another snowplow would be sent to dig out the first and sometimes that got stuck, too.

Somehow the adventurous crews would show up eventually with the caboose tied on and parched and tired passengers gasping for a drink. The train stopped regularly in McCarthy for about a half hour. Not only was mail delivered, but the passengers leapt from their seats and made the four-hundred-yard dash up a hill into town where each man could seek out his favorite den of destruction and grab a quick thimbleful of grog. The train pulled into the depot and Bud made the run into town. Dodging the crew, he quietly disappeared from sight and dug himself into a hotel room. A little later, when the locomotive bell began its impatient clamor, and after a decent interval allowing passengers time to return, the train began chuffing up the steep grade to Kennecott.

Bud lowered his barricade and set about organizing himself for the walk to Chitina. He briefly shopped at O'Neill's store, stocking up on items lost in his luggage. Most surprisingly, Bud picked up the information that Kraemer, the Chitina superintendent, was not at the mine, but was in town. This was quite unusual because Kraemer rarely left the mine during the season. Bud tracked Kraemer to his hotel room and told him his story, truthfully, including wanting to jump his Kennecott contract and work at Chitina instead.

Kraemer listened gravely to this tale and then sat quietly for some time. He knew that one man made little difference to Kennecott, where five hundred to seven hundred were employed, and where workers came and went every day. But he was sensitive to the prepaid traveling contract. The copper mine rightly had a claim on Bud since his expenses to Alaska had been covered.

Kraemer decided to give Bud a chance, with an if. "I'll get in touch with the officials at Kennecott and see what they have to say," he said. "I'll try to raise them on the telephone. Drop back here in an hour."

When Bud returned, Kraemer was brief and blunt. "Kennecott has agreed to cancel your contract," he said. "I have arranged to pass your transportation charges over to them. That amount will be deducted from your earnings when I make up the payroll at the end of the season."

It was late when Bud finished his story. The rest of the camp had been in bed for an hour or more. There was a spare bunk in one tent for his use that night. The next morning he was moving on to the Upper Camp, three miles up the creek. We were going to be much closer together for socializing than we thought.

The night air was chilly when we started for bed. I remarked to Bud that he had come off lucky in scuttling the contract. Otherwise he might have been tied up in underground work for a year. Bud's hackles stiffened and a bleak, faraway look came into his eyes. "I hope those bastards at Kennecott don't throw my blankets away," he said. "Those blankets and clothes will come in handy in this frozen bitch of a country. Besides, there's a good pair of shoepacs rolled up in 'em that I paid two dollars for in a secondhand store in Lewiston."

7

The Country

The dead work at the Lower Camp was drawing to a close. The sluiceways were readied and workers blocked the out area which lay on the opposite side of the creek approximately two hundred feet wide and a thousand feet long. The depth of the gravel varied, but averaged about twelve feet to bedrock with very little topsoil or other overburden and no permafrost. Those favorable conditions were offset by the quantity and hugeness of the boulders.

Putting in the sluiceways took about a week and it was a tough job since there was still considerable surface frost which required blasting. Before mining could start, arrangements had to be made for stacking the tailings which would be pouring in a steady stream down the sluice.

The real mining was about to begin. However, my education about Alaska's wild country had already started.

Since arriving in Chitina, I had heard some interesting stories during the evening chat sessions and they were not the kind associated with tall tales like wifflepoofs. They were more stories about mining experiences during the Shushanna stampede. Most miners at Chitina had spent a season or two camp-mining and prospecting. Their stories impressed me as being out of the ordinary. They were certainly different from the ones I heard as a kid back in Zion, Illinois.

Cheechako that I was, I knew that one does not risk his neck on glaciers or in storm-swept mountain passes, and do it repeatedly, as a matter of course. The place names themselves these men spoke of were flavorful. They mentioned Solo Mountain, the Goat Trail, Canyon City, Ping-Pong Mountain, Ptarmigan Lake, or the Homestead. Other names had the air of desperation, such as the Jump-off or the Glory Hole.

I listened to vivid descriptions of glacier trails where blizzards struck without warning, trails that were mantraps. I learned there were mountains so high a man had to lie on his back to see the summits. The wild goats that inhabited the region had to go in reverse to climb the steep foothills, the storytellers said. In some high mountain passes the trails were so narrow the packhorses traveled on clouds to get around the tall peaks.

The accounts seemed to originate in some rarefied atmosphere. One of the boys had a Geological Survey Bulletin with a topographical map of the region, and I borrowed it to study the landscape's features. This fabulous region lay north-ward in the Wrangell Range, with the White River and Shushanna country lying just beyond. From all accounts, the country was as isolated and difficult to access as any place to be found in the North. Great ice fields lying across the height of the Wrangell Range guarded it on the coastal side, and in all other quarters there were forbidding distances of rough, trackless wilderness between the upper White River–Shushanna country and the nearest settlements.

The leading roles in the epochal conquest of the region had been played by dog drivers and packers who had been freighting into the gold camps since the mineral's discovery. For more than a decade they had been carrying on their ac-tivities in a matter-of-fact way, moving freight in tonnage quantities across glacier-locked heights which by any logical and sensible estimate were properly termed impassable. The routes were often condemned in that vein. Even the boys in camp who had survived the ordeal of crossing the range some of them several times—declared no one in his right mind would tackle such country, much less freight on the trails year after year. They said one thing, but did another.

One characteristic of the White River–Shushanna country was the infor-mal way it neglected national boundaries even though the International Bound-ary Line connecting Alaska and Canada crossed the White River. Considerable country lying beyond the White River watershed was often referred to as "The White." A mineralized belt lay across the upper White valley with part of it on the Canadian side. The region was as large as a good-sized state and was regarded by early prospectors as kind of an autonomous domain, with its sovereignty invested in an impregnable mountain barrier on one hand and a periphery of impenetrable wilderness distances on the other. The area's autonomy was evident even in official affairs, for though much of the country being prospected on the upper White was within Alaska, the recording office for the district, until the Shushanna stampede in 1913, was at Forty Mile in the Yukon Territory.

The character of the region stamped itself strongly on the men, superseding na-tionality to an extent. Those who came to know the area intimately by living in it were known as "White River men." This was a fraternity whose hardiness and competence was above average and was recognized as such by others who were no strangers to rug-ged wilderness travel either. Such distinction was well earned. The White River coun-try was notoriously tough on Cheechakos and on occasion took its toll on veterans.

The Creator had designed the White on a grand scale and those broad dimensions began right at the river's source. The river headed into ice fields which flowed down from a mountain range where peaks rose to heights of ten thousand to sixteen thousand feet. Immediately on leaving the glaciers, the river entered a wandering course with many channels straggling across bars and winding back and forth across flats, which in some places were several miles wide. After entering Canadian territory, two canyons were encountered within a dozen miles of each other. These were the only places where the stream limits were confined and each time the river boiled through the canyons and burst out upon broad flats.

Beyond the lower canyon, the White continued its wandering, rushing sweep. Timbered islands parted its channels and the brawling river, grown to a turbid flood through its many tributaries, swept down the broad valley, strewing debris on the shifting bars. Its roiling current was slowed only when it joined with the Yukon River, 230 miles from the White's head.

The White was legendary for its bounty of wildlife. Sportsmen prized the magnificent trophies of grizzly and black bear, moose, caribou, mountain sheep, and goat that lived in the area. During annual migrations, the caribou numbered in the hundreds of thousands and for several weeks the river bars would be alive with the moving animals and the river itself choked with swimming herds. Shortly after spring breakup, the river bars were a busy concourse with thousands of Canadian honkers promenading and sunning themselves. Other wildfowl were also plentiful, and ptarmigan, spruce hen, and willow grouse often fell into the White River man's skillet. The lakes and clear-water streams also provided mainly grayling, whitefish, and trout.

No, the White was no miserly, picayune country by any standard. And the men who lived in it had much the same qualities of the country. Beneath a breezy, easy-going manner, they were tenacious and obstinate in overcoming odds, yet with a resiliency that pushed through trails when others turned back. They knew the White River intimately, from source to mouth, and knew the routes which led in and out of the region as one knows the paths in his home backyard. In traveling over glaciers and mountain passes they were uncanny in their knowledge of weather and trail conditions. They took chances almost daily, but calculated chances. They were unpredictable in their tactics for outmaneuvering natural obstacles and the many hazards that beset the trails.

These were the top hands, who spent their lives prospecting, mining, and freighting tons of supplies across the ice fields in the Wrangells. But the outstanding feature about these fellows was not so much what they were doing under impossible conditions, but the gusto and apparent ease with which it was done. The exploits of these dog drivers and packers in the course of an ordinary season's work taxed credibility. They would get up to their necks in some catastrophic situation that every minute threatened to annihilate them, but by the breadth of a hair it never happened. Whenever they failed in a venture, it was failure on a grand scale and soon enough that too was bruited up to a notorious, howling success.

They were busy lads, these nephews of Paul Bunyan. There were only a handful of the boys, but their foot tracks are on the pages of history, between the lines of print telling of minerals being uncovered, trails being blazed, and settlements rising in the wilderness. They were freighting in supplies when the International Boundary Line was cut and they were freighting in supplies when gold was being mined.

My first acquaintance with dog drivers who freighted across the Wrangell Range came about during the latter part of May, about the time active mining commenced. The spring thaw had knocked out the bottom of the snowy trail and made it impassable for our freighter Jim Murie and his buckboard. The camp was without mail and had been for nearly two weeks.

One evening after supper the boys began talking the situation over. "The way things are now, we miss out on a lot of 'sassiaty's' doings," remarked the skinner, "not having the McCarthy newspaper. Why, the Prohibitionists might knock over the town and have everybody locked up in jail and us not hear a word about it!"

The mail had gone as far as the roadhouse six miles away and the suggestion was voted upon that someone should "sashay" down to the roadhouse to retrieve it. Conversation next turned to who might "volunteer" to trek down the trail and bring back the mail. Thoughtful glances turned in my direction. With knowledge derived from past experience of how things turned out, I knew what was coming next. Without words wasted in useless argument, I reached under my bunk for my packsack and a few minutes later I was out the door.

The trail was a morass and that made six hiking miles seem like sixty. For most of the distance I kept to the woods where the walking was fairly good on timbered flats. Eventually, I slogged into the roadhouse yard. I was muddy, but not terribly tired.

I quickly caught a glimpse of two large dog teams sprawled out in harness near the kennels. The teams were double-hitched on long towlines and the sleds were the long, low-slung basket types common to the freighters in this locality. Immediately I forgot my errand and turned aside for a closer inspection of these phenomenal dogs. I was puzzled. Where had these outfits come from? What was the urgency for them to be traveling over flooding streams and trails that were bottomless bogs? The last ice had gone out from the river three weeks earlier, and snow had disappeared everywhere except on the higher mountain slopes.

One team had nine dogs and the other eleven. They were big, muscular fellows, and as rangy as foraging wolves. They were wet, muddy, and disheveled, but looked powerful enough to pull stumps out by their roots. At the moment they were taking life easy, and with an air of aloof dignity managed to convey the impression that they were important fellows and had seen better times. They were utterly bored, so they informed me, with traveling in all of this mud, and heartily wished that dog drivers would show the good sense of dogs.

Upon introducing myself and explaining that there were no dogcatchers in my family, I went about carrying on doggy conversations with the big fellows. They appeared to be friendly without wishing to become too intimate while flopping their tails on the ground. The lead dogs eyed me impersonally and asked where I had come from in my imagined conversation. I was no dog musher, and they knew it. I was just a tender chicken. I could see them thinking, why didn't I amount to something and learn to swear and spit tobacco juice?

While moving around and carrying on a running conversation, I was not only studying the dogs, but also the harnesses and towline rigging and finally the sleds. What sleds these were. One of them appeared to be all of twelve feet on the bed and they were both sturdily constructed. They gave the impression of being light and lithe as a whip. Their weathered and trail-battered appearance could not conceal the rakish, smooth-flowing lines which started at the high bow piece and ran through the basket railings, struts, and runners right to the footplates in the rear. These sleds were aristocrats and they would be so, even after being dumped on the scrap heap with all of the other old, used sleds.

I stood, spellbound, looking the outfits over from the lead dogs to the sleds' handlebars and back again. There was an appeal in these trail-worn, mud-splashed outfits that went far beyond anything of the storybook variety with their spangled, prancing dogs, enameled carioles, and silver harness bells. There was a coldly efficient and sparing quality in these outfits, as purposeful in their class as battle cruisers stripped down for action. Here was mystery and meaning. The mystery was where these outfits came from and why they were traveling in summerlike heat, in water and mud. The meaning was harder to define, for it touched on the inward nature of things, and carried within it the significance of why one thing appeals to us and another repels, and why we choose to live our lives one way and not another, and are often unhappy if it turns out otherwise.

Why had I not chosen the high road to the cities, or gone to the tropics, or sought some easy passage through life, possibly beachcombing in some South Sea island paradise? But no, the smell of spruce borne on some vagrant breeze was in my nostrils and I had come north seeking the answer. Now as I stood in the roadhouse yard looking at these battered, mud-splattered outfits, I had the same feeling of exaltation and thrill as I had experienced once before when I had sighted the forbidding Alaska coastal range from the forepeak of the steamer.

Reluctantly, I turned from the dog teams and walked into the roadhouse.

8

The Roadhouse

There was some kind of merrymaking going on inside the roadhouse and while scraping mud from my shoepacs I could hear shouts of laughter coming from the kitchen. Opening the outer door—insurance against the winter weather—I passed through the storm porch to the open kitchen door and found myself standing directly behind a man who could have passed as a survivor of a shipwreck. His clothes were mostly rags. His old woolen shirt and breeches were patched with canvas and he wore waterlogged moccasins which oozed water all over the clean kitchen floor.

But that fellow was not the only survivor. There were two others in the same condition seated at a table with Murie. A gallon demijohn was set in the middle. It was evident the three strangers had been someplace in glaring sun on ice and snow. Their features were burned black except for large white circles around the eyes where snow goggles had been worn. The weird effect gave the appearance of specters that were around in broad daylight. Had it not been for the hilarity of the party, one might have suspected that these fellows had fallen into a glacier crevasse and barely escaped with their lives.

Whatever the circumstances were, at least it was not worrying them. The man holding forth on the floor had a water tumbler partly filled with liquor in one hand. He was mincing around daintily and talking in a whining voice, initiating some bawdy story that the others seemed to know. The performance was greeted with roars of laughter. I set my packsack by the door. After a minute or two Murie came over and lent one ear for my errand, keeping the other open to the high jinks going on. When there was a break in the affair, Murie introduced me around. I heard names that were somewhat familiar. They were dog drivers who freighted on the glaciers, the demigods I had heard so much about.

My mind was seething with a dozen questions. I was prepared to listen while ponderous strokes of history were related by men whose fame had spread from the Copper River country to the Yukon. Murie encouraged my line of talk by placing a water tumbler in my hand. Words flew at the table and I tried to take it all in while wondering if I could stay sober enough to complete my return to camp. The demijohn came my way and I poured a small drink. I waited for someone to join me, but when no one did, I said, "Well, here's good luck," and bolted the teaspoonful of mule.

During the course of conversation I learned that these fellows had been working on one of the creek claims near Shushanna. Toward spring two of the men had left off mining to hitch the dogs and move some freight across glaciers. It appeared three tons of supplies, bound for the trader at Shushanna, had been sledded up-river by horse and double ender, and landed at the foot of the Nazina Glacier. The dog drivers had relayed the freight across the hump and landed it at Shushanna just prior to spring breakup. They joined the other member of the party in sluicing the winter's dump. After cleanup, the three men with the two outfits made the return trip across the glaciers, headed for McCarthy.

The ice travel had been good, but naturally so late in the season they had encountered a spring flood in the Nazina Valley. They had to work their way down the valley to make stream crossings with drift logs lashed to the sides of the sleds to keep them afloat. The men forded the river waist deep and the dogs swam. The rest of the time they traveled on river bars and barren flats. One dog driver referred to this method of travel as "dry sledding," but I thought that was inappropriate for travel better accomplished with a rowboat.

The talk of this adventure that had me spellbound went on for an hour before discussion turned to the pay itself for such hazardous work. "It looks like you're rich when you sack it up, but the stuff won't go far," one driver said of the cost of living. "By the time you're through paying the bills and getting some more dog food there isn't enough left to buy a decent round of drinks. I don't think this stuff will go more than fourteen dollars to the ounce." The man, named Scotty, reached under his chair and came up with a large moose-hide poke which plainly showed weight. He worried that the weight owed more to quartz than to pure gold.

One of the other men spread a large bandana on the bare kitchen table and the contents of the poke were emptied out in a heap. Roughly the pay amounted to two thousand dollars, representing the larger half of the cleanup. It appeared the remaining portion of the poke was out on one of the sleds.

Much of the pay pile was in coarse gold. Scotty flushed his hand through the pile, picking our certain nuggets and handing them to Murie. "Like that," he said, indicating this hunk of mineral was more quartz than gold. "And that one, and this. Those slugs are more quartz than pay."

Mrs. Murie had been working in the kitchen and she leaned over the table to take a look. "My, but they certainly are pretty," she said.

The comment made Scotty moan. He was less interested in appearances than values. He threw his hands in the air. "Me, I like the solid slugs, the ones that smash toes when the poke falls on 'em," he said. "You can get someplace with the hefty slugs. They're the ones that pay the bills."

The sight of this raw gold as it came out of the ground was thrilling to me. Even though I was working in a placer gold mining camp I had not yet sighted so much as a bit of color. The only nuggets I had ever seen were displayed in shop windows after they had been made into jewelry. My eyes were probably sticking out a foot, for one of the men who glanced in my direction jerked a thumb and said, "Go ahead, pick up some of the stuff and look at it if you want to. Hell, nobody can eat it. I tried that once myself and nearly starved to death with ten thousand bucks wrapped up in a gunnysack on the sled."

It had never occurred to me that gold had no value unless you could find someone who was foolish enough to pay for something they might not be able to use. But such a technicality did not dampen my interest in the fascinating metal, and I picked up several sizeable nuggets for closer inspection. They were slugs two or three times bigger than my thumbnail. As I replaced one of the slugs in the pile, Scotty reached for the nugget. He hefted it lightly in the palm of his hand. "Now there's one loaded with quartz," he said. "Nearly all of the big ones are. This one is not worth ten dollars."

One of the partners broke off conversation with Murie and turned a sour look on Scotty. "You wasn't kicking so much when we was digging the stuff," he said. He turned back to Murie. "By sufferin' damnation, every big boulder we ran into Scotty would get down on his belly with a tablespoon and start gouging under it to see if there was any more pay to be found. And that wasn't enough. He goes out and cuts himself a long willow and ties that onto the spoon so he could dig all the way under. He wore out so many spoons digging holes in bedrock that we ended up eating beans with our jackknives. Yeah, no foolin', by God we did."

Scotty snorted and passed Murie a sly wink. "He's just loading you," he said to Murie. "Pete, he's never 'et with anything but a jackknife. He can't handle a spoon even when he has one." Scotty looked at me. "I'll give you a good tip," he said. "You just might have use for it sometime. The gals like to get hold of this quartz stuff on account of they like to have it made up into fancy junk. You've seen 'em. Stuff like necklaces and earrings, and belt buckles, Jesus Christ, big enough to choke a horse! Just remember that when you're out studding around. Hell, there's more romance in a few lousy no-account nuggets than a man can put across with a handful of twenty-dollar bills."

The party was on the verge of breaking up when I got the mail and left the roadhouse. Murie had suggested the boys stay over for the night, but they were not persuaded. "Daytime travel is too hard on the dogs this time of year," one said. "We laid over at Dan Creek cabin on that account. If we get started now we'll be in McCarthy before the sun gets too hot."

Trudging toward camp that cool, twilight evening my mind was bursting with rehashing the details of the happenstance meeting with the freighters. I felt a little bit disappointed that I had not heard tales of more derring-do, of greater adventure. The dog drivers appeared to be no more than rough, plain-spoken, unpretentious fellows, just the same kind of men I was already acquainted with in the mining camp. But one didn't get to know these trail men by meeting them casually in a roadhouse or around town. One had to travel with them, to live with them on the trail. It was only by being with them when a crisis rose that one could discover their exceedingly tough and resourceful nature.

But, as so often happens, history was being made right under one's nose without it being recognized as such until sometime later. In this instance, the history of the glacier trail was closing. It was unknown to me at the time (as it was to the men concerned) that this party of three men with dog teams that I met in the roadhouse was going to be the last travelers ever to use the glacier trail to Shushanna.

Changing conditions made it impractical to maintain the trail any longer, and beyond this time in the spring of 1926, the trail was abandoned. The alternate route was Skolai Pass, but that was to have a short lifespan. The era of prospecting, mining, and freighting in the White River–Shushanna country was closing in less than a quarter of a century and only shortly after I showed up.

9

Forest Fire

The warm month of May passed into the hot month of June, bringing with it the seasonal mosquito plague. When the first early ones arrived I brought on ridicule by batting vengefully at the few big fellows flitting around on a reconnaissance job. Those big ones, I was told, were of the tame variety. Just wait till the man eaters arrived! Well, the man eaters now arrived in force.

There was scarcely any escape from their tormenting stings short of wearing a head net and head gear of the sort that was too hot and stifling to be endured on the job. The bunk tents were not mosquito-proof either. I was always secretly delighted when the rhinoceros-hided skinner was moved to crawl out of his bed and, kneeling in his long-handed underwear, offered up prayerful imprecations.

Throughout June the days were clear and cloudless, with scarcely a cooling breeze to break the heat, although the nights were cool and refreshing. The sun was wheeling an unwearied circuit, barely dipping below the northern horizon for a few night hours before it was on another day's round. The sun poured a merciless heat upon the freshly green countryside, which less than two months before had been a frozen, lifeless land buried deep in snow.

The burning sun beat into the mining cut. The heat was reflected from the bare bedrock and the bull gang gasped in the torrid oven. Sweat stung the eyes and ran in rivulets from the end of one's nose. Shirts were soaking wet and the hot sweat coursed down one's legs into one's rubber boots. The men on the bull gang cursed, cursing the heat in this usually frozen land more than they ever thought of cursing the winter cold.

Cool night shifts were now the favored time for working. No one who had worked the night shift before in a northern summer had escaped the transcending spell of peace and quietude, nor overlooked the matchless beauty which comes with the midnight hours. Those night hours were never completely dark. At Chitina, during the midnight hour, there was a bright twilight glow on the northern horizon, a glow which soon broke into dawn and full daylight. The midnight hour was a moody, contemplative hour in the wilderness. It was then that Nature wore her magic curtain of cerulean, violets, and deep purples, with the hills and distant mountains cast in as many changing hues as a temperamental lady in a dressmaker's shop. The sky and earth brooded over the matter of a common palette, while wisps of foglike smoke rose from the valley bottoms, softening the contours of timbered hills and sharp-ridged mountain slopes.

They were mysterious hours, too, those midnight hours. They were hours when the eternal spirit of past eons seemed to rise and cast their shadows over the land. The endings and beginnings of all past ages were signified in the fading sunsets, which at the self-same hour was not departing daylight, but arriving dawn. Even the birds hushed their twitterings while Nature changed her translucent hues and continued concerning herself with the makings of another day.

June's air was parched and dry and the new green leaves on the willow trees hung listlessly. They were tinged yellow from drought. The rutted trail, so recently a bog, was dried out. The moss in the woods was dusty. The camp was mindful of fire hazards. We knew if a conflagration got started it could hardly be stopped without the entire countryside going up in smoke. The parched valley needed rain badly. After the spring runoff, the creek had dropped to such a low level that every dribble of water was being used for mining operations. Had it not been for the melting glacier at the head of the creek, the hydraulics would have been shut down.

On the late afternoon of June 17 smoke was observed rising from the distant hillside on the left of the creek upstream. When first discovered, the flames amounted to little more than a brush fire, but it already covered a considerable area. Its progress downcreek was slow because a light breeze was quartering against it. Nevertheless, the fire was making progress. To attempt a back fire was out of the question, for there was only one team of horses in camp and there was no suitable equipment to make a fast ditching job. Starting a back fire without adequate control meant simply starting another conflagration in the immediate neighborhood of camp.

Work continued in the mining cut, but with a watchful eye on the column of smoke. The Upper Camp was relatively secure, since it was situated in open country, where there was little combustible material. But the Lower Camp was in a dangerous position. It was hemmed in closely on both sides of the creek, with hillsides timbered with spruce and birch, and the undergrowth was a veritable jungle of tinder. Fortunately, the pipeline flume and other mine installations were on the creek side away from the blaze. There would be little chance of saving the camp if the fire jumped the creek.

The breeze blowing upcreek blew steadily all day. Through the night the fire made little progress towards us, but it spread in the brushy hill country and blanketed the countryside with smoke. The bull gang worked shorthanded. Two men were assigned to patrol the mine's equipment, mindful of stray sparks. The situation changed little until about noon on the eighteenth when the wind moved in the opposite direction. Within a few minutes the fire had leapt into dry undergrowth in a dozen places. From there it swiftly evolved into a forest fire of dangerous proportions.

The fire was now sweeping towards the placer cut, on the creek side opposite camp. The furious blaze created one enormous draft and gained ground by the minute. A fearful roaring mingled with hissing bursts and cracklings. The noise carried a half mile as timber crashed. Leaping tongues of flame licked upwards into lurid, boiling clouds of smoke. The entire timbered hillside upstream on the creek was sheeted in flames. The air was heavy with smoke, blotting out views in every direction. The small bull gang continued with its work, stoically doing the job as sparks and hot ash drifted down and sizzled out in puddles of water standing on the bedrock.

Work in the cut did not go on very long, however. The sparks and ash thickened and the forward wall of the fire was no more than a quarter mile away. Heat from the blaze was starting to be felt when the foreman signaled a thumbs-down order to button up the operation. Tools were picked up and cached at a distance.

The camp was up and stirring. The night shift had abandoned the bunks. With sleepy interest the workers sat on tent stoops, idly watching the progress of the fire. Snippets of conversation mentioned weather conditions and wind shifts, but scarcely a word was said about what we all dreaded most—that there seemed to be an excellent chance that the fire would jump the creek and wipe out the camp.

Superintendent Kraemer enlisted men from the Upper Camp and using a mining monitor they set up to protect the Lower Camp, ready to spray the fire. It was midafternoon when the fire swept across the hill slope on the opposite side of the creek. A light wind quartered across the creek in the camp's favor, otherwise red-hot debris would have showered all over us. The Chitina miners watched in silence as the forest of living spruce and birch melted in towering sheets of flame. There was a pang in the heart for the nestlings, and the grouse and rabbits, and other living creatures that we knew must be caught in the inferno.

The forest, which represented at least a century of uninterrupted growth, was destroyed in a matter of minutes. The seething cauldron of flame parched the face, and even at a quarter of a mile gave off heat that was unbearable. There was a hurricane roaring as timber crashed to the ground and was swallowed up by the flames. The sound of rendings and angry hisses, and staccato reports like rifle fire beat against one's senses. Wary eyes followed the charred and singed pieces of ash and other fire remnants as they landed within a stone's throw of camp.

By the standards of forest fires, this was not a large one, but its destructive force was nonetheless impressive. It was awesome and appalling. The hills, all of the way to the ridge, were a white-hot furnace with whirlwinds of flames and burning brands rising upward into roiling clouds of smoke. A hellish red glare lit the undersides of smoke clouds and spread an ever-thickening pall across the sky. A bloodred sun shone wanly. It was a ghastly sun, which in one's eye symbolized apocalyptic wars or plagues. The atmosphere was supercharged with portentous feeling. This was destruction on earth, a pitiless doom for the forest and living creatures caught within range of the all-devouring flames.

The fire did not pause long in one place. The tremendous draft created by the awful upsurge of heat was hurling brands and burning spruce tops at distances far beyond the main fire front. Leaping flames were constantly outdistancing the main conflagration.

The area over which the fire had passed was desolate beyond description. Within a few hours the entire countryside had been transformed from a cheerful, living creation into an unrecognizable ruin. The blackened wreckage of fallen timber lay smoldering in red-hot ashes, with here or there the smoking skeleton of a tree still standing erect. Sparks of fire played fitfully in the blackened rubble and every light breeze stirred new life under dying embers. A thousand thin columns of smoke rose like wisps of vapor issuing from fumroles in a volcanic valley. Fire, man's most useful gift, had run amuck.

In camp, work went forward to prepare for firefighting. We did not know which way the wind would blow. All inflammable brush was cleared from the area. Coils of hose were retrieved from a warehouse and made ready to connect to the main pipeline. There were tubs and many buckets of water placed at critical points around the mine's installations for quick use in dousing a small fire just getting started.

The crest of the fire at its nearest point opposite camp passed quickly. There had been no serious damage to equipment in the cut. But the heat had been intense enough to melt the pitch coating on the heated side of branch pipelines despite the ice water coursing through them. The heat from the smoldering hillside was still intense. The boys spat tobacco juice disgustedly when they gazed at the scorched forest.

Through good fortune and favoring breeze the fire was confined to the other side of the creek and was now sweeping across backcountry. The camp had come through unscathed, but the miners remained uneasy. The hazard from sparks was present in the nearby smoldering area and we were all aware that the air had been dry anyway. It was a dangerous situation and would remain so until soaking rains fell. The superintendent kept patrols of two men going as the shifts returned to work that night.

The morning of the nineteenth dawned with a pallid sun showing ruddily through the smoke haze. The rising day shift sniffed the murky atmosphere, wet their fingers, and held them up in the stagnant air, and decided the present weather would stay put. A fine black ash was rinsed from the water basins. After breakfast, the rubber boots were pulled on and the day shift went to work.

The expected calm weather took a turn in the early afternoon. Turbulent air currents rose undoubtedly from the fire raging in the backcountry. There was a rising wind straight across the creek from the burned area to camp. It stirred new life in the wreckage and streamers of smoke drifted across the water.

It was at the upper canyon, where the penstock and dam were located, where the fire jumped the creek. A member of the bull gang returned to camp on the run. Before he could issue a warning a column of smoke was seen rising from the ridge above the canyon. It was a blaze that was out of control from the moment it was sighted. In ten minutes, less time than it would have taken to reach the site at a dead run, the entire ridge was a mass of flame and smoke. Mining work was shut down at once and preparation to fight the fire was taken up in grim earnest.

Two monitors in the cut were hurriedly dismantled and hauled into camp by the teamster. Spaced about fifty yards apart, they were set up in front of the camp, ready to spray water against fire instead of sluicing. They were positioned to allow the high-arching streams to be swept back and forth over the tents. The deluge of spray falling from such massive streams of water was enough to keep the camp drenched. In addition, there were a couple of hose lines laid out to protect the rear side of the tents, where the heat would be intense. Two men patrolled the flume while other men were sent with tools and water buckets to maintain a close watch on wooden benches and blockings supporting the pipeline. Every man was hard at work. While we prepared, the fire worked its way downstream towards us. But the advance was slow now with the wind quartering across the creek. The shift in wind drove the fire towards the backcountry and was a strong point in favor of saving the camp. Our firefighters might only have to fight the flank.

By midafternoon the fire was closing down in a wide arc upon camp. The atmosphere was stifling and dense. It was difficult to tell what the general situation was for the narrow valley was blanketed with thick smoke. Yet we came out all right. For the most part the fire spared us. The fire overspread the timber country beyond the lower canyon, but the camp survived with but minor damage.

Amazingly, by the time it was determined that the fire was a half mile past us, mining was under way again. The fire continued down the creek and it burned fifty square miles. We kept a close watch on the camp for several days and we wetted surrounding areas with water from the hose lines. Gradually, the heated hillside, knee-deep in hot ash, cooled off. Days later, when it rained, we felt safer than we had since the fire erupted.

The total loss to the mine from the fire was merely a few lost hours of production. But Chitina was a different place following the fire. Everything that had made for pleasant surroundings, from the verdant landscape to singing birds, had gone up in smoke and flame. The hillsides were a blackened ruin. The creek ran black with ash. There was ash in the drinking water, ash in our beds, and the very air was tainted with the smell of ash and soot.

The one advantage gained from the fire was that it had scotched the mosquito plague.

10

Mining Something Else

Fourth of July passed quietly at the mine. Work went on if it was a national holiday or not. The casual dismissal of the holiday did not hold true for McCarthy, however. The citizens of that redoubtable village were still fighting Tories and upheld the Fourth in a manner reminiscent of the rebels at Lexington and Bunker Hill.

Time had not tempered the spirit of independence, but in McCarthy the Liberty Bell roared rather than rang. Even dogs took to their holes while the residents embraced open hospitality by the jug-full and kept in battle practice by indiscriminately blackening one another's eyes.

A week or two after the Fourth, Murie showed up on one of his regular buckboard trips carrying mail and camp supplies. He also brought some news. He announced that a fresh stampede was under way near McCarthy. The roadhouse man didn't seem to know a great deal about the affair, except scraps of information he had heard in town. But the gist of his report was that an oil strike had been made in the Nazina Valley flats. The entire town was streaming out to the scene and staking the countryside for miles around.

The strike's location was not far from Chitina. It was only about ten miles as the crow flies or twelve miles by trail. The boys in camp got together to talk things over. They were familiar in a general way with the geology of the locality. In years past there had been reports favorable to oil in the lower part of the valley, but the reports had never been substantiated by the filing of a discovery claim. The Chitina miners were skeptical about the discovery. They expressed the opinion that the swamps in the area would never produce anything except mosquitoes. The confab ended with the boys turning thumbs down to the proposition and no one left camp to join the ranks of those hoping to become oil millionaires.

No knowledge was to be gained from the McCarthy newspaper except who had filed claims. No one seemed to know who the original locator was. More than three weeks passed before Murie had all of the facts lined up. When he did the news caused enough of an uproar to tear the bunk tents down. The circumstance starting the stampede began in Murie's own roadhouse. He hired a roustabout mechanic to work on his machinery. After ten days, around the Fourth of July, the man took some days off on unstated business.

After his brief disappearance, he showed up in town at a bar and ordered a drink. When it came time to pay he reached into his pocket and unloaded a multitude of odd items, some nuts and bolts, and his change. Mixed in was a small glass vial that rolled down the bar containing a dark, viscous liquid. It rolled right under the barkeep's nose. The mechanic pounced on the vial and quickly stuffed it back in his pocket. After this mishap, the man left the bar promptly, forgetting in his haste to put the other odds and ends into his pocket. The hastiness of his departure was seen as evidence that he had been flustered unduly by the small incident, something he clearly did not want to talk about.

The barkeep was an astute businessman who didn't believe in letting grass grow under his feet where a fast buck was to be made. He did a quick job of running some notes through his mental adding machine and since he knew of the reports of oil in the Nazina Valley he wondered if a strike had been made. It was no surprise that the mechanic wasn't talking. Under the local law he had thirty days to file a claim, which would provide the location to the public. If he waited till the last minute he could file the claim, rush back to the site, and file a second claim before anyone was the wiser and before he would be shut out of the area by others' claims.

Assessing the situation, the barkeep put on his hat and departed his work station. He borrowed a jitney and followed the mechanic being driven in a Tin Lizzie down the trail to Kennecott. Upon the car's return to McCarthy, the barkeep corralled the driver and plied him with drinks. The driver knew only so much, but the barkeep concluded that the mechanic was staying at the mine until he could get the contents of his vial tested.

He rounded up his cronies—other barkeeps—and they hatched a scheme to waylay the mechanic on his way back from Kennecott and overload him with corn liquor in hopes he would spill all he knew. The theory sounded good, but the plan did not play out as planned. Upon his return to town the mechanic avoided all bars and took a little-used trail to his cabin. It was late evening when the conspirators learned they had been outmaneuvered. When a couple of visitors with a jug called at his cabin the loud sounds of snoring drowned out any sounds of knocking on the door.

The mechanic was not to be found the next day because he had departed early for the roadhouse to resume work for Murie. That evening the barkeeps fired up an impromptu party and in the course of affairs the celebrants picked up the assayer from Kennecott and brought him to town. The bartenders plied their guest with choice private stock and explained they had always considered him to be just one of the boys. The assayer did not allow any choice refreshments to get past him as he listened gravely to the shop talk.

Finally, the barkeeps felt their guest of honor had been loosened up enough and started asking him questions. The assayer was a professional man and not given to talk overly much about confidential matters related to his work. But in short order he had exhaled the one word they hoped to hear. "Oil!" he said with gusto and raised a significant look in the group.

The first hurdle had been cleared. Yes, there had been a discovery. But they didn't know where and they had to locate the site to wisely stake the surrounding area. Then, by the time the stampede started they could control the discovery. They could sit back with shears in hand and clip dividend coupons.

The next morning the barkeeps took a sudden interest in healthful outdoor activities. They pulled on rubber boots, rigged themselves with fishing gear, and stuck a large number of brightly colored flies in their hatbands. One of the town's jalopies was chartered and as soon as they made known the purpose of the excursion was fishing they headed off to the Nazina flats. The trail ended in the area of where oil seepages had previously been spotted. After parking the jalopy the boys began thrashing around through several square miles of muskeg flats, with a cloud of hungry mosquitoes following them to see that they didn't get lost. The expedition showed no lack of perseverance, but a couple of days passed without the party finding a single claim corner to reward their sweaty efforts.

The spade work necessary for becoming oil magnates proved to be such a rough chore that the barkeeps finally gave up on the muskeg swamps and fell back on routine formulas. They knew that the mechanic had returned to the roadhouse, so the boys cranked up the jitney and took to haunting the roadhouse with a cargo of corn juice. But the mechanic was as shy as a gunshot goose and unaccountably disappeared every time the fishing party roared into the yard. The barkeeps' junket bogged down in despair.

Meanwhile, the bartenders' sudden yen for outdoor exercise did not pass unnoticed in McCarthy. An ugly rumor began that the expedition had nothing to do with trout and grayling fishing. "It was oil the fishing party was on to, the lowdown rascals, now wouldn't you know it?" it was said. They were accused of being sly varmints who were staking every bit of land without saying a word about it. Word spread and the town buzzed like a beehive. Oil! Someone had struck oil on the Nazina flats!

At once, everything with wheels had been rented and those who either couldn't obtain a vehicle or afford one loaded up packsacks and walked. The exodus from

McCarthy was complete. There was hardly anyone left in town to feed the dogs. There was considerable doubt where to set up claim corners, but some leading citizens of the town demonstrated knowledge of the geology of the region and settled the discussion. Within a few days the entire area had been solidly staked. The stampeders' mission complete, they drifted back to town to recuperate and await further developments.

The week that followed was a tense period of watchful waiting. As yet, no one had come forward with the all-important oil discovery claim. The townspeople conjectured, bet, argued, and spread rumors. Everybody watched the bartender clique and the barkeeps watched the mechanic. But the mechanic seemed oblivious of the whole affair. In between unexplained disappearances into the Bush, he was quietly absorbed in overhauling the rear axle of Murie's old truck.

Before another weekend passed, the affair had broken down into acrimonious debate. No one knew for certain whether the staked area was within the discovery region that had supposedly been made. During the rush, no one had thought to carry on a close search for discovery claim corners. Now, with claim corners sticking up like matchsticks all over the area it was virtually impossible to locate what may have been the original discovery claim posts. Then, too, some claims had been improperly staked, with lines overlaying each other in some instances.

The situation left a bad hole for litigation later on, if the ground proved valuable. There were enough technicalities lying around to keep a dozen lawyers talking for a year. Who was the discoverer anyway? Where was he? And how did everybody get involved in such a mess? The roused citizenry jumped on the barkeeper clique. The bartenders squirmed and tried to explain their unbidden interest in the mechanic's affairs, but the explanation only raised the ire of the worthy citizens to a higher pitch.

They began talking of ropes and guns, but a tamer compromise was reached. A delegation was sent to the roadhouse to enlist the mechanic's friendly counsel and aid. But the mechanic had left only the day before for a fishing trip, without saying where he was going.

Now the rumor had come full circle, indicating that the vial never contained oil in the first place and the mechanic had been prospecting a copper lode. The vial, it was said, contained sulphide concentrate from one of the several known outcroppings in the valley. This new information directed the ugly finger of suspicion on the bartending coterie. Half the citizenry stoutly maintained that the bartenders had been caught red-handed in a scheme for unloading worthless oil claims on the public. Others contended that the chuckleheaded rumdums couldn't tell oil from wild goose grease.

With the mechanic nowhere to be found, the only way to prove or disprove the oil rumor was to trot out the assayer. The bartenders fixed up another impromptu party. The assayer arrived in town according to plan, but scarcely had time to be primed on plain cooking liquor before the barkeeps plunged in. "We thought you told us that fellow's sample was oil," they quizzed the assayer. "Now they say the stuff was something else and the town is threatening to hang us. How about it? We want the lowdown on this business. Was the sample really oil, or not?"

The assayer was astounded that his veracity would be questioned, and questioned so rudely. There was a sternly reproving look on his face as he turned on his inquisitors. "Certainly it was oil," he retorted. Drawing himself up with his utmost dignity, he added, "Crankcase oil. It came out of an old Ford truck."

That put the kibosh on an oil stampede near McCarthy.

11

Prohibition and No Inhibition

McCarthy was too close to the frontier to be class conscious. When viewing the obstreperous affairs that sometimes took place, one would be in error to conclude that serious factional differences existed between the townspeople. McCarthy's history during the Volstead era was an open denial of any such theory. Bud and I were puzzled by the open flouting of the Volstead Act from the moment of our arrival.

Judging from appearances it seemed the citizens of the town had never ratified the Eighteenth Amendment, or else had not heard of it. We were amazed at the wide-open, unabashed manner in which a dozen or more bars dealt in bootleg liquor. In addition, there were hotels and other businesses where one could buy a drink, including not less than a dozen houses of prostitution. It was a standing joke that the only place in town where one couldn't get a drink was the post office. And that narrowly missed being an understatement. The post office was located at the rear end of the drugstore and the pharmacist was known on occasion to tipple with a customer.

Bud and I knew that such carrying on was decidedly wrong. We had been raised as good boys, been dressed up, had our hair combed, and went to Sunday school. And during our grade school years we had both passed civics tests. So we recognized that this activity was breaking the law.

McCarthy's war rose directly from the frontier philosophy for living as based on the egalitarian principle. The frontier element had no use for demagoguery in any degree. In common with other communities, McCarthy had no use for Prohibition on any count. The Eighteenth Amendment was viewed as aggression on natural rights. McCarthy's attitude was less than that of violating the law than as a refusal to recognize the existence of the Eighteenth Amendment.

Resolute McCarthy's stand brought down the wrath of all political hell. The town was blacklisted and castigated from one end of the territory to the other and even Alaska's delegate to Congress took a hand in the recriminations. The determined villagers loaded their guns and those guns stayed loaded all the years of Prohibition. In the end, attacks were limited to mudslinging. The location of the town favored the situation, for it was in an isolated inland position, backed by a high mountain barrier. McCarthy was an easy place to barricade. In the matter of law enforcement, McCarthy called the tune.

The pro-Prohibitionists were soberly aware of this fact. They knew the town intimately, and they knew its deadly temper when aroused. They also knew every pertinent detail concerning the errant bootlegging, and the name of every person who was involved in the smallest degree. They couldn't help learning it unless they plugged their ears. It was common talk, all up and down the railroad, and in every roadhouse, mining camp, and town throughout the Copper River country, and along the coast. A McCarthy resident traveling almost anywhere between Seattle and Nome usually found that the hardy reputation of the place had preceded him.

The Probis sat tight through it all. They had no stomach for making the moves that would inevitably end in shooting. So officials restricted their activities to visits once a year and with no attempt to conceal their arrival, presence, and departure. Signals were developed to alert businessmen and lodge owners along the rail route between Cordova and McCarthy as to the advance of the government officials. Word on their progress was flashed up the line and the liquor business would be suspended. The townspeople went into a familiar routine with all of the cool precision of a fire drill.

Changeovers were completed within a few hours and even bartenders drank water when the officials were in town. Although McCarthy had enough secret tunnels under the main business block to turn the area into a large rabbit warren, places of concealment like that were regarded as good for emergencies only in case of open hostilities.

Still, occasionally the agents stumbled upon poorly concealed caches of liquor in a gunnysack, perhaps near the railroad bed. They announced a full-dress investigation to determine who the culprit might be that dared violate the law of McCarthy. As news of the search passed around town there would be much tongue clucking and head wagging. Then the residents chimed in with many confidential tips to "help" out the agents. Confusion would be rampant and by the time the investigation closed everyone in town was under suspicion, most of all the agents themselves for being alleged to have planted the sack.

The agents always seemed to be about as happy to depart from the town as the town was happy to see them leave. As for all of those scandalous reports of bootlegging going on, there was no tangible evidence to support such contentions.

Most notable events took place during the years McCarthy was wearing the war paint. One such affair took place a couple of years before Bud and I arrived in the country and the story was told in roadhouses and mining camps so often that it became a trail classic. The incident concerned the activities of a couple of McCarthy dog mushers.

The dog drivers engaged in the rum-running business from inside Canada. Worse, they had the bad taste to carry out their errands under the watchful eye of officials in both countries. The villagers tended to regard the affair as McCarthy's contribution to the field of international goodwill and neighborly understanding. Officialdom took a dim view of that attitude. They let it be known that the two dog drivers were ministers without portfolio and definitely in the doghouse.

The base for securing the bonded stock had been Dawson, in the Yukon Territory. The round trip between McCarthy and Dawson was upwards of a thousand miles, the larger part of which was through trackless wilderness. The fact that the route cut across glaciers and Skolai Pass, reputedly the most rugged and difficult trail in the North, did not faze the stubborn ingenuity of the lawless fellows.

Despite being weighed down by cases of booze, the dogs and drivers made the return run in record time. For good reason. On the way back to Alaska, the mushers had the Royal Canadian Mounted Police on their trail.

As counsel for the defense, it must be pointed out that the rum-running expedition had come about through a combination of circumstances, all of which were beyond human control, an act of God as it were. The trip occurred at a time when the Shushanna was falling off in gold production. As they were going broke, the dog drivers faced the hard alternative of feeding their crack, hard-working teams, or disposing of them by shooting. The latter was scarcely to be considered.

The dog drivers had been drinking bad bootleg whiskey during jaunts into town. The rank taste of the fuel oil convinced them the local moon-shiners needed a shaking up. The mushers decided business was best done by introducing a couple of sled loads of good bonded stock into the camp, thus raising popular taste to a higher cultural level. This matter of placing an ostrich egg in a hen's coop was considered a worthy objective by anyone acquainted with McCarthy hootch.

The dog drivers threw light outfits on their long freighting sleds, hitched up their trail-tough dogs, and quietly disappeared from McCarthy. Nothing more was heard of the boys for several weeks. The newspaper in the Klondike reported the arrival of two well-known Alaskan dog drivers. The boys dug themselves into a hotel room and occupied themselves with renewing old friendships and making a lot of new ones. This was all part of the good-neighbor policy, and not incidentally helped provide the needed quantity of booze.

Liquor sales in Dawson were restricted to government stores and a limit was set of one quart per day per person. So friends of the dog drivers could purchase the liquor needed to make the run worthwhile. The mushers made the trip to the liquor store for their own share, but also passed out greenbacks to old friends and new ones alike, to buy for them.

This continued until they filled 120 cases stacked up in their hotel room.

This did provide a sudden upsurge in business at the territory store. The McCarthy dog drivers were on the verge of successfully completing their transactions when they became aware of the quiet surveillance of the Royal Canadian Mounted police. Until that point the Alaskans had not broken any law. The Police wanted to wait until they loaded up the sleds to catch them with the goods red-handed. The booze would likely be confiscated and the men would probably be blue ticketed out of the territory and asked never to return.

The threatening situation was coolly weighed by the imperturbable dog drivers. These two rascals did not go about preparing confessions. They looked upon the circumstance as a legitimate sporting venture. The affair was a necessary chance taken to carry through their enterprise. The dog drivers' main concern was the three-hundred-mile dash to the border and how their heavily loaded sleds could outrun the lighter RCMP sleds.

To the average onlooker the odds were so great as to make the situation appear hopeless, but the McCarthy dog drivers were famed for dealing with the odds. Their years spent in freighting over some of the most rugged terrain in the North gave them the ability beyond the ordinary in wilderness travel and their sorcery in the art of dog driving was proverbial. The men added up all of the points and laid all of their money on gaining the boundary at least one team length ahead of the Mounties.

Late one night the Alaskans slipped out of sight and hitched their teams to sleds previously loaded without anyone being the wiser. They put their lead dogs' noses to the upriver mail trail, which followed the Yukon River, a trail hard-packed from considerable usage. This matter of handicapping the police with a few hours' head start was considered only fair since the Alaskans were handicapped with such large cargos of pedigreed booze. The liquor was hidden under sled tarpaulins piled higher than the basket railings.

On the trail at night the outfits slogged along at a leisurely gait, sparing the dog teams' energy as much as possible. A couple of hours before dawn the drivers pulled off the trail to give the dogs a brief rest. The dogs were unharnessed, bedded down, and given a light meal. Shortly after daylight the dogs were put back in harness and swung onto the trail. Now the pace picked up to hard-pounding running. It would not let up, except for short rests, until they reached the international boundary line.

Meanwhile, in Dawson, the RCMP was not aware their men had taken it on the lam. The situation was discovered during the forenoon. The police dog teams and toboggans were kept in readiness for patrol duty at all times during the winter. One of the teams was soon on the trail in hot pursuit of the missing men. The flight of the lawless and the pursuit by the law took on something of the character of the All-Alaska Sweepstakes, that grueling four-hundred-mile cross-country dash.

As the hard-driven dog teams pulled into, and almost immediately out of, Yukon River points, old Sourdoughs shucked their reading glasses. Soon, they gathered together in the quiet corner of roadhouses to exchange notes. Taking into account trail and weather conditions, the age and physical conditions of the drivers, the physical condition of the dogs, and the comparative weights of the sleds, the Sourdoughs placed bets on who would make it to the border first.

Still following the mail trail, the Alaskans were putting distance between themselves and the Mounties. The rum runners held a slight edge after 140 miles of Yukon River travel. Then they veered off the mail trail at the Wellesley Cutoff and headed into the backcountry. The cutoff at the White River marked the shortest way to reach the boundary. Most of the way was trackless wilderness, however, except for short, sketchy portions.

The mushers swept up the valley toward the head of the stormy White River country, a stern region of glaciers and peaks that these obdurate men regarded as their home stomping ground. The wide slash through timber where the international boundary line lay was their goal line, with safety on the other side for the Alaskans. For once, the Mounties failed to get their men. But the RCMP, once it has taken up the trail, does not let down so easy. When it became evident the rum runners had won the pennant, the police team turned back for a fast return to Dawson. A quick wire was sent to Juneau, the territorial capital of Alaska, informing federal officials of the affair. This resulted in the U.S. Deputy Marshal in McCarthy being alerted.

Ordinarily, the role played by the marshal in McCarthy was that of peacekeeper. Matters of Prohibition enforcement were left to federal agents. On this occasion, the marshal was given specific instructions to bag the offenders with their contraband the moment they showed up. The marshal was able to calculate how soon the miscreants would arrive and he was surprised how swiftly they were moving. It was plain they weren't stopping to moose hunt. He had to set a trap without delay.

There were too many roads and dog-team trails scattered around for him to watch. He also knew the canny traits of those fellows. After the chase the RCMP gave them they would be wary approaching McCarthy and undoubtedly would have a watcher keeping the marshal in sight. The marshal could take no chances with a slipup. To make certain of nabbing his men it was going to be necessary for him to get out on the trail and surprise them where his presence was unexpected.

The marshal quietly left town and took quarters at the Nazina Roadhouse, ostensibly on a short visit to get away from humdrum affairs for a few days. As a further precaution he deputized one of his friends in order to put eyes on the trail twenty-four hours a day. There was a fair amount of dog-team travel going on between McCarthy and the surrounding countryside and occasionally dog teams going one way or the other would simply drive past. Among the dog-driving fraternity were several who knew the purpose of the Yukon expedition and carried a blueprint in their heads of how it would pay off.

These mushers took notice of the marshal's trip to the roadhouse and they realized it could inconvenience the boys should they pull in with sleds loaded to the handlebars with prime Canadian booze. Accordingly, one of those drivers made a fast run up the valley twenty miles beyond the roadhouse, to a homestead cabin situated at the foot of the Nazina Glacier. The cabin served as a trap-line headquarters and the trail passed its door. The trapper's aid was enlisted to warn the boys of the trap set at the roadhouse.

Within a couple of days the two dog teams pulled into the homestead cabin yard. The trapper was right on the spot. While pouring buckets of hot tea into the boys and filling them with mulligan, bannock, and beans, he recited a horrible tale of vice and how the world had gone wrong. After escaping the RCMP the two dog drivers were indifferent to the ordinary hazards of life. They handed the trapper a quart of whiskey to cheer him up.

Only then did they huddle to hash out a plan to undo the roadblock at the roadhouse. Within the time it takes to skin a rabbit they had roughed out a plan whereby an impossibility could be turned into a probability. Given the right twist of the tail it would unquestionably work. In the part of the valley where the mushers were located stood a rugged mountain barrier with peaks reaching to between four thousand and five thousand feet. There was a divide between the Nazina Valley and McCarthy Creek lying about six miles distant across the ridge. A copper property known as the Green Butte Mine was located on McCarthy Creek and there was a good trail between the mine and the town. The trail led into McCarthy from the rear.

Major difficulty lay in negotiating the high ridge, for the country was not only steep on both sides, but was exceedingly rocky and rough. The ridge had never before been crossed by dog team for the going was difficult even for packhorses which did sometimes use the route. But these were the kind of odds these fellows pitted their wits and skill against for years. Now, with the law enforcement blockage barring further travel down the valley, this served as the most practical alternative route.

The dog drivers sorted out a trail in the steep, rocky mountainside and by dint of much arduous geepole work succeeded in relaying their loads to the top. The loads were reassembled and the downhill pitch began, with much vigorous use of the brake and with rough locks being used in the runners from time to time.

It was gee and haw and easy lads, take 'er easy. And hold up there. Whoa! We're doing fine. Everything's jake. Let's get moving now. An easy pull and we'll be out in the clear.

The boys had the job licked when they reached McCarthy Creek and connected with the Green Butte trail. The last few miles slipped by smoothly and soon the rum-running dog teams were entering McCarthy through the back door. News that two sled loads of bonded stock had hit town caused as much commotion as if a gold strike had been announced. The dog drivers had scarcely unharnessed their tired dogs before the stampede started cash in hand, for scotch, rye, or rum— Who comes first? The stuff unloaded at twenty dollars a quart.

Cases of choice pedigree booze were sold swiftly down to the bare sled strips before the dog mushers had a chance to change their worn socks. McCarthy never lacked a feeling of appreciation for the dog driving clan, and on this occasion the lid bounced off the town and bounced higher than ever before. Corks popped, and there were sounds of revelry through the night and into the next day as the town ruffled its hair, stomped its feet, and whooped.

Meanwhile, out at the roadhouse, the marshal was pacing the floor and expecting any minute to hear word of the dog-teams' arrival. Not until a couple of days after the rum runners reached town did the moccasin telegraph pass on the news. The marshal hurried back to town in time to witness the aftereffects of the appalling coup.

It was one of the few times in his harassed career that the marshal found McCarthy orderly and utterly peaceful. The booze was given credit for bringing about this gratifying condition. The town had been knocked completely out and just about everybody was sound asleep.

The marshal now had only circumstantial evidence to bring charges. There was plenty of that around aside from the empty bottles and the rich aroma hanging over the town. But he was confronted with a different situation than if he had caught the dog drivers cold turkey. To secure a conviction he would have to subpoena unwilling witnesses. Under the circumstances he decided to retain his personal dignity and the respect of the town, and he dropped the matter entirely and returned to his routine duties as peace officer.

12

Finishing the Season

At Chitina mining went on without intermission during the hot days of summer. The cataract roar of the monitor stream pounding gravel could be heard day and night. The labored puffing of the donkey engine and the occasional fusillades of high explosives breaking up the larger boulders were sounds as familiar on the creek as the roar of traffic in metropolitan centers.

Nature does not always use caution when constructing a landscape. In designing Chitina Creek the retreating glaciers left an uncountable number of large boulders behind. The bull gang felt that more economy might have been shown in that respect. The boulders were as thickly clustered as eggs on a dinosaur farm, but the boys could clear a face of boulders in little more than an hour. Chitina was a hard camp on dynamite and every member of the bull gang was a powder monkey as a matter of course.

The largest monster boulder encountered that summer was eight feet through the middle in height and breadth and not less than twelve feet in length. A full box of 120 sticks of dynamite plus an additional twenty sticks were used for the initial shot. The load was placed on top of the boulder and packed heavily with mud. The shot went off like the Fourth of July in McCarthy. The night shift had to pick itself up off the floor. They stood in a frazzled row, dusting off their long underwear and wondering whether Mount Katmai had blown its top again with another volcanic eruption. The day shift swore to get even by blowing something up.

Wet weather arrived with August. Ragged gray clouds scudded low across the sky, bringing sweeping rain that soaked the fire-blackened countryside. The black water in the creek soon went up to flood level. A frothing dark current raced down the sluice. The bull gangs went about their work dressed in sou'westers, rubber raincoats, and hip boots with the tops drawn to the thighs. The rubber armor made for awkward working, but even with seemingly complete protection the driving rain penetrated in places and soaked through to skin. The evenings in camp were rank and steamy. Drying garments hung around and over the stove and the close air was pungent with the smell of tobacco smoke mixed with the acrid odor of drying footwear.

I was told the gamy atmosphere was healthful. It was supposed to grow hair on the chest and make men out of boys. I was not convinced such strong measures were necessary to achieve voting age. All-night daylight was slipping away and we now needed floodlights for night work.

A melancholy feeling permeated the stormy night shifts. A feeling of loneliness crept in with the dampness. A feeling of utter isolation, with us just barely set off from the dark landscape by the floodlights, and of separation from all other life, was almost overwhelming. But this was the miner's life, the Sourdough's usual circumstance.

The Sourdough might not speak English correctly in an English-speaking country, possibly no English at all. And his formal education may not have gone beyond the three R's. But all of that is no barrier to integrity in character and a sound intellect. It was difficult to determine sometimes just how much formal schooling a Sourdough had, for his broad experience, his self-education, and his lively interest in affairs often belied his brief formal education. He read a good deal during his leisure time, which was mostly during the winter months. Aside from newspapers, magazines, and current books, his reading covered most everything under the sun.

It was not uncommon to find such diverse works as Shakespeare, Plato, the Bible, Voltaire, Darwin, Tom Paine, Melville, Nietzsche, Thoreau, Mark Twain, Homer, Conrad, world history by various authors, principles of modern science, home medical advisor, World Almanac, and the latest mail order catalogue, all struggling to reconcile one another's company in the same box of books under a Sourdough's bunk.

Visitors and visiting writers have typed the plain old chap known as Sourdough Bill for being the character most representative of the North. The nomination is probably fair enough. At least there is no real harm in Bill, except for the predilection of keeping people awake at night listening to tall bear stories.

The Sourdough was generally a fairly comfortable person to get along with, and wore well with time. He was an excellent neighbor, minded his own affairs, and was kindly and honest in dealing with others. He was easygoing, reflective, tolerant, had a genial disposition, and viewed affairs broadly, sometimes too philosophically for his own good. He knew what steadfast friendship was—friendship unmoved by adversity or success. Friendship with the Sourdough was a mutual affair that was held in common trust, rather than being a sordid device to be prostituted and traded upon for mercenary self-interest.

He was chary of accepting favors from anyone, unless such favors could be returned in kind. The Sourdough's friendship was based solely upon character, not according to one's bank account or position in life, for both are superficial standards that can go up or down at the turn of the dice. So long as sterling character was represented in the person concerned, Bill showed no distinction in his friendship whether white-collar worker, or common laborer in overalls, whether janitor, mayor, or governor. That is a classless society, but it is not a society of ditch diggers.

Just as the Sourdough knew how to be a steadfast friend, he could also be an implacable foe to those who were bent upon destroying his free manner of living. He was a shrewd judge of character and not easily taken in by sham and deceit. In times of distress, accident, or illness, the Sourdough could be helpful without being intrusive. In doing a good turn he was apt to take a roundabout course, often preferring to remain anonymous as a donor. He could be peppery, sometimes did much growling, but was a poor hand at holding a grudge.

It was the Sourdough's character to be forthright and outspoken in matters of general concern. He was reluctant to attempt forcing an opinion or a decision upon others, but when he felt matters of importance were not as they should be, no one needed to ask where the Sourdough stood. He stated his conviction with a firm, level look in his eye that invited no argument.

After three weeks of almost constant downpours on us, the skies began to clear. The change in weather brought the first sharp pinches of frost. Along the creek, the willow and alder that had escaped the fire were turning crimson and other colors, though it had seemed as if only yesterday they had arrived in smart spring dress. Clustering groups of swallows sallied about the flats, chattering excitedly over the coming adventure of making the long flight south. High overhead, winging their way in a straggling procession, were long files of geese returning from the arctic coastal rim, where winter had already touched down lightly.

The annual migratory process, which had burst so suddenly upon the North with the advent of spring, was reversing itself in step with the receding sun. Thoughts of the miners also began turning to wintertime activities. Camp talk mentioned the caulking of trap-line cabins, laying in stocks of provisions and wood, and sinking prospect holes on creeks that looked likely to pay. There was even some talk of a trip Outside or to Iditarod if perhaps a partner was there. At least one worried-looking fellow canvassed the camp wondering if anyone could sell a couple of dogs.

Fall weather arrived swiftly and spread itself in glory, with cobalt skies and clear, frosty night when the aurora spread lightly on the northern horizon, beginning its first rehearsal for winter's full-dress orchestrations. The gray fugue of August disappeared from the mind as a phantom disappears at daybreak. The air was spiced with a heady tang that raised the spirit.

These clear, frosty mornings made the boys flex their muscles, pound their chest, and occasionally turn loose a lusty war whoop. There was no mystery why moose chose this time of year to do their fighting and rutting. Two weeks of superb fall weather passed. Willow and alder dropped their leaves. The ranks of migrating waterfowl thinned to a few hard-bitten stragglers that would need a boost of hard freezing weather to urge them on.

The days were still warm, but temperatures dropped considerably below freezing every night. Sheets of ice formed on standing pools of water, and in the morning a half inch of ice would be thrown out of the water buckets standing on the porch stoops. The earth was gradually yielding its surface warmth and the lower valleys were often wreathed in their layers of fog during the cool morning hours. At the time of fall equinox the northern climate is changing hands, and the retreating sun can no longer undo the work of advancing winter.

During the last week of September the superintendent appeared on the scene. He looked around the bedrock area, where ice was forming on pools of standing water, wet his finger in the chill air, and decided it was time to shut 'er down. Should an unpredictable cold snap come on, followed by an early freeze-up, it might easily seal the sluice box riffles.

The water was turned off at the monitors for the first time in months, which made the creek sound strangely quiet and after the long season of it throwing off a thundering roar. The final cleaning of the gold was a tedious process due to the large amount of copper residue mixed in. The job was taken over by the superintendent himself, assisted by a couple of the older hands. Magnets were used to iron out residue commonly called "black sand." Other foreign material was washed out or picked out with tweezers. Some of the finer gold was picked up with mercury. When all of the gold was cleaned, it was placed in a strong box and shipped to a government mint in the States.

At the mint the raw gold was melted and formed into bullion along with the residue from hundreds of other cleanups in different parts of the country. The annual production totaled about eighteen million dollars. Thus the annual gold return alone more than doubled the original purchase price of Alaska.

Throughout the mining season we saw much native copper—termed free copper. Nuggets ranged in size from small particles to big slugs weighing several hundred pounds. The copper was corroded, which gave it a greenish cast, and many of the larger nuggets looked like green-hued boulders. However, often scratching the surface with a knife showed pure metal as bright as a new penny. Several dozen nuggets taken from the ground that season weighed from twenty to one hundred pounds. The single biggest slug weighed two hundred pounds and required three men to carry.

When the last day's work was drawing to a close, the boys began dropping into the office to get the paycheck for a full season's work. As everyone packed up, the last ones remaining were the cook and the superintendent, plus two workers. Taking in the silence, the cook declared, "The bloody place sounds like a funeral!"

Bud finished work at the Upper Camp the same day I finished work at the Lower Camp. But we did not go into town immediately. We had seen little of the surrounding countryside during the summer and we planned an outing to neighboring Young Creek lying across the ridge from Chitina. The cook scrounged up some grub for our packsacks and we headed up the creek, crossing the ridge near the head of Calamity Gulch, a Young Creek tributary.

The country was mountainous and good sheep country. We had our rifles, which had been shipped from Montana during the summer, but after looking at the steepness of the country more closely we abandoned the idea of sheep hunting. We were not feeling ambitious enough to pack meat for twelve or fifteen miles back to camp.

We were happy without mutton chops anyway. On reaching Young Creek Valley we found plenty of spruce hens and willow grouse for the frying pan. We had a gold pan with us and as we moved downstream we did a little panning here and there. Young Creek, however, had been well-prospected twenty years before our arrival and had not shown enough pay to make mining profitable.

But gold is where you find it, and we found ours in the countryside. The valley was pleasant country to travel. It was well timbered with spruce, poplar, and birch. We camped under a light tarp each night, bedded on spruce boughs. The weather remained perfect, and after a leisurely outing of several days we headed back across the hills for Chitina.

The camp was still open. The final cleanup was still under way and the cook thought it would be several more days before the job was done and the camp closed for winter. So we ate again, and like Sinbads related our adventure. The cook shook his head. He was of the opinion that a man got enough exercise in a placer mining camp without going out of the way to make the season longer. "I get fallen arches every spring," he said, "just lying in bed thinking about it before the work starts."

We remained in camp that night. The next morning we bid farewell and set off on the trail for town. Our Chitina days were over, but we were not certain of that at the time. We had no definite plans for the future, nor did we have any idea we would remain in Alaska for several more years.

Bud and I still retained the perspective of looking at Alaska as an outsider, quite curious about northern life. We were not yet northerners ourselves because we had no vital interest that bound us to the country. The north is not a place that yields itself to easy acquaintance. We had yet to put taproots down into the Alaska soil.

13

Off-Season

McCarthy was dozing quietly in the early October sunshine on the afternoon Bud and I arrived. We turned in at the Golden Hotel and got the same room I stayed in before. After tidying up we went to O'Neill's store to cash our paychecks. Except for about $180 for current expenses, we left our money on account at the store since the town had no bank.

Before leaving, however, we outfitted ourselves with new wardrobes, from underwear, socks, and shoepacs to Filson breeches with shirt and jacket to match. The comfortable green outfit was almost standard apparel with northerners for informal dress. The comfortable and well-tailored suit was often worn too with a regular suit, but its informal tone would sometimes result in a cold stare from headwaiters in smart cafés. More than one Sourdough returning north from a trip to the States laughed at the darned fools that couldn't tell the difference between a twelve-dollar shirt and a white-collar job bought for sixty-nine cents at a fire sale.

Back at the hotel we took turns with the bathtub and shaving mirror. That removed some of the spruce pitch from our hair and when we got dressed up in our new clothes we felt so civilized we shook hands with each other just to get acquainted again. We went up the street to a restaurant and ordered a steak dinner and later met a couple of our Chitina friends. That in turn led us to making the acquaintance of several bar owners. Everyone we met was friendly and said howdy. There was no evidence of the riot and mayhem for which the town was famous.

For a moment we were disillusioned that McCarthy did not live up to its reputation, but the next day we noticed a man with a black eye and a swollen welt on the cheekbone. Heavens to Betsy, this character was one of our peace-loving Chitina miners. He was a big Swede who worked in the Upper Camp. It seemed that he had invested a large portion of his paycheck with one of the girls on the line and her rival had wrapped a mop handle around the delinquent's ears, poor man. Most of the Chitina men had left town. Those that remained stretched their luck playing poker and pan games.

During the summer at Chitina I learned something of the man who had staked me to twenty dollars and a hotel room when I arrived broke in McCarthy. He was W. E. "Dud" McKinney, an old frontiersman of the original breed that had arrived at Fortymile Camp before the Klondike Gold Rush. He prospected and mined and later operated a roadhouse. He married a Native woman from the Yukon and had a son. After his wife died, Dud returned to prospecting in the White River area. When his body began showing its age he invested in the hotel.

I found Dud at his usual place behind the bar and thought it a good time to repay the loan. I stepped up and began counting out greenbacks and he reached for a bottle of whiskey and a glass. "That's all right, too," I said, "but first I want to square up on the hotel bill and the twenty dollars you loaned me last spring."

Dud ceased polishing the bar to look at me closely with a blank expression. "Me? Loan you twenty dollars?"

"Yes," I replied, surprised that he didn't recognize me. "You must remember it."

There was no sign of recognition in Dud's eyes. He looked me over impersonally, as if I was a strange dog. "Why man, I've never seen you before in my life," he said, "let alone handed you twenty dollars. I have enough trouble hanging on to twenty-dollar bills myself without passing them out to every Tom, Dick, and Harry that comes in here."

I swallowed hard, counted to ten, and recounted my story of walking to McCarthy. Dud listened as if he was hearing an account from a drunken man. And then he pushed the money back to my side of the bar, walked to the end, and stood with his back to me, staring out the window. The rudeness of the man was infuriating and for a moment I was speechless. Abruptly, I pushed the money back. Once again he said with a scowl on his face, "I don't know what you're talking about." He said it with heat in his voice. "I keep track of everybody who comes and goes in this dump."

I was equally hot. He demanded my name and when this event supposedly happened. He picked up a ledger and looked through it, then slammed the cover shut. "You don't owe anything in this house," he said, "or otherwise it would be in the book."

I shouted back that I didn't care if it was in the book or not, I owed the money. Finally, steaming, he stepped forward and scooped the bills from the bar. Then he jabbed his finger at the bottle and said, "Now drink. Drink up and that's on the house."

It was more than a year after this incident that I made the surprising discovery that some old frontiersmen had their own methods for investigating character. If you passed muster it was impossible for others to discredit your integrity through malicious gossip or rumor. Apparently, this was how Dud did it.

Bud and I encountered one of the old-timers as he cleaned out his cabin. He unloaded a bunch of literature on us, but before we got too immersed in get-rich schemes for Alaska, we tore ourselves away and threw it in the rubbish. Instead, we took on the job of painting Bob Marshall's store. While Bud and I painted we discussed the idea of taking over the old-timer's cabin for twenty dollars a month.

The cabin was located on the outskirts of town on the Green Butte Trail and was the only one around except for an unoccupied cabin next door. We were only a ten-minute walk from the main street of town. The cabin had two rooms, one a large front room with a wood-burning heater, and a couple of bunks on one sidewall. Several chairs and a table were also included. The kitchen was small, but adequate for our needs. The cabin contained a small cookstove, cupboards, and an inside pitcher pump.

We had worn our new Filson duds for about four straight days, but now we laid them aside for work clothes. The old iron pants and canvas-patched shirts were not less comfortable, anyway, and were appropriate for the next few days of mopping and scrubbing. A new stovepipe went into the heater. Pots, pans, dishes, and kettles were washed. We stockpiled groceries and set up a sourdough crock for flapjacks. A load of wood was landed in the yard and sawed to length and stacked behind the house. Oh, we also bartered a gallon jug of bootleg liquor from one of the bar owners. We considered this a necessity in case somebody's St. Bernard had to be rescued in a blizzard.

There was no official housewarming party, but whenever any of the neighbors or one of the Chitina boys showed up we pulled out the jug with the gusto of proud hosts and sat around discussing local affairs, Prohibition, or mining with the air of experienced hands who knew their way around. Strangely enough, since moving to the cabin, rather than looking for something else to occupy us, Bud and I were contented with our routine existence. While living at the hotel or anywhere else we had been restless and talked vaguely of plans. We didn't think we were cut out for a country where we had to spend six months in town doing nothing in order to work the same job each summer.

We felt we would get in a rut following such a course and although we enjoyed it, the move to the cabin had not solved the problem. At the moment we were simply coasting. Still, we were becoming part of the community, taking an interest in small affairs, acting more like residents than tourists. We were now beyond mere spectators looking on at the game while others played it. The conditions of life in the North, whether we understood them yet or not, were becoming a matter of vital concern to us.

There were midterm elections that year and as usual McCarthy was the bone of contention for many politicians. Oh, there was mudslinging and name calling and Prohibition enforcement headed the list of issues for some politicians. McCarthy was the whipping post where political issues were flogged. What a damnable viper's nest of iniquity, with its cribs and bootleggers and uninhibited lawlessness—and its loaded guns! One had to keep up with the electioneering handouts to learn about all of the scandalous affairs allegedly going on in one's front yard.

Then, from the midst of this recriminatory shelling and political battle smoke stepped forth a hero. A staunch defender of McCarthy's insurgent stand, he was a Fairbanks attorney, running against the incumbent Republican delegate. The territory's delegate to Congress had not been sparing in his castigation and condemnation of McCarthy. The town embraced the upstart when he sailed into port bearing the legend, "It is a foul bird that dirties its own nest!"

Despite the high tide of public approbation, the political rally held in the Arctic Brotherhood Hall was orderly. The only incident was the late arrival of a sporting couple twenty minutes into the proceedings. Clearly, he and his lady friend had thrown the logbook overboard and were navigating by the stars. All would have gone well if there had been room for them to dock midhall. But the place was crowded and the only seats available were down front, directly under the speaker's stand. The couple was on their last tack for those seats when the gentleman quietly folded his sail and fell in a heap in the aisle within three paces of the platform. The lady weaved around unsteadily, a glassy stare fixed on her helpless partner. Reaching down, she made an ineffectual attempt to drag the unconscious gentleman to his feet. But the effort was too much. After a couple of tugs, she too folded, and fell in a shapeless heap across the other's inert form.

From his place on the platform, the defender of McCarthy's honor was ogling the scene taking place directly under his nose. His words seemed to be coming from a very great distance and were trailing off into hesitant sentences, with long spaces in between. It made no difference as no one was any longer listening. All eyes were turned on the unfortunate couple, some in amusement, some in anger, and some in disgust. As the speaker came to an abrupt halt in his discourse, a half dozen men rose from the audience, picked up the vanquished pair, and neatly removed them feet first into the cool night air.

The candidate poured a glass of water, took a long, studied drink, and allowed enough time for the stunned expression on his face to change to one of calm resignation. Then with Olympian concentration launched forth into higher affairs of state and avoided any comment on McCarthy's bootlegging business.

Bootlegging was McCarthy's avocation. Its occupation was freighting and its profession was driving dogs. There were few places on earth where dog-teaming was followed with more avid interest than this frontier town.

The sled-dog population numbered around two hundred dogs. This was a low figure for McCarthy. In previous years, when freighting into Shushanna was at its peak, there had been more than four hundred dogs quartered in or near the town. Frosty fall weather put the dogs in concert form. The air was filled with their barking and howling and bickering complaints at being chained to their kennels. No one in town seemed to mind the racket. They had grown accustomed to hearing it for years and scarcely noted the noisy bedlam at feeding time each evening.

Old hands at dog-teaming actually claimed they had insomnia when the dogs were not howling a dirge. There was probably some truth in this. One could develop an ear for this wolfish plaint, just as some people acquire a taste for the wailing and sobbing of modern jazz. All night long, every night, the dogs rehearsed their repertoire in resonant sharps and flats. The malamute chorus was the recurring theme not only in McCarthy, but in every village and river settlement. Future composers will have to reckon with that wild refrain of wilderness solitude when scenes are written for northland overtures and symphonies.

Hard October frosts had seared the countryside brown. Ice was beginning to form along the edge of the rivers and the moist earth was frozen with a solid crust already several inches thick. The retreating sun in its shortening daily circuit was losing its daytime warmth and night temperatures dropped as low as zero. The air changed from clear and crisp at the start of the month to fretful near the end. The skies clouded and a chill north wind swept down from the glacier country, bringing with it the first snowfall of the season. When the storm clouds cleared the drab earth had been transformed as though by magic into a strange new world glistening pure white.

The morning after the first snow there was merry bedlam at the kennels. The dogs were hitched for the first workout of the season. From our cabin on the other side of town Bud and I were on the lookout for the first passing teams. Soon we sighted them, several dog teams racing pell-mell through the streets as if they had been shot from a gun. The sleds were careening in wide arcs as they swept around corners and the drivers swayed and balanced on rear runners like ballet dancers. The oncoming teams hit straightaway on the Green Butte Trail.

They approached us at breakneck speed and swept past. One, two, three, four dog teams closely spaced, with the drivers riding the runners with a jaunty air as though these unleashed hurricanes were controlled at a word. The running dog teams seemed to confirm the fact that we were living in the North. We stood in the yard, staring after the disappearing teams until they passed from sight around a distant bend.

The full-dress procession returned in a couple of hours. The hell-bent-for-leather pace had slowed to a jogging trot and the dogs' tails were down and their tongues lolled. Now the dogs were content to be headed for their kennels. Despite being weary at the moment, we knew the same cannonball rush would happen all over again the next day. Within a couple of weeks they would settle down to a normal pace.

Winter transportation depended largely on dog teams, and the work of hauling mail, freight, and passengers continued through the deep cold, the gales, and blinding blizzards. Throughout the North, within a month, a veritable spiderweb of trails would lead through mountain passes and along frozen river courses, and across trackless tundra. Dog-teaming would go on without respite until the hot sun of late spring gutted the river ice and wiped the snow trails out of existence.

14

Dog-teaming—Origin of a Mistake

An old dog driver said this: "I swear by Christopher it was the worst mistake I ever made the day I hitched up my first dog team. If ever I had this life to live over again I'd stay clear of dogs, even if I had to tie myself to a stump with a logging chain. For more than twenty years now I've been running my legs down to nubs and nearly every season I come out on the short end owing bills. A man is a fool to keep going like that year after year. But once you start in driving dogs you're plain ruined for living like a civilized human."

It is a mistake, chorus all the dog-driving hands, to be everlastingly caught up with feeding a pack of howling malamutes, to be eternally patching up busted harnesses, wiring smashed sleds, cleaning kennels, doctoring cuts, trimming toenails, and forever be breeding, raising, and breaking in another litter of pups. You just keep on going further and further into the hole and the harder you try to pull yourself out, the deeper you get in.

Trouble is, a man makes the mistake the first day he starts driving dogs, and anybody with a lick of sense would never let himself in for it. The experiences of those professional pessimists served as a warning to Bud and me not to get messed up in dog-teaming affairs. There was no need for it, either. We were comfortably settled in our cabin and we had not a worry in the world. We got up in the morning when we felt like it, ate two, three, or four meals a day, took the occasional hike around the countryside, and spent half the night reading books borrowed from neighbors.

Bud had a sudden stroke of ambition one day and talked of continuing a correspondence course in chemistry, which he had let drop in Montana. However, he was back to normal the following day and returned from town with an armful of normal books. Things might have gone on in this leisurely fashion if it had not been for fate.

On an evening several days after the first snowfall we were lying in our bunks reading when there was a knock on the door. Destiny does not always use Morse code and we failed to recognize this as being anything more than a normal knock. Of course, it turned out to be. Upon opening the door we found one of our Chitina friends, Fred Trustad, sweeping fresh snow from his shoepacs. Fred was a sturdy Norwegian and a hard-working Sourdough. He was quiet and reflective, a man with an easy smile, and inclined to sober habits. For more than a quarter of a century in the North he had followed prospecting and trapping with the seasons, and mixed in occasional summers in placer mining camps. We considered him a special friend and in our enthusiasm to do the right thing we pulled out the visitors' jug to make him feel perfectly at home.

For half an hour we sat around talking about mining and other things, and on the second or third, or maybe even the fourth, round of sipping from the jug, Fred came to the point of his visit. He had a small problem that gave him some concern, he told us. He explained that he had a partner prospecting in the Tonsina Valley about a hundred miles distant in another part of the Copper River watershed, and his partner had been carrying on negotiations to take on certain mining claims. They looked as if they might show fair pay. The claims, located in the area where his partner prospected, were owned by a party in the States. Negotiations had been going on for some time and only that morning Fred had received a wire from his partner informing him the deal had been closed.

Fred hoped to catch the train leaving Kennecott the following morning and join his partner waiting for him at Chitina. However, it looked as if he might be delayed because he had a small trap-line outfit that he wanted to dispose of before leaving town. He had trapped the Upper Chitina Valley during the previous winter and the outfit consisted of two young dogs, a sled, and a considerable amount of trail gear. Fred thought we might be interested in taking the outfit off his hands to do a spot of trapping, or just to get around the countryside during the winter.

The outfit was out at the Nazina Roadhouse where the dogs were being boarded and their board bill was paid to the end of the month. It was Fred's idea that we take the outfit, but if we decided not to keep it we might sell it as opportunity offered and even make a little profit on the deal. Given his circumstances and his need to hurry, he was willing to accept half price on the approximate full value of the outfit. It was in his interest to make a quick cash sale. If we gave him $150 we could take the whole outfit.

Bud and I took the offer under consideration, in the meantime not forgetting to pass the jug around and around. Our reticence to cut a deal was not unlike the kind of maidenly modesty that is surprised when the proposal is forthcoming which had been considered all along as the inevitable outcome of wooing affairs. Bud and I were not sure we were ready to become wedded to a dog musher's life.

We realized we knew nothing about the inter-related affairs that were linked to dog-teaming and lack of that knowledge in the wilderness could prove fatal. The simple fact that one owned a dog team did not make one a dog musher, for anyone could learn to drive a dog team on a well-traveled trail as easily as one learns to drive a car. Such runabout travel close to town was simply another form of outdoor sport like skiing or skating, and had little relation to dog-teaming insofar as general utility was concerned. For all practical purposes, dog-teaming was not a field for novices.

Mushing required ability to get around in the trackless wilderness, to break your own trail, to find your way through the hills, to live partially off the country, to survive emergencies arising from weather conditions and natural hazards of various kinds. Old dog mushers with wide experience usually considered their first three or four years at dog-teaming being an apprenticeship. That was confirmed by Natives who since time beyond written record had lived in the wilderness. Although they knew the country intimately and had adapted to its conditions, they were sometimes caught in death traps or otherwise perished through starving or freezing in the common course of hunting, trapping or traveling. The wilderness presented problems that were so elementary that one either solved them or died because one didn't.

Classrooms did not offer the type of education one needed for the trail. The dog driver started in where even woodcraft books left off. And no matter how long he stayed with the business he was always learning a few more things and developing new ideas. The dog musher's handbook was never complete where one could slap an index at the end of it. He was still writing new chapters when airplanes took over as the main means of transportation in the country.

Conditions varied greatly in the North, all according to terrain and climate at different localities, and the problems encountered were numerous and diversified. How did one live in a place where treacherous ice fields had to be crossed as a matter of course year after year, and where a musher knew others had lost their lives? By what sorcery was tons of freight hauled by dog team through incomparably rough country, where foot travelers with only a packsack on their backs had been known to give up in despair and return the way they had come? How did one survive storms of the utmost ferocity when caught in an emergency affording no protection?

What was the gauge of a man's ability to overcome every natural obstacle and make his way through wilderness, sometimes for hundreds of miles, where others attempting the same route failed to get anywhere, and sometimes perished? How did a man find his way unerringly across confusing divides, where others strayed and became lost? How did one travel with certainty in thick weather and blizzards when others, even though having lived in the North for years, had been known to stray from a village, lose themselves, and freeze to death within rifle shot of their cabins?

What incantations were invoked in making camp on the trail where one sat around comfortably in weather that was fifty degrees below zero? What sort of crafty insight enabled a winter traveler to negotiate hundreds of miles on rivers, which in places were only partially frozen over, without once finding a concealed weak spot for a fatal breakthrough into the swift current?

These were some of the problems that Bud and I had been turning over in our minds in connection with dog-teaming affairs. Each problem represented situations in which we knew lives had been lost either through lack of know-how or through accidents occurring due to carelessness. Yet those conditions had to be overcome if one's life was not to be confined to the vicinity of towns or restricted to such travel as was offered on beaten trails. Only through experience did one gain proficiency in overcoming natural odds.

But in gaining experience we inexperienced Cheechakos came directly up against the problems requiring experience. In our minds the entire matter was a vicious circle, with no logical or safe beginnings. The northern wilderness was the kind of country that did not allow for a blundering course of trial and error. In this country one made mistakes at risk to life or limb, with the odds as a rule against the gambler. Such a direct challenge as we anticipated was made in the face of a dire dictum which warned that the first mistake could easily be the last.

When we admitted to our lack of confidence in undertaking tackling of the Bush by ourselves, our Sourdough friend smiled. "You fellows are in the same shape I was in nearly thirty years ago when I first came north. I found out the only way to get experience is to go out and get it. I know a lot of fellows don't see it that way. Valdez was full of them, hundreds of fellows. They were husky fellows, too, some of them, but they hardly got one foot off of the beach. Plenty of big talk and noise, but they were scared, every one of them. They lay around and rotted, got scurvy, and most of them ended up going right back Outside again."

The Sourdough's comments were hitting pretty close to the bull's eye. Bud reached for the jug on the floor and took a long swig before passing it over to me. Fred continued talking. "Of course you'll have to break your neck a few times," he said. "Everybody does that when they're first getting started. But you've got to use a little good judgment, too. After you've been through a couple of jackpots you begin to catch on and don't make as many mistakes. That's the important thing about learning. Don't ever be caught making the same mistake twice."

Bud gazed at Fred thoughtfully. "What if you don't live through the first mistake," he said. "A fellow doesn't gain much by killing himself off."

Fred issued a bemused smile, but didn't answer directly. He took the jug and lifted it for a pull and absently passed it back to Bud again. "After you've lived through your first year in this country," the old Sourdough said, "you'll find that things ease up a little. It's the first year that's rough and that's the time you're doing most of your learning. I've noticed that most fellows that go belly up do it in the first year, and then they give up trying. But you don't want to do everything all at once. Take it easy for a while until you get the hang of the ropes. Then the next thing you know, you'll be spitting snoose, and kicking dogs around, and telling the other fellow how to do it."

Bud and I had been in the country for a bit and worked through a mining season. We were not complete tenderfeet. We felt we were starting to understand the North a little bit.

"Getting started isn't half as bad as it looks," Fred said. "But you don't get anyplace just sitting around talking about it. Sure you take chances. Everybody does. Look at all of the people that get killed just trying to cross the street in cities Outside. It never gets as bad as that up here, even at its worst. A man has to take chances, no matter what he does. Some fellows take their chances playing poker. I'd rather take mine doing some prospecting. The odds are about the same either way. But a man gets more enjoyment out of life following prospecting than he does losing his money at a card table."

Then he reminded us of what Bud and I had already learned. The North was different. It was darned difficult to make a living year in and year out just working for someone else.

"If you figure on working just for wages," Fred said, "you might as well throw in the towel right now. It costs you everything you can make during the summer season just to keep yourself alive during the winter. And what for? Just so you can go back and do it all over again next summer? And sometimes you don't even make that much. There's fellows here in McCarthy and in Cordova that end up owing bills every spring. It isn't because they aren't careful, either. They aren't even living good. You fellows don't want to do that. You're young. You've got your lives ahead of you. If you use a little head work you can rustle some kind of proposition for yourselves.

"There's much more to it than that, too. If you don't rustle something up where you can make your own living you'll find yourselves being kicked all around by the big fellows. Being your own boss is pretty important in this country, and if you aren't your own boss it can be a pretty mean hell. If you have something of your own, even if you go to one knee sometimes and take wages to grubstake yourself, you always have something to fall back on if it gets rough."

The big outfits, he said, would treat us like dogs, or not even as well as dogs get treated. He made a convincing case for us to think about. "So you fellows have nothing to lose, even if you lose everything making a try," Fred added.

His pep talk, or sales pitch, however you want to look at it, was winding up. "Go out and get the experience so you know what you're doing. That's the only way you'll ever have any independence in this country. You'll not be tied down to town life and you can come and go as you please. Of course it will be rough for a while, until you get started. Later, you'll find out that you had the most valuable experiences life can offer."

15

Adopt-a-Team

It was late the following morning when I began returning to consciousness. My throat was parched and my head was pounding like a cost-plus-ten-percent riveting job. The atmosphere reeked with the stench of stale alcohol. While trying to recall where I was and what had happened my meditations were disturbed by the funereal tolling of a bell. I knew then I had been caught making my first mistake and fell into a small panic.

The devil had been on the job and without giving me a chance to explain the error he had pitch-forked me straight into hell. It was a frightful jackpot and I began to consider the possibility of prying my way out through a ventilator. Realizing that I would need assistance to jimmy the joint I raised myself to one elbow and turned loose a shout: "Hey, Bud! Are you here?"

There was silence for a full half minute. Then came a stirring from the other bunk, "Whash a-matter with you?" was the muffled reply. "Can't you shleep?"

The sound of the tolling bell was interrupted by the short blast of a whistle. "It's time to get up!" I shouted. "The train from Kennecott is just pulling out from the depot."

Bud dozed for a while longer before turning over in his bunk for a look at the clock. "Criminy," he said sleepily. "We forgot to go down and see Fred off. I hope he shucked the sheets in time to catch the rattler." And after that showing of consciousness Bud turned to the wall again, pulled the blankets over his head, and went back to sleep.

The outlook for the day seemed bleak as a hobo's Christmas. Propping myself up on one side of the bunk I discovered that I had gone to bed with my clothes and shoepacs on, which saved me the trouble of getting dressed. There was nothing I needed so much as a good drink of water, and feeling my way out to the kitchen, I drank half a bucketful before hanging up the dipper.

Since I was already on my feet I decided to establish a few control points and went about getting a fire started in the kitchen stove for making coffee. I was fanning smoke up the chimney when Bud began stirring in the other room and I could hear him talking to himself about having lost one of his shoepacs. Served Bud right. If he had kept his shoepacs on his feet where they belonged, he wouldn't have to be looking for them.

By the time Bud staggered out to the kitchen I had one lid off the stove and the coffee pot was setting on a roaring fire. Bud reached for the dipper and drank the rest of the water in the bucket. We wondered why we hadn't thought of buying aspirin at the same time we bought the bootleg. We washed our faces in cold water, but that didn't seem to improve the day. When the coffee boiled we sat down at the kitchen table to drink a couple of cups apiece. We should have felt better after that. But I knew I didn't and Bud looked worse, so we pumped another bucket of water and put on some more coffee.

Bud was using thumbs for fingers trying to roll a smoke and after lighting up he turned a puckered eye in my direction. "What time did Fred leave last night?" he asked. I had no more of an idea of how or when the party ended than Bud did, and I replied, "How should I know? I was already in bed."

"You were?" Bud said. "Where was Fred then?"

"Fred? Don't you remember? You were sitting there talking to him when I turned in."

Bud looked at me unbelievingly for a moment, and then gave up the thought. We had another cup of coffee and cooked up some flapjacks and fried eggs for breakfast. We were still sitting at the table when Bud had another thought. "Didn't we buy a shotgun, or a toboggan, or something like that last night?" he asked. "Seems to me I remember Fred writing out a bill of sale."

"If he did, I don't remember it," I replied, my speech still a little bit thick. "Look in your pocket. You probably have it if there's anything like that around."

Bud went through his shirt pockets, his pants pockets, then pulled out his billfold and searched through that. "We must have bought something," he said darkly. "All I've got here is six bucks. Yesterday, I had seventy or eighty dollars."

I reached for my billfold and examined the contents. I found no more than twenty dollars where there had been something close to a hundred dollars the day before. "There must be a bill of sale somewhere," I said. "Look in the other room. Maybe it's in the writing tablet."

While Bud was doing some further searching in the front room I found what we were looking for in one of my shirt pockets. The folded piece of paper was rumpled since I had slept on it. I announced my discovery and Bud and I pushed aside the breakfast dishes and smoothed the paper out on the table. In bold, firm handwriting (must have been Fred's) the particulars of the sale read:

To Whom It May Concern,

For cash in hand the following trap-line outfit has
been sold to George Guiler and Ted Lambert, to wit—
1 black dog. Name Rex, 2 years old.
1 brown dog. Name Spike, 2½ years old.
2 sets of dog harnesses new.
1 Yukon sled.
1 8 x 10 trail tent.
1 Yukon stove and stovepipe.
1 .250 3000 Savage rifle new.
1 .22 Winchester repeating rifle.
3 dozen traps various sizes.
1 box pots, pans, dishes, etc.
1 pair snowshoes.
1 pole ax.
1 gunnysack containing parka, cartridges, tools, snare wires,
   sled riggings, repair kit, and other misc. items.

Fred Trustad.

The discovery that we had one foot in dog-mushing affairs came as an intrusion
to our leisurely existence and forced us to make a decision that otherwise might
have been delayed indefinitely. We wondered vaguely what we were going to do
with the outfit. Two dogs were not enough to make a team and we had to consider
buying more dogs or getting out of the business by selling the two we now owned.
We talked things over and in the end decided to keep the outfit.

During the afternoon we rustled up a couple of unused kennels and moved
them into the backyard. The kennels were cleaned, sprayed with disinfectant, and
given a good bedding of straw salvaged from packing cases. We bought a pan for
cooking dog food and a couple of tin wash basins to serve as feeding pans. We
also bought a bale of dried dog salmon, some tallow, and a hundred-pound sack
of cornmeal for dog food. By the end of the day we had added another $30 to our
original investment of $150 and we hadn't even seen the dogs.

Early the next morning we set out on the trail over Sourdough Hill, heading
for the Nazina Roadhouse. We stepped along briskly for it was our intention to
return to town with the dogs and sled before nightfall. The new snow was already
packed into a dog-sled trail by teams traveling across the hill. But as yet the snowfall was light and the sled runners were piling onto the bare ground in places. We
made good time on our hike and around 1 P.M. turned into the roadhouse. Murie was
out in the yard splitting wood and seemed surprised to see us. "You buckos are a

little early to start another mining season," he said. "Thanksgiving and Christmas have to come around first, and then New Year's and St. Patrick's Day. But I've got a lot of wood to cut in case you need some exercise."

"Thanks," I said, "but we're not looking for work. It was such a nice day that we thought we would come this way and pay you a friendly visit."

The roadhouse man smiled expansively. "Oh, fine," he said. "Meals one buck and three dollars for the bed. But tell me, what are you sports really up to? Is town life really so bad that you had to come all of the way out here just for some fresh air?"

"Our trip," Bud replied importantly, "has to do with business affairs. We are now dog mushers and we came out here to get our dog team." He took an impressive pause and Bud added, "That is if two dogs make a dog team."

An incredulous look came across Murie's face. He passed the look from one to the other of us, and then broke into hearty laughter. "Ha, ha, ha," laughed Murie. "Ha, ha, ha. And there I was all of the time thinking what nice boys they were. Now look at them—dog mushers! Ha, ha, ha."

Murie's attitude was no surprise. We were well aware of the long-winded debates that went on between dog drivers and teamsters. The teamsters claimed they could do more freighting at half the cost with their horses than a half-dozen dog drivers working relays. Actually, there were little grounds for argument. The horses and dog teams had their respective places in winter transport.

Dog teams could move supplies into remote localities that were ordinarily inaccessible to horse-drawn sleds. And most of the mail on winter routes, as well as much incidental freight, was hauled by dog teams. Still, for heavy work around the mining camps and settlements and on winter stage lines where barns with hay and grain could be provided, the horses were used.

Not wishing to disclose our plans for competing with the rival teamsters we explained to Murie that we had bought the outfit as more or less a matter of speculation. While the conversation continued, Bud fished into his billfold to withdraw our crumpled piece of paper.

"Maybe you got it," Bud said.

"Got what?" I said.

"The bill of sale," Bud said. "Or maybe we left it behind in the cabin."

Murie waved the idea aside and laughed some more. "I know the stuff you're looking for," he said. "The sled and the rest of the outfit is over at the cache. As for the dogs, anybody can have them, bill of sale or not. I gave up driving dogs years ago when I learned better. But I'll swear that running a roadhouse is nearly as bad sometimes as dog teaming."

Murie led us over to the cache where he pointed at a Yukon sled leaning against the building. We pulled the sled into the yard. Then Murie took us inside the shed and showed us where the rest of the outfit was stacked against the wall.

The plunder seemed like quite a load for such a small sled. The sack of traps was heavy considering the light snow on the trail. We talked the matter over and decided to take only the rifles and the tent, leaving the rest of the outfit for Murie to bring on his next trip to town.

"A hundred pounds or so extra makes no difference to the horses," he said. "Always glad to help out my friends."

When we finished sorting through the trail gear, we went across the yard for a look at the dogs. They had been sitting on top of their kennels while the palaver was going on, but seeing the sled pulled into the yard they began showing keen interest in the proceedings. As we approached they jumped to the ground and pranced around exuberantly, stretching their chains. The actions invited us to roughhouse with them. They were fine, big dogs, not the least mean or surly. It was easy to tell they had been given good handling.

"I wonder which one is the leader," I said. "I can't remember if Fred told us or not."

Murie had the answer. "He [Fred] worked the black fellow in the lead," he said. "There were four dogs in team when Fred came off the trap line last spring, but I don't know what he did with the other two. He must have sold them or their harnesses would be around."

We figured out which dog was Rex and which dog was Spike. We stood in the yard for a while talking about dogs and things in general. But time was pressing and I thought Bud and I had better get started if were going to make it back to town before dark. Murie said, "Oh, you've got lots of time. You'd better come in and get something to eat before starting back. The dogs will make it to town, all right. Don't worry about that. It's you fellows that are liable to play out."

"Oh no, we won't," we both replied. "We're going to ride."

Murie let loose a wild whoop. "Oh, merciful Lord," he shouted in laughing mock horror. "May heaven help the poor dogs."

We intended to take turns riding the sled just the same. That was the reason we were leaving most of the outfit. What was the use of having a dog team if you couldn't ride? A little later Bud and I went back to the cache to stow some of the duffel's contents. We washed up and sat at the table where Mrs. Murie was putting out a lunch. Murie sipped on a cup of coffee. Mrs. Murie had a sly look on her face as she said, "Murie tells me you boys are going into the dog-driving business. I thought Murie was going to stay with dog-teaming when I married him, but now he spends more money buying hay and grain to feed his horses than it ever cost us keeping dogs."

A surprised and alarmed look spread across Murie's face. "Hey," he said, "whose side are you on, anyway? We skinners are outnumbered badly enough without you joining the opposition."

After lunch we prepared to go. The rifles were wrapped in the tent and lashed onto the sled. We laid out the tow line with the tug lines and neck straps attached.

Meanwhile, the dogs watched the proceedings and the moment we started toward them with the harnesses, they exploded in a frenzy of excitement. They barked and plunged around so much that we wondered how we were ever going to get them harnessed. We chose one dog apiece and moved in. At the end of a two-minute tussle the dogs had unconditionally won the round. The harnesses were in a hopeless tangle.

We laid the harnesses on the ground and began patiently rearranging. The more we passed single lines through back straps and traces over collars, the more involved the mess became. It was difficult to conceive how much of an incredible tangle could develop in two minutes. We knew that dog drivers harnessed a dozen dogs in a jiffy. But how it was done was a mystery to us. After working for ten minutes without success, we finally untangled the harnesses by unbuckling the tugs from the collars.

For our next harnessing attempt we moved in on the dogs cautiously, taking care not to get the harnesses snarled. The dogs had quieted after the last rumpus, but the moment they saw the harnesses again the riot started all over. Bud grabbed his dog and I grabbed mine. There was a brief scuffle mingled with grunts, strangling sounds, and a dog's yelp from a cuff on the nose. The frantic dog between my legs struggled loose, tangled my feet in the chain, and threw me sprawling on the ground.

After freeing myself from the chain I peered over the kennel to see how Bud was making out. On first sight it seemed he had done better than I had. He had succeeded in getting the collar over his dog's head, but the feat had been his undoing. Bud was on his back, feet in the air, with the rest of the harness wrapped around his neck. The dog was frantically trying to free itself from Bud and the harness and Bud was trying to get away from the dog.

We finally got the dogs harnessed by combining our efforts and harnessing one dog at a time. The chains were unsnapped from the kennels and the dogs fairly dragged us across the yard to the sled. Murie was standing by the woodpile with a choked expression on his face. He could see that things had not proceeded by the rules, but offered no advice or assistance.

Bud and I took the chains off the dogs and rushed them into position, hitching the black dog Rex into the lead. I had just hooked Spike into wheel when both dogs lunged, knocking the legs out from under me. Before either Bud or I could make a grab, the dogs and sled were gone. They raced across the yard, tails in the air, with the sled bouncing behind them. Ten seconds later the outfit, dogs and all, swept around the bend and disappeared onto the trail to McCarthy.

Murie was strangely silent and when we looked, we saw him doubled over in throes of laughter. In a moment his head came up, arms flailing in the air. "Oh, ho, ho, ho, oh, ha, ha, ha," he cried. "I never thought I'd see the day—oh, ha, ha—when dog mushers got themselves into a jackpot mess like this."

On the run, we bade Murie farewell with a brief glance and we took off across the yard in hot pursuit of our runaway dogs.

A wedding portrait of Ted and Lovetta Lambert. (Photo courtesy of Pat Lambert.)

A happy family. (Photo courtesy of Pat Lambert.)

Lovetta, cradling infant Pat. (Photo courtesy of Pat Lambert.)

A beaming father Ted, wife Lovetta, and daughter Pat. (Photo courtesy of Pat Lambert.)

One Lambert's favorite painting subjects, an Alaska husky sled dog. (Photo courtesy of Pat Lambert.)

Doting father with baby Pat on his knee. (Photo courtesy of Pat Lambert.)

Artist Ted Lambert taking a smoking break. (Photo courtesy of Pat Lambert.)

Lambert the outdoorsman, equipped with hunting rifle and wearing warm Eskimo mukluks. (Photo courtesy of Pat Lambert.)

A thirty-something Lambert at his easel. After his early days in Alaska working in mining camps and driving dogs, Lambert traveled back to Illinois to study art, then returned to Alaska to paint full-time. (Photo courtesy of Pat Lambert.)

Cordova Express 1908 (1939), 9 × 12 inches, oil on Masonite. (Courtesy of Braarud Fine Art, La Conner, WA.)

Tundra Homestead, 7¾ × 12 inches, oil on Masonite. (Courtesy of Braarud Fine Art, La Conner, WA.)

Goodnews Bay, Winter (1937), 7½ × 10½ inches, oil on board. (Courtesy of Braarud Fine Art, La Conner, WA.)

The Freighter (1947), 16 × 20 inches, oil on canvas. (Courtesy of Braarud Fine Art, La Conner, WA.)

Long Day Ahead (1948), 14 × 18, oil on canvas. (Courtesy of Braarud Fine Art, La Conner, WA.)

Golden Autumn, 8 × 12, oil on board. (Courtesy of Braarud Fine Art, La Conner, WA.)

Camp at Mt. McKinley (1943), 10 × 12 inches, oil on Masonite. (Courtesy of Braarud Fine Art, La Conner, WA.)

Yukon River Fish Camp (1948), 16 × 20 inches, oil on canvas. (Courtesy of Braarud Fine Art, La Conner, WA.)

16

The Dogs Teach Us to Mush

The first mile was covered in record time. We were starting on the second mile when we caught sight of sled tracks abruptly leaving the trail to enter the brush. The dogs had given chase to a rabbit and we found the outfit hung up in a clump of willows. The two vagabonds showed no remorse for their misdeeds. Instead of apologizing, they were tugging energetically on the tow line, expecting us to release them so they could continue the chase.

We collared the dogs, turned the sled around, and marched the dogs back to the trail. When next they started to lunge forward there was order in the affairs. Already we had learned what one mistake could produce. Now we were both riding on the sled.

The dogs tugged along stoutly for a while and even managed a run down the easy pitch. But after traveling a half mile or so they began casting sidelong glances and passed understanding looks between one another. The steady pace began to slacken. We jerked along hesitantly for a ways, made a few tentative stops, and then came to a standstill entirely. Turning around in their harnesses, the dogs eyed us blandly and sat down on their rumps. Apparently, they were through traveling for the day.

Bud and I remained on the sled. "Just because they got away from us at the roadhouse," I said, "they think we're going to let them do it again. Let's teach them a lesson."

So we sat there in one place and taught them a lesson. We spoke in quiet tones, explaining that time was passing and if they wanted any supper they had better get moving. The dogs showed no interest in the conversation. Nor did they pay any interest when we began shouting and waving our arms around threateningly. Our demands to mush went unheeded as though the word belonged solely to pulp fiction. There was only one tactic left in our repertoire.

We took a long breath and cut loose with a lurid vocabulary that we had learned from old Montana mule skinners. These were the kind of blazing oaths that set prairie grass afire. The terrible verbal barrage brought a flicker of recognition to the dogs' ears, but earned not one step of travel.

The hour was getting late and the air chilly. There was nothing to be done, but arrange a compromise where one man would ride the sled and the other ran along behind. We felt this arrangement would keep us attuned to any changes in the dogs. Should the dogs take sudden flight in pursuit of rabbits or ptarmigan at least one of us could report the position of the outfit by sending up a smoke signal.

The one-man riding arrangement seemed to be just what the dogs were after. When the sled started with a push, the dogs jumped to their feet and set off down the trail at an easy lope. The hard-jarring run continued across the flats and over the bridge. While ascending the hill the dogs pulled the sled unburdened, but upon reaching the crest of the hill, we began taking turns riding again. Several miles were covered and we were a little more than halfway to town when the dogs began holding conversations again. Having successfully unloaded one man they conspired to unload the other. Bud and I discovered what their conversations were about when they jumped the trail and dove into some brush. The action plainly implied that they had done their share of the work and now it was their turn to do the riding.

Now we were really in trouble. Our main trouble was that Bud and I were not really dog drivers. We knew nothing about handling sled dogs and the dogs had known it from the first minute they laid eyes on us.

Bud and I talked the situation over and we decided this sort of rebellion had to be dealt with firmly. I cut a willow switch and collared the lead dog first, then grabbed the other. I gave both of them several good swats on their rumps. The dogs were pulled back to the trail again and ordered to mush. The unruly pair took one sidelong look at Bud sitting on the sled and they promptly dove into the willow patch again.

We were already disgusted with dog-teaming. Throwing the switch away, I sat down on the sled with Bud and rued the day we ever thought we might take up mushing. After a while Bud stood up and pounded his arms around his body in order to keep warm. It was already dark and we were six miles from town.

"It looks like we're going to have to give up riding the sled," Bud said. "Otherwise we might as well walk back to the roadhouse and get a fresh start in the morning."

Grudgingly, I conceded that the dogs had won the contest. We tied an extension cord to the short tail rope so both of us could hang on if the dogs should take a notion to leave us behind. The dogs were pulled onto the trail again and to get them started Bud ran ahead, shouting and whooping. I gave the sled a push. The dogs started hesitantly, traveling with a sideways trot, all the while casting suspi-

cious looks around to see if our intentions were on the level. Then they straightened out and broke into a hard loping run. Bud's feet were already flying when the
dogs passed him and he just managed to catch hold of the tail rope.

The remaining miles were covered at a man-killing marathon pace that would
have given old grandpa Pheidippides trouble. We were still doing a mild six miles
per hour when we rounded the hill above town. We threw ourselves on the sled
for a ride down the grade to the bridge spanning McCarthy Creek. Our outfit
straggled in a disorderly file through the streets of town. But at least we arrived as
one party, dogs, sled, mushers.

Bud and I were stretcher cases, but the dogs were in finest fettle. They were enthusiastic over the social possibilities offered in town life and inspected their kennels with busy snuffings and wettings. As for Bud and me we were less enthusiastic
about becoming dog drivers than we had been earlier in the day. After feeding the
dogs and eating supper downtown, we pulled off our clothes, dosed our stiffened
joints with liniment, and straightaway went to bed.

Our days of carefree leisure before we got mixed up with the dogs seemed to
be a year ago, not merely a day before. We knew now we had made a mistake, but
we didn't realize how much of a mistake it was. Had we known then we would be
involved in mushing for the next seven years we might have given it up right then.

Or yet again, perhaps not.

The day after we brought the dogs to town we should have had a doctor help
us out of bed. We were stiff and sore in every joint and we were saturated with liniment. We smelled like a family of skunks that had lost a shooting argument with
themselves. But the liniment may have helped our recovery. On the second day at
home we were limbered up enough to hitch up the dogs for a short run.

Thereafter we made almost daily runs around the countryside. It was the peak
time of year in the rabbit cycle and Bud and I began picking off rabbits with a .22
for cooking in the dog food. The dogs enjoyed these excursions and at every opportunity they took off in chase of rabbits themselves. We envied the dog drivers
whose teams were well behaved and seemed to take work seriously.

Bud and I decided we were using too many words and not enough English to
point our dogs in the right direction. When Murie brought the rest of our outfit
to us, we rummaged around and found a whip. The whip was of a very junior size.
It was just a whip stock removed from the kind stout matrons carry to keep stray
terriers from mixing with their poodles when the pets are being aired in the park.
The next day we brought the whip out and showed it to the dogs. Thereafter they
showed some moderation in their pranks.

Bud and I took our daily hunting trips, but when we retreated to town we
prowled around looking for some more dogs. We were up against it as the fall
work season was beginning. There were scores of dogs in town, but none were for

sale. In dog-teaming a good lead dog is invaluable and seldom does such a prized dog change hands. Other dogs pinch-hit in lead occasionally, but the best true leaders were born, not made. As a rule, if a man considered selling his leader, the other dogs and the rest of the outfit were sold, too.

The price of a good sled dog was commonly fifty dollars. Some of the top freight dogs were valued at considerably more, if they could be purchased at all. I heard of instances where seventy or one hundred dollars had been paid for such a dog. A full-blood timber wolf, reared from a litter of pups captured in a den in the wild, was occasionally kept by dog drivers for breeding. The offspring of a wolf crossed with the better sled-dog made for some of the toughest and best draft dogs in the North.

The wolf itself is a temperamental animal and not generally to be trusted, even when raised in captivity. A well-matched sled-dog team of superior dogs could move almost anything that wasn't frozen down. Nearly all northern sled dogs of the better stock have a touch of wolf blood in their makeup. The purpose for breeding the timber wolf was to obtain large, powerful, clean-limbed, big-chested dogs that were strong-winded, tough, and displayed endurance under all conditions. The most important quality might have been the offspring having clean, tough feet. The timber wolf had matchless strength and endurance, but could not be worked in harness. The killer instinct in the wolf was not to be trusted around humans or dogs. There were rumors from time to time about tame wolves working in dog-teams, but it is doubtful that ever occurred.

Dog drivers are confirmed innovators. They are not content unless they are inventing, experimenting, rebuilding, or improving something. Over the years, dog drivers, individually and collectively, originated and put into use several kinds of harnesses, and devised the double hitch knot. They invented the "weegie board," something shaped like a sawed-off surfboard, so drivers could stand more comfortably on the back of sleds. The dog-driving clan either originated or improved upon at least a half-dozen different types of sleds and toboggans. The dog driver often incorporated his own artful ideas.

Nearly all dog drivers carried rifles as part of their regular equipment. The .30-06 and the .30-30 caliber were the most popular for general use. Nothing was more important than experimenting with the breeding of dogs. It cost no more to keep a good dog than a bad one and since dogs were expensive to keep no more were kept than the minimum needed for actual use. Breeding made mushers hesitant to sell good dogs, so there was little dealing.

Before the age of air transport, dog-teams played a vital role. The existence of many settlements depended as much upon dog teaming as such localities now depend upon the bush pilot and his plane. Mushers sought pure-blood Siberian huskies and a freighting dog known as the McKenzie River husky. That dog, however, has almost disappeared because of cross-breeding with inferior stock.

There were many Outside dogs imported for cross-breeding with northern sled dogs. Among those guests present were: Newfoundlands, staghounds, St. Bernards, German police dogs, retrievers, and setters. All this cross-breeding did much to improve the general quality of northern sled dogs.

Dog-team racing was a highly specialized field in itself. Races of thirty to forty miles were held on single days. The most capable lead dog I ever owned, a dog named Yukon, was the offspring of a half-blood wolf bitch crossed with a registered bloodhound. He was willful and inclined to wildness whenever he got off his chain. But he got right down to business when in harness, and in following a drifted, windswept trail he was unexcelled.

Racing was not just for professionals. As much enthusiasm could be shown in small races as in the big ones. Many northern communities held an annual sporting event. There were shorter races yet for the junior mushers, with both boys and girls competing. The biggest races were the All-Alaska Sweepstakes in Nome and the results were recorded in newspapers, magazines, and books.

The list of famous dog drivers includes Scotty Allan, Iron Man Johnson, Leonhard Seppala, Fox Ramsey, and Charlie Johnson. These men were so well known to northerners that they ranked with baseball heroes to sports fans Outside. The mushers won their honors and their reputations on the longest and roughest course, going 408 miles.

The Sweepstakes records will undoubtedly stand for all time, for the enterprise shown in dog breeding passed with the heyday of dog-teaming. In recent years the entire concentration has been on races of about thirty miles and something is missing with no races in existence for these marvelous dogs with such stamina.

17

Beefing Up the Kennel

We had been scouting around town looking for more dogs for a week when a dog owner gave us a tip. He told us one of the senior freight dog drivers, Andy Taylor, was going out of business. He had already disposed of most of his dogs, but kept some around to howl at night to prevent him from being lonesome. Now he was ready to swear off dogs entirely. He was leaving town to work at Kennecott and didn't want to spend the money to board his dogs.

Andy Taylor's cabin was only a three-hundred-yard dash from where we were standing and we were pounding on the door in no time. When Andy answered the door we asked breathlessly if it was true he wanted to sell some dogs. The old dog driver looked us over in a friendly way and invited Bud and I inside. This was a serious transaction and one didn't sell dogs with the dispatch of someone rushing to a three-alarm fire. We sat at the kitchen table and Andy brought out a couple of bottles of double-strength home brew and poured it foaming and over-flowing into water tumblers.

Taylor was a well-known figure in McCarthy and we knew of him by report. This was our first meeting, however. He had been absent throughout the summer and had only returned a few days earlier. He was a mild-mannered, unassuming man, not physically large, but wiry and of tenacious character. A Chilkoot Trail alumnus, class of '98, he had been in the White River country before the Shushanna strike. For a decade following the gold discovery, he had divided his time between mining, freighting with a dog team, and convoying travelers to and from the gold camp with pack horse trains. He was a licensed guide and had been active in handling various hunting parties. More recently, he had turned to guiding mountaineering parties.

Andy had a speech impediment and camp raconteurs widely imitated it when telling anecdotes about his life. Andy never seemed to mind, but on occasion during a long, hard winter he made an effort to correct the problem by signing up for a correspondence course guaranteed to stop stammering. Andy continued to stammer and joked that the course had helped out a lot, but he hadn't had time to finish it.

After taming a couple of bottles of wild home brew, talk steered around to the two dogs we wanted to buy. "I really don't have any further need for them," Taylor said. "I'm away from here so much of the time I can't take care of them."

We could and we told him that. "We can sure use them," I said. "We're stuck. We've been trying for a week to rustle up a couple or three more dogs. The only thing we've run into is offers to buy the two we have. How much are you asking for the dogs?"

Andy pondered the question. He said he really didn't care to sell them. He had kept them for company. Then he offered them to us for free. A gift of two dogs? Bud and I nearly fell out of our chairs.

We sat at the table talking a while longer, and then Andy took us around back to look at the dogs. There we got another surprise, for aside from a pert-looking husky, there was a Siberian bitch that Bud and I were well acquainted with. The bitch recognized us at once and began wagging her tail and nuzzling our hands affectionately. The dog's actions surprised Andy. "Nora seems to know you fellows," he said. "I have never seen her do that with strangers before."

Laughing, I turned to Bud. "So Nora is her name," I commented. Then to Andy I said, "She knows us all right." There was a story behind our connection with his dog. The previous spring Andy was leaving McCarthy to guide a mountaineering expedition to Mount Fairweather in the St. Elias Range. He made arrangements with a McCarthy dog driver to board his two dogs. A few days after Andy left, the Siberian broke her chain and disappeared from the kennels. After nosing around Andy's cabin she vanished from town. The operator of the kennels theorized she had gone off to Shushanna on the trail she was used to running.

But the dog didn't go to Shushanna. In late May at Chitina I noticed a white dog digging into a tent. We asked around, but no one knew where the dog was from. I grabbed the chain to take a closer look at her. She was disheveled and muddy and moved around uneasily, casting timid glances at us. I tied her to the tent stoop and rustled up a plate of meat scraps from the cook. The dog remained uneasy and we thought she might be sick and injured. We couldn't find evidence of anything wrong, but tied her up to watch for a few days just in case.

Due to my boyhood companion of another dog that I had left behind when I left home, I took a strong interest in the lonely white dog. I began pampering her, obtaining materials for a kennel, badgering the cook for food, and lining her bed with straw. But to my dismay, the next day, the dog was gone, having chewed through her tie rope. I looked for her intermittently, but could not find her. Two days later one of the teamsters reported a sighting. She had dug herself in at the warehouse. I went over bearing a flashlight in search of the missing dog and to my surprise I found her nursing a sole black-and-white pup.

I was baffled. I had never heard of a litter of one. I had seen eight in one litter and heard of twelve once, but never just one. I searched the area, but found no other puppies. The arrival of the pup caused a stir in camp. All of the expert dog drivers that had examined the mother for injury or illness had missed that she was pregnant. Everyone voted to keep the dogs until the owner could be located and the mother now seemed perfectly content. The pair quickly became camp mascots and were allowed to roam free of the chains.

After the pup's birth a discussion was held about naming the dogs. I had been thinking about it for some time and immediately recommended "Nanook" for the mother. No competing nominations were offered. Several options were mentioned for naming the pup. The majority liked the name of the camp itself as a name for the dog—"Chitina." I carried on a losing campaign in favor of "Chinook." An elderly Swede from Cordova piped up and said the pup should be called "Sooner." There were arguments against it, but the Swede said, "Vell, dey pup come sooner dun ve all ogspected, didn't he?" The awful pun won out.

When the mining season ended and when Bud and I took to the trail to McCarthy, the dog and her four-month-old pup were trotting companionably at our heels. When we got to town we talked to one of the dog drivers who recognized the mother and he offered to turn her over to the man responsible for her care. We gave Nanook and her pup a fond farewell.

Nanook disappeared from our affairs, but on several occasions when we were out for a tramp around the countryside we picked her up at the kennels and took her for a romp. Not until this day had we learned where the dogs belonged. Andy never knew the dog had spent the time with us, only that it had been at the mining camp.

The other dog Andy was giving us was called "Chief." Andy explained that he was of somewhat doubtful caliber. It seemed that when Andy experimented with different breeds he crossed a German police dog with the Siberian. Chief was part of that litter. He was an important-looking dog with a stocky, well-furred appearance, and the bushy, erect tail of the Siberian, but with the color markings of the police dog. He had a friendly disposition. The Siberian breed is generally regarded as a shy, temperamental dog and difficult to handle for drivers used to handling rough-and-tumble common sled dogs.

Andy had been trying to breed some of the Siberian's native shyness out of the litter when Chief was born. Women seemed to take to Siberians, and the famed dog driver Leonhard Seppala showed that Siberians could out-point the field by winning the Sweepstakes and other races with crack Siberian teams.

We asked Andy how he thought the cross-breeding had worked out and he said, "It might be all right with some further breeding. As it stands now the damned dog is so smart you have a hard time getting him to do any work." Andy paused and added another thought, as if considering that the breeding had been too successful. "Another thing you have to watch for, he's a fighting sonofabitch with other dogs. You'd better work him in the wheel where you can keep an eye on him. Give him a boot when he takes to cutting up."

We went back into the cabin and Andy opened another bottle of brew. Shortly afterward, when we were leaving, he pulled out a couple of sets of dog harnesses, and threw those in with the dogs. With that gesture, Andy's long career as a dog driver was over. Bud and I little realized at the time what poignant memories must have been passing through his mind as he stood in the doorway of the cabin and watched us lead the dogs away. He had been associated with dog-teaming for more than a quarter of a century.

The introduction of two new dogs to the team was appraised in a discriminating way by the originals Rex and Spike. Nora seemed to be granted the prerogatives of her sex. She was accepted with an indifferent air, as though they had known all along that something of this sort was bound to happen and nothing could be done about it. The easy attitude did not go for Chief, however. The arrogant half-police dog was greeted with snarls and raised hackles and that was ominous of feuding yet to come. In our double-hitch lineup we kept Chief in the wheel position next to the sled as Andy suggested. Spike was worked in swing directly behind the leader Rex. Nora could be worked either in the wheel or swing position, but was usually paired with Chief. If we tried to work Chief with spike a battle would result.

The extra dogs put some ginger in the team. Daily runs soon settled the dogs into a working unit and within a week we noticed a certain team spirit beginning to show. Rex plumed his tail and strutted pridefully in his position as leader and it was evident from his actions that he thought these four dogs would whip the hell out of any other dog-team in town. That Napoleonic attitude had to be watched. We always cleared our dogs bodily off the trail whenever we saw another team approaching.

Although we made trips of six to ten miles every day, the dogs really didn't get enough work to hold them to a steady pace. Our uncontrolled flights when we took off from the cabin each morning began to assume importance with the town folk. The small Yukon sled had no brake and from the moment when the tie rope was slipped our rush through town was an uncharted affair, depending entirely on the lead dog's whim. Elderly citizens watched these takeoffs with sober-sided mirth.

On occasions, we learned later, quick bets were made as to whether our outfit would go around the street corner or shoot through some narrow passage between buildings midway in the block. It was a fair enough gamble, as we didn't know either, and the lead dog wasn't doing any talking. After we had torn boards loose from the sidewalk, overturned dog kennels, and crashed head-on into the Chinaman's chicken wire fence, we decided to work at gaining more control and holding it down a little bit on the speed.

Bud and I found an old sled brake in the junk pile in back of the blacksmith's shop and rigged it on the rear of the sled with a couple of door springs to store it when not in use. The brake brought some semblance of order to our outfit. The team eventually learned that when we shouted "Whoa!" it meant to stop right then instead of continuing on for a quarter of a mile until we bodily wrestled the team to a standstill.

The lead dog did not like the brake for it curbed some of his strong-headed designs for doing things at whatever time and place he took the notion. Rex had been showing obstinacy in gee and haw, although he knew the difference between right and left as well as we did. He tried all types of artful dodges for evading the issue when we ordered him to go in one direction and he wanted to go in another.

He would jerk and pull and swing the team in every direction. He would start in the right direction and then when the brake was eased, swap directions. Failing in those maneuvers he would turn around with an imbecile stare as though he lacked understanding and was appealing for advice. It took a good deal of patient insistence and the threat of having his rump tanned with the whip before Rex conceded the point that we were running the outfit. We finally convinced him that no traveling would be done at all unless he followed orders. Things went along better after that.

Gradually, we came to understand that we were driving trained sled-dogs and they knew what they were supposed to do. It was Bud and I who were learning. In our outfit it was the dog mushers who were undergoing training rather than the dogs.

18

The Education Continues

Mid-November temperatures ranged from around zero to occasionally twenty below. Days of clear weather alternated with spells of steely-gray skies with raw winds blowing down from glacier country. Snow squalls accompanied the strong winds. It was excellent weather for mushing with just enough snow on the trails to make good sledding. Every day teams traveled the countryside on one errand or another.

There was little freighting going on yet, however, except to some trap lines or scattered prospector camps. Dog drivers were having a hard time making ends meet. Only this season freighting ceased to Shushanna. Winter freight moving had been the mainstay of dog-teaming out of McCarthy for thirteen years. It turned out the two teams I encountered at the Nazina Roadhouse back in May were the last ones to cross the divide on the glacier trail. Since that time some of the bridges spanning the larger crevasses had fallen in, making the trail impassable.

On a couple of trips out in the countryside Bud and I had traveled as far as Kennecott. The country beyond the mine was a region of glaciers and naked high mountains, ice locked and uninhabited. The country seemed fascinating and we set out on a trip well beyond the mine.

It was a bright, sunny morning for our outing. A light outfit with a tea can, a primus stove, and a lunch was lashed to the sled. The trail dropped away from town to wind leisurely along boulder-strewn flats and began a gradual ascent toward the mine. About two miles from town the trail turned at a sharp angle for a short distance. There, briefly, all view of the trail ahead was cut off. Suddenly, a dog team burst into sight, coming at breakneck speed right for us. The team had nine dogs and a big driver riding the rear of the sled. Before we could move our team out of the trail the teams collided in a snarling sideswipe and piled up in a glorious battle.

In one awful moment I saw our lead dog go down under a welter of slashing fangs. Without thought of the consequences I dove in after him, hoping to salvage the hide, if not the harness. Abruptly, two large hands attached themselves to my person and I was bodily hurled through the air. I landed hard and saw stars. For a moment I pondered delightedly the wonders seen on a dog-team trip and then I realized again where I was. The dog fight was still going on, but it was being brought under control.

The big driver was standing beside the sled with a long bullwhip in hand laying the leather across the backs of the fighting pack. Judging from his cool actions there was no great urgency, for even as the whip flicked back for another stroke there was time for a squirt of tobacco juice from between his teeth. Each blow of the whip was vicious and coldly efficient. The squalling pack was quieting and a fear was taking hold of them that exceeded the lust for battle. Dogs were unscrambling themselves with frightened, whimpering yelps and cowering on the sidelines. Our dogs were already separated from the others and Bud was herding them into a ditch well away from the other team.

The blows ceased the moment the dogs dispersed. The dog driver flicked his whip into a coil and stepped in among the dogs. Growls stopped at a word, and if they did not, a sudden, savage blow of the whip commanded no further nonsense. Two of the dogs at the bottom of the heap were still locked together. One dog's jaws were tightly clamped to another's throat. The insensate fury of battle was still in this pair, the kind of unfeeling, insane fury that gives no quarter and is insensible to the whip short of being used in a knockout blow across the nose. The driver moved in swiftly on this pair. Dropping the coil to the ground he seized the top dog's head firmly behind the ears, at the same time ramming the butt of the whip into the dog's tightly locked jaws, forcing them open. The instant the one's grip was released from the other's throat the two dogs were thrust apart. The entire operation had been done so deftly that it seemed to occur almost as a single sweeping movement.

That ended the battle. The dog that had been gripped by the throat took a bad mauling. He struggled to his feet with an effort, blood-flecked, stony-eyed, and looking considerably the worse for wear. The driver now moved easily in the midst of the team, soothing the quivering dogs with quiet words, straightening harnesses, and tacking together broken neck straps and torn harnesses with pieces of twine from his pocket. In a few minutes the damage had been repaired enough that the outfit could make it the rest of the way into town. The lead dog was stepped ahead, straightening the tow line, and bringing the team into orderly formation again. The driver returned to his sled, started the team, and pulled past our outfit for a short space down the trail. There he stopped and throwing his tie rope round a stump, he came back to give us some attention.

In the meantime I had recovered from my status as a dazed observer and joined Bud with our outfit. This was our first experience getting tangled in a dog fight and we thought the war was over when the other driver moved on with his team. But the big dog driver didn't appear to view it that way. There was a mean look in his eye as he approached us.

"You!" he snapped, looking directly at me. "You will get your goddamned arm chewed off one of these days jumping in on a dog fight like that." He glowered at both of us, then demanded, "Don't you bastards pack a whip with your outfit?"

The language was disrespectful but not having had the brigand's background I blew my lines. Instead of asking the man to smile when he called us that I retorted angrily. "Certainly, we pack a whip. Do you think we are such dumb dog drivers we don't know what a whip is for?"

The big dog driver did not reply. He passed a dirty look from one to the other of us and scowled. Bud, by way of supporting my truthful contention, reached into the rummage sack and brought out the mail order catalogue whip, the one that had come with the outfit. I knew it was the wrong thing to do, but Bud did it anyway. He passed the whip over for the man's inspection and the big dog driver nearly blew a gasket. He took one look at the whip and slapped it down with a curse. He was packing his own long whip, slung in a coil with the thong around his wrist. In an instant he dashed the coil to the ground. Flipping the thong loose he thrust the butt of the whip directly under our noses, shouting, "This, goddamnit! This is what I mean!"

We looked at the whip butt. Bud's solemn eyes met mine, and then transferred their attention back to the whip again. Slowly, Bud reached out and took the whip from the driver's hand, a hesitant action like a chary customer examining a bill of goods. Bud hefted the heavy shot-loaded butt and his hackles began to rise. "This," exclaimed Bud, a strident tremor in his voice, "why this, holy Jesus, my grandfather used to skin the hides off mules using a whip like this!"

The dog driver fixed his hard, expressionless eyes on Bud, and then shifted the look to me. It was plain he thought we were pulling his leg and for a moment it looked as if the dogs would get a turn at breaking up a man fight. In the end, we were given the benefit of the doubt. That is, we were considered just a pair of jugheads that didn't know which end of the dog went into the collar. Snatching his whip away, the driver rasped scathingly, "You don't use this thing for driving dogs, goddammit. You use it for stopping dog fights."

The big dog driver eyed us angrily for a minute, then turned and started for his outfit. After a couple of strides he paused to growl a warning. "You bastards had better get yourselves a whip if you're going to travel these trails around here," he said. "We aren't going to stand for having dogs cut all to hell in dog fights, not anymore than can be helped. Get a whip and use it when they pile up in a tangle."

We didn't take our intended trip beyond Kennecott that day. The dogs had been roughed up considerably in the squabble and Spike had taken a hefty gash on one of his forelegs. After traveling a little bit farther along the trail we called the trip off and returned to town.

We gave the dogs a layover the following day. They still showed cuts and bruises. When next our outfit took to the trail we were sporting a $12 whip as insurance against being run over by any more tough dog drivers. We felt self-conscious about the thing and kept it out of sight in the rummage sack. The whip was longer than our dog team.

Our light Yukon sled had seen hard usage even before we bought the outfit. Since then it had been bouncing over rocky gravel bars and across fallen timber and had crashed into enough stumps and other obstacles to be wrecked completely. Now its rheumatic joints were loose. There were a couple of gaps on the bed of the sled where slats were broken and hay wire was holding several joints together where bolts and braces were missing. Furthermore, the steel shoes had been worn to paper thinness and threatened to give way at any time.

Neither Bud nor I were rolling in riches, but we had to do something about the sled or otherwise we would have a dog team with nothing to pull. We decided at the least we would put a new pair of shoes on the sled. The homemade brake was taken off the sled and we pulled the sled to the blacksmith shop. The black-smith was located close to the bridge over McCarthy Creek. The blacksmith was busy at the forge when we dragged our sled inside.

Harry Mudge was the village blacksmith, an Irishman as solidly constructed as a reinforced concrete pier. He was not only a top craftsman, but he knew dog-teaming from first-hand trail experience. When Mudge took a break from the forge he looked over our sled. As he examined the Yukon he dished slivers of tobacco with the point of a jack knife into his muscular jaw. Mudge reached out and seized the seven-foot sled in the middle and flipped it over. An awed look passed between Bud and me. We had enough trouble picking up one end of the sled when throwing it around.

When Mudge finished the inspection the blacksmith spun the sled around and dropped it at arm's length flat on the floor. Crash! We were glad it was the sled getting new shoes and not us. There was a thoughtful frown on the blacksmith's face. "This rig isn't worth shoeing," he said.

He proceeded to list a number of things that were wrong with the sled that would prevent us from acquiring any heavy-duty freighting work. However, he said the sled should be OK for light hauling or narrow trail driving. "Light haul-ing is about all we figure on using it for anyway," I said. "Unless we decide to go trapping later on."

Mudge was still skeptical that we would be OK. "You might get by with a rig like this if you're just traveling the trails around here," he said. "But that doesn't get you anyplace unless you just need exercise. If you get out and do any traveling on your own you'll need something better than a Yukon sled. There's a big difference between the kind of average traveling dog drivers do in the Interior and the kind of rough side-hilling the boys are doing around here. You've got too much dodging around to do in this country."

The blacksmith ran a critical eye over our old battered sled and gave it a disdainful push with his foot. He predicted bolts would come off and steel braces would come loose. "Sleds in this country have to stand up under some pretty hard punishment," Mudge said. "There must be a couple of dozen of these Yukon sleds lying belly-up in Skolai Pass and scattered in the moraines on the glaciers. That's as far as they ever get on the way to Shushanna. Around here the boys build their own sleds, or if they're too busy with other work they get someone here in town to do the job. There's quite a knack to building a good sled."

Mudge recommended against putting new shoes on the sled and talked about replacement models. But Bud and I didn't see it that way. We thought the sled would last a while longer considering the type of running around we were doing. After buying the outfit we were not well disposed to making an additional investment.

19

New Equipment

On the afternoon of the second day we returned to the blacksmith shop. The man was shaping heavy steel for a coupling on a bobsled and we watched the showers of sparks as the anvil humped under the measured heavy blows and offbeat ring.

While Mudge was busy, we glanced around the shop for our sled, but didn't see it. When Mudge stopped his pounding I asked about our sled. He nodded at a Yukon sled upright against a wall, but obviously that was not our battered old rig. It was a new sled painted red. I looked to Mudge again, but he was busy, so we investigated.

Bud and I had some trouble identifying the sled as the one we pulled into the shop. The old rig had been given a complete overhaul and sported a coat of bright red paint. It was not surprising that we failed to recognize it. Aside from the new shoes, there was a new crossbar strut replacing a cracked one that had been held together with wire and friction tape. All the missing and broken steel braces on the runner struts had been rebuilt with babiche [rawhide] rope. A new half-inch rope tug line led from the bow piece along each side of the sled and was firmly secured with a hitch on each runner strut. The new tug line replaced an old one that had merely been tied on without concern for stress on the sled. And there were two new strips on the bed of the sled replacing broken ones.

The transformation was amazing. The job surpassed our idea even of a general overhaul. In effect we had a brand-new sled. The work must have taken five hours of the blacksmith's time and we expected a sizable bill. "That sure is a good job you put into our sled," I told Mudge. "How much do we owe for the job?" Mudge did not immediately respond. He shoveled some coal into the forge and shaped it, then put the blower to the fire. Then he named the price. "Five bucks," he said.

Five bucks! We knew that price was the standard rate for shoeing a sled without any repairs. We talked the matter over between ourselves. We couldn't believe it. Five bucks, we thought, that was cockeyed. I stepped back up to Mudge and said, "How about the other work on the sled? The repair work, how much is that?"

Mudge seemed to be annoyed at the question. But the blower ceased and he focused his attention on shaping the steel. After the steel went back into the fire, the blacksmith turned to us. "That rig wouldn't have lasted you two weeks the shape it was in," he said. "You wouldn't get up the glacier or anyplace else with a siwash outfit like that. You'd just get yourselves in a jackpot and be sitting around with hay wire and pliers like crippled squaws mending a fishnet. Then I'd be the one to blame."

We didn't exactly share Mudge's viewpoint on the fixing of responsibility, but we knew by report that the blacksmith was not a man who went in for philosophical debate. I took the course of assuring him the job was entirely satisfactory, only we wanted a price for it. Mudge frowned and said, "I told you once. Five bucks." That was the end of it. We promptly dug up five dollars and handed it over. The blacksmith crumpled the bill into his pocket under his leather apron and went on with his work. Bud and I crossed the shop and carried the sled to a place where we could set it on the floor. As we turned to leave, the blower ceased for a moment. "You fellows," Mudge said, "would do well to rustle yourselves a good sled if you figure on doing much dog-teaming. You're always up against it whenever you try getting anyplace with those dinky rigs. They don't pack enough dog food to keep you two weeks out of town. And you're lucky even when that much of a load isn't falling off and getting scattered around."

We dragged the sled from the shop and we trudged up the street in silence. We were halfway home when Bud spoke. "You never know if these fellows are doing you a favor or are jabbing you right up to the neck," he said. I agreed. We thought it was possible the blacksmith was trying to unload a sled on us that was no better than the one we had. But Mudge was not viewed as a man who practiced such tricks. He had known all along what was in our minds. But we had received a very good deal on the repair work.

The sled incident stirred some latent brain cells into action. It was not long before the blacksmith's sound advice was given serious consideration. Mudge was right that sooner or later we would have to get a sled that was suitable for handling a bigger load. The Yukon sled served our present purpose of knocking around the countryside on short trips. But when we really got down to business, whether it was traveling, freighting, or working a trap line, it would be necessary to have something better.

The problem of us obtaining a good sled would be fair to difficult, much as it had been in obtaining dogs in this dog-mushing town. We did not feel we were good enough craftsmen to make our own and having one built required a full year's notice. The town's best craftsmen were dog drivers themselves. They considered sled building to be only an off-season job when they weren't out with their dogs in winter.

Furthermore, the select materials for sled making had to be ordered in advance and laid aside for seasoning. Native birch was commonly used for building sleds in the Interior, but the sled builders in McCarthy considered that wood too soft. Tough-grained hickory and oak were the only materials that stood up to the kind of rough-and-tough sledding in this region. Other than having a sled built to order, the only alternative was to watch for an opportunity when a sled was put up for sale. We decided to scour the town in hopes of finding an unwanted freight sled.

We talked to several dog drivers and teamsters and to others around town, but they all shook their heads. Better plan on having a sled built, they said. Or else find an old, discarded sled someplace and have Mudge rebuild it as only a blacksmith could. We seemed bound to lay out the cost of a new sled at a couple or three hundred dollars. Ouch! Our casual search went on for a week. One morning we were talking to a neighbor and he mentioned that he saw a business card sticking in the back bar mirror at the Golden Hotel. The writing on the card read SLED FOR SALE—SEE DUD. "That was two or three days ago," our friend said. "I don't know whether the card is still there or not."

The Golden Hotel, of course! We should have thought of that sooner and advertised our wants there. Dud's bar was not only a bastion of anti-Prohibition activity. It was also a kind of board of trade for the town's business affairs. If you lost a dog or wanted the wood saw rig to show up, or wanted to repay a loan to somebody who was seldom in town, or if you wanted to know the present whereabouts of someone within a hundred-mile radius of McCarthy, you stopped at the Golden Hotel to see Dud. Sooner or later all answers were provided. So we hustled downtown to see Dud.

Dud was out for a few minutes, but the card was still stuck in the mirror so we hoped the sled had not been purchased. We joined Shorty Gwin near the big heater. Shorty was a teamster who took a dim view of society's more elevated graces. He had been riding the range for decades in Wyoming and Montana and his language still smacked strongly of the camps. One of Shorty's peculiarities was traipsing around with his shoepacs unlaced. The laces trailed a foot behind him and were a standing invitation for those inclined to upset Shorty in the middle of what he called "argoofying." Such happenings never cured him of the shoelace habit, but only entered him into additional arguments.

Shorty was dozing and his unlaced shoepacs rested high on the iron fender around the stove. A dilapidated fur cap, which looked as if it had been trapped out of season forty years before, rested on the back of his head. Every once in a while Shorty shifted to one side or another and shot a salvo of tobacco juice into a spittoon. Shorty awoke briefly to direct a disparaging comment at a salesman at the bar who had been arguing noisily and non-stop. Finally, an hour and a half later Dud appeared.

Dud informed us the sled was owned by Scotty Anderson and it was unlikely it had been sold because he was out of town on a freighting trip. Dud gave us the key to the dog driver's warehouse and told us to go look at the sled. Bud and I found two sleds, one a long, rangy freighting sled that was partly covered with a tarpaulin. The other, standing close to the door, appeared to be the right one. It was a neat basket sled of standard width, almost new. It measured about seven feet on the bed.

The sled displayed skillful and painstaking craftsmanship. It was a beautiful sled and would be wonderful for Bud's and my needs. The elemental question was how much it would cost. We returned the key to Dud at the hotel and left the message that we would like to talk to Scotty Anderson when he returned to town.

A couple of days later Scotty showed up at our cabin. We put on our mackinaws and caps and returned with him to the warehouse. Scotty was talking sleds in general and explained some of the fine points that are taken into consideration when sleds are being built and how that fits in with the purposes they are used for. Conversation narrowed to the sled that was up for sale.

"That sled will likely be large enough for all the knocking around that you fellows want to do at present. It isn't a long sled, but it's built skookum. It will handle any kind of load you put on 'er and stand up under any kind of travel. She holds the trail well and is easy to handle. When I built the sled last year I figured on using it for passenger trips and light hauling. But there hasn't been much work of that kind going on and my other two sleds handle all the freight that comes my way. So I really don't have much use for this rig. I wouldn't figure on putting together another sled like it for anything less than $250. But since I've had a few runs out of 'er, I'll make a price of $150 if you fellows want to make a cash deal."

It was a great sales pitch and we didn't need to be sold too hard. The deal was closed on the spot. After we counted out the currency into the dog driver's hand our attention went over to the long freighting sled sitting near the opposite wall. The sled was all of ten feet in the bed, with a low-slung basket, and the rakish lines of a racing sloop. We remarked admiringly upon the strong construction of the freighter. While talking with Scotty I learned that this sled was one of the two battered dog sleds that I had seen standing in the roadhouse yard in May. But since that time it had been given an overhaul and a coat of shellac, making it look almost new.

"That sled," remarked Scotty, "is the real McCoy when it comes to tonnage hauling. I can load anything up to a ton of freight on that rig and still have plenty of room for my own grub box and other stuff. It handles easy, too, considering her length. A sled like that is worth between four and five hundred bucks, without any fancy trimmings. Right now I'm not doing any work with 'er. There's no freight going over the hump like there used to be, and my smaller sled does all the hauling that needs to be done around this locality."

Bud went over and hefted the sled by its handlebars. "How many dogs do you use when you're freighting with a sled like this?" he asked.

Scotty laughed. "All the dogs I've got myself and everybody else's that I can borrow or steal," he said. Then seriously, he added, "It depends on the job. Usually I have fifteen dogs on the tow line for that rig, but I have used as many as twenty-one. An average trail like you have around here, you can load a hundred pounds to the dog, maybe a little better. But you don't get the average trail for any distance in this part of the country. Most of it is rough and standing on end. There are places up around the glaciers and Skolai Pass where a man is lucky if he can split the load in half and boost it through with a single relay."

The glaciers and Skolai Pass again! We knew from camp tales that the place was indescribably rugged. But since we had been running around with a dog team the place had assumed more than passing interest. It had become a place of special mystique.

The stocky dog driver passed us a warning look, with a glint of amusement in his eyes. "Take my advice," Anderson said, "and never go near the place. Not unless the marshal is on your trail. And even then you'd be ahead by cutting a deal and spending your time in a nice warm jail. You'd be showing more sense than some of us fellows have been showing the past ten or twelve years climbing that Skolai Pass with a dog team."

20

Early Winter

The short, gray days of late November were blustery and cold. The north wind sweeping down from the glacier country brought occasional snow flurries and whenever the sky cleared the temperature dropped to minus twenty or even minus thirty. But the weather gave Bud and me little concern. We had lived through it all in Montana.

We busied ourselves with our routine existence. We took care of the dogs, cooked, and handled the few chores around the cabin. We were content. The basket sled was in use as part of our daily runs with the dogs and we were delighted with its performance. It was a little bit heavier than the Yukon sled, but it pulled just as easily and the substantial brake gave us better control. The sled was a pleasure to handle on the trail.

Our outfit was gradually being worked into shape. We were trying to find one more dog to put into swing position with Spike. Without one more dog we could not handle a full load on the sled. Besides, the prevailing opinion in McCarthy is that nobody had a dog team unless they had a minimum of five good dogs. Since Bud and I got one foot into dog-teaming we felt we should get both feet in and qualify in every respect.

On Thanksgiving Day, we picked up a rumor that there was a spare down at the kennels not being used. Our tipster suggested we go see the owner, but no one knew his whereabouts at that moment. He had last been seen navigating between various bars taking on a cargo of corn juice. On Thanksgiving, business at the bars would be booming. It was a bad day to try to find anyone in a sober state.

Still, Bud and I decided to lose no time in tracking down the report of a possible available dog. We chucked our caps and coats and headed downtown, not in observance of the holiday, but in quest of the dog man. We wanted to intercept him before another dog driver bushwhacked him.

In McCarthy, three days a year stood out on the calendar where every man, according to his course, chose a celebration. The Fourth of July, Thanksgiving, and Christmas marked the days when the residents imbibed more freely than usual. New Year's was considered superfluous. It was too close to Christmas to be good for much of anything besides ingesting bromo-seltzer. It was into this kind of holiday atmosphere that we stepped seeking to do business.

Upon entering the head of Front Street we noticed the area was strangely silent, especially on a late afternoon on such an important occasion. There was no one to be seen the entire length of the street and for once even the dogs weren't barking. We commented on the unusual scene as we marched along the frosty boardwalk. Bud and I craned our necks, searching for any reason for such quiet.

Approaching the end of the street near a restaurant, our attention was drawn to an object lying in the middle of the street. It was a large heater, a hundred-gallon oil drum converted into a stove with the fittings of a fire door, air vent, and stovepipe collar. It normally occupied the center of the floor in the restaurant. Now it was lying upside down in a scattering of soot and ashes with a curl of smoke rising from it like an expiring dragon in a Norseman legend. There was no legend about this affair. Since the heater was too large to come out through the door, it must have come out by way of the big plate-glass window. And it had—violently. The shattered window was strewn in pieces across the sidewalk and into the street, almost as far out as the heater.

Bud and I looked at the stove, the gaping hole where the window had been, and then at each other. Cautiously, we moved toward the restaurant door. The interior of the place looked as if a locomotive had jumped the tracks and run through the dining room. The center of the floor was a shambles of trampled stovepipe and soot, broken counter stools, splintered hat racks, smashed chairs, shattered parts of tables, with the whole mess of wreckage topped with a couple of booth partitions torn from the walls.

Through some unfathomable oversight the plate-glass mirror in back of the service counter was still intact. That was a mere technicality and it reflected the magnitude of the disaster. Everything else in the place was ripped asunder, smashed up, torn apart, and distributed in the most unusual of places. The sight of the catastrophe seemed to be deserted.

Bud and I stood in the doorway of the disaster for several minutes, silently scanning the wreckage. Then we set a tentative foot inside. The flood of water thrown across the floor from the overturned water cooler was just starting to freeze. The evidence indicated the eruption had taken place not long before our arrival. While we were nosing an inquest, uncertain as to causes, we heard the back door open and close and footsteps moved cautiously through the kitchen. In a moment, the head of the Oriental proprietor peered around the corner of the kitchen door.

The man wore an over-sized fur cap which fell misshapenly down over his ears and an old mackinaw coat pulled on over his white cook's uniform. The coat was apparently borrowed since it was big enough to be wrapped around him twice. The cook proclaimed that "It's that goddamn Harry," referring to the indestructible blacksmith. Bud asked what he meant, but no immediate answer was forthcoming. The cook's eyes dolefully surveyed the wreckage in a vain attempt to identify anything familiar and still useable. He shuddered, and then turned to the kitchen range and began lifting pots and pans to sniff and to determine if they smelled of burning.

After some minor cleanup it became clear what happened. From the cook's account, the blacksmith had been in earlier in the day and ordered a turkey dinner to be set aside for him in case they sold out while he was working. That was standard procedure for such citizens. There had been a strong stampede to the restaurant, more than the cook could properly accommodate, and the roast turkey had been scratched from the menu in early afternoon. When the delinquent blacksmith failed to put in an appearance by midafternoon, and it was reported that he was out on the town getting drunk, the cook sold the last order of turkey in the house. "I didn't think he would show up," the cook said, wiping his hands on his apron as he looked again at the rubbish dump in the kitchen.

"What did he do?" Bud asked, pressing for more details, as if the evidence on the floor didn't offer information about one aspect of the story.

The cook repeated his shuddering shake, as if he was trying to remove all remembrance of the incident from his head. "He put his foot against the stove and pushed it over," the cook said. "I didn't know what happened after that." He left the restaurant and retreated to another nearby owned by a friend. The cook lapsed into silence, a foreboding silence like that hanging over the rest of the town. His eyes somberly surveyed the debris, but a wary glint shot to the sidewalk. We were well aware of the portentous situation surrounding this cataclysm.

It did not happen very often, possibly every two years or so, but when the blacksmith of this village rose from his anvil to give destiny a twist of the tail, it made carnage and history. The event usually ran its predictable course for a day or two and then a hardy soul at a bar reached out unseen and parted the villain's hair with a gallon jug. But the strong arm was a risky procedure where the blacksmith was concerned. The town's citizens, through long association and habit, usually conceded that valor lay in leaving bad enough alone and took to the cyclone cellars while the blow lasted. The blacksmith would be in a sober state of mind in a couple or three days and be back to the place where relief work was needed to pick up the tab, no questions asked.

The marshal would be called in if the state of siege ran too long and the flag of distress was raised. But that was considered to be something of an indignity in a place where mayhem was turnabout and few real grudges held. It was part of the independent character of McCarthy that it preferred solving its own problems without official aid or interference.

Still, bad news traveled fast and the hatches were battened down until it was safe to show above ground again. Bud and I glanced at one another, expressed our sympathy to the cook and said farewell. We stepped carefully through the rubbish and paused long enough at the door to take in the entire mess of a scene. It was getting toward sundown and Bud and I had not eaten since breakfast. We had been on a dog-team run down the river during the day. There was another restaurant just around the block. Presumably, it was still in action. "There's no use trying to find anybody in this type of situation," Bud said. "Let's eat and go home." We called it a night.

The day after Thanksgiving, Bud and I picked up the trail where we left off. The dog's owner was located, but the situation turned out to be a little bit different than originally reported to us. The dog had broken loose from its chain the week before and while philandering around the kennels had its belly slashed in a dogfight. The owner put several stitches in the gaping wound, and although the dog had worked a couple of the stitches out, it was on its way to recovery. The dog was a convalescent and not a spare dog.

A couple of days later we were passing the restaurant that had been so recently decommissioned when we were called inside by the cook. The local carpenters made temporary repairs pending arrival of more permanent replacement parts from the States. The restaurant had re-opened for business the day before. The cook had recovered his usual debonair manner and was in a pleasant mood. "Somebody was telling me you fellows are looking for dogs," he said. "Maybe I got a dog you might want to buy."

We passed a questioning look to the cook indicating we wished to be further enlightened. We knew that he boarded dogs as a profitable sideline. "He is out in the backyard," the cook continued. "He is a fine dog, a very good dog, one-quarter wolf from Bob Marshall's dogs." At the mention of Marshall's dogs, we perked up our ears. We were well aware of the breeding strain he had been working at and several of the largest and best freighting dogs in McCarthy had come out of that stock. We wondered how the cook came to be offering such an outstanding dog for sale.

The cook baited our interest by remaining silent about how he obtained the dog. It appeared he knew dog trading as well as his chicken consommé and was on his way to driving a hard bargain. There was a somber look on Bud's face. "Let's have some pie and a cup of coffee," he said. "If Walter doesn't open up after that we'll order a turkey dinner ourselves next Thanksgiving."

The cook smiled cryptically as he set out our pie and coffee. Then he reached for an envelope on the counter behind him, removed the letter, and laid it before us. The letter was dated a week earlier from Seward. The contents made it appear that the owner, who had boarded the dog with the cook the previous spring, had changed his plans about returning to McCarthy as originally intended. He had joined up with a couple of partners who had a gold quartz prospect that looked promising. He decided to stay on the Kenai Peninsula and develop the property.

To that date the dog's board added up to forty-five dollars. Essentially, the chatty letter was really a bill of sale, informing the cook that by way of settling the board bill he could sell the dog, and retain for himself the full amount of whatever price the dog would bring. We returned the letter, and after finishing pie and coffee, we went out to the backyard to look at the dog. The cook had not underestimated the dog's worth, for he was the equal of the best dogs in the locality. We were told the dog's name was Sam. After making the formal presentation the cook talked business.

Sam was a big, rangy dog, three years old—in his prime—and weighed about one hundred pounds. Sam was black with white markings on his broad, powerful chest, and was well proportioned with large, muscular legs. Sam was larger than either Rex or Spike and they were good-sized animals. Sam came across as friendly despite his wolf ancestry. He pranced playfully at the end of his chain and seemed anxious to show the world that all he needed was a harness to pull as much as any two average dogs.

When we completed our interview with Sam we went back inside to begin negotiations. The cook said, "Good dog, huh? You don't see dogs as good everyday as Sam." The dealing promised to be tough. The cook was out to make some cash and we were determined to have that dog regardless of cost. Approaching discussions in a low-key manner, Bud and I admitted that Sam was a pretty good-looking dog and we would be happy to take a chance on him and take the dog off his hands for the cost of the board bill.

The cook ignored the offer and countered with a dark hint that he would definitely sell Sam elsewhere. "I have not talked to any of the other fellows," he said, "but I bet they would give me ninety dollars, maybe even a hundred dollars for such a good wolf dog as Sam." Bud reached across the meat block for a large butcher knife and began caressing it suggestively. "Now, Walter," Bud said, "you know that's too much to ask for just one dog. Why even if Sam was all wolf, he would be worth only the fifteen-dollar bounty."

The dickering went on for a half an hour until we brought the price down as far as it would go. The deal was closed for sixty-five dollars with the harness thrown in. We felt satisfied with the deal and the cook seemed satisfy to clear twenty dollars over the board bill. We went out to notify Sam of his change of address and he seemed satisfied with the deal. He trotted along amiably next to us when we headed back to the cabin.

Sam's purchase rounded out our dog team. The two originals, Rex and Spike, greeted the new arrival with a decent display of fangs and growling to put him in his place, but it was really unnecessary. The big dog had a good-natured disposition, minded his own affairs, and was a demon for hard work. Those sterling qualities were just what Chief was lacking and it seemed to irk the police dog beyond reason. As far as Chief was concerned, Sam's entry into the team meant an unending feud.

Adding Sam affected the positioning of the team dogs. Sam joined Spike in swing. Chief and Nora ran in wheel. A quarrelsome dog is a nuisance in any dog team and had there been another good dog available to buy we would have parted with Chief. His genius for creating a ruckus within the team and getting them all into a fight while escaping unscathed himself was what eventually finished him.

December showed up on the calendar almost as a surprise. We had been so busy we barely noticed the days slipping by. In six weeks Bud and I had accomplished a lot. It seemed only yesterday we had gone out to the Nazina Roadhouse to get the first two dogs. We were rapidly approaching the point where we were being confronted with the larger problem of putting the outfit to practical use.

Novice dog drivers gain their experience in degrees and in the course of routine activities learn their way around the hills by traveling with veterans. But the situation placed us in a position where we had to cut loose and make our own way with little trail experience. We had been eyeing this step with some misgivings. The region was not a placid country of easy trails, but a rough, mountainous country of fierce glacier winds, sudden blizzards, and partially frozen watercourses fraught with ice traps. We had just enough experience to estimate fairly well what we were up against and we were feeling none too confident about tackling the odds.

The field of trapping was open to us if we chose to head for the mountainous country on the farther side of the Chitina River. But that did not appeal to us. We were offered a trap line for eight hundred dollars, but we did not wish to settle down and work it for years to make a profit. We were sniffing the wind of Interior places. We didn't want to be tied down to McCarthy because it was feeling the pinch since Shushanna freighting had ceased. We wanted to be free to pull up stakes.

Meanwhile, we could not afford to sit idle. Keeping a dog team added to the sizeable food bill and our expenses kept apace. The initial cost of outfitting had cut a good-sized swath through our seasonal earnings and there was considerable trail equipment yet to be purchased. If we did not bestir ourselves to produce some income we would end up flat broke. We felt we had to restake ourselves and took note that Kennecott had been hiring a few men in recent weeks. Taking a job at the copper mine seemed the most logical way to remain solvent until spring.

We made arrangements to board the dogs with Walter and warehoused much of our gear at the cabin. The dogs seemed puzzled about this change and Bud and I were not too happy about it either.

It was a raw, bleak December morning when we trudged the trail to Kennecott without the dog team. Our thoughts were as bright as the toneless gray sky and wintry landscape.

21

Kennecott

In the great horseshoe-shaped valley of the Copper River, whose watershed nearly encircles the Wrangell Mountains, the history of copper is no less intriguing than the history relating to gold discovery in the North. It is the history of intrepid individual enterprise. It is also the history of monopoly, of politics and ruthless plunder.

Free or Native copper was known to exist in the Copper River basin since the early days of Russian occupation. Copper tools and the like were items of trade between the local Native population and coastal tribes. Prospectors had already entered the valley by 1885. That year Lt. Henry Allen led an exploratory mission through the Copper River country, down the Tanana and Yukon rivers to St. Michael's on the Western Arctic Coast. Many samples of high-grade copper were encountered.

It took until 1899 for prospectors to stake the area and they named the region the Nikolai Mine after the local Native chief. A mountain of copper had been discovered, one of the richest deposits in the world. Competing claims and federal court battles ensued. In late fall of 1903 matters were decided and the newly organized Kennecott Copper Corporation was set up to develop the site. The name Kennecott came from early naturalist and explorer Robert Kennecott. Kennecott's name was also attached to the river and glacier in the area.

New York economic powers, named "The Syndicate," (headed by millionaires J. P. Morgan and Daniel Guggenheim), took control and guided the building of a railroad to the mining camp. That was an adventure in itself, in part memorialized in Rex Beach's famous novel *The Iron Trail*. A railroad 196 miles in length was constructed with steel being laid across rocky terrain, mountainous country, necessitating piling bridges, and crossing three rivers. It took until 1911 for the railroad's completion at a cost of $23.5 million. The production of high-grade copper ore easily paid off the establishment of the Copper River and Northwestern Railway. As a bonus, the rail line was used for freighting, mail, and passenger service.

Various reports show that during the life of the mine, copper extracted topped two hundred million dollars in value. The owners ran a company town and controlled the railroad. The Syndicate did not lose money on Kennecott. The worst aspect for the public was that owners issued shares of railroad stock for numerous lines with the promise that they would haul coal that citizens bought and which were then manipulated into being worthless. There was also supposed to be a commitment to a "public service" branch of the railroad to Kennecott that was never built.

The construction of the Copper River railroad was an achievement that deserved a more enduring life and creative purpose than a brief existence for looting a mountain of copper. In 1938, when the ore at Kennecott was exhausted, the railroad was shut down. It had operated only twenty-seven years. Within a couple of years after rail transportation ended the town of McCarthy virtually ceased to exist. Chitina was a ghost town. And it was reported that more than a hundred families left Cordova. In a brief period of four decades from the time prospectors discovered the fabulous lode, the region of the Chitina Valley passed through the climactic cycle of discovery, exploitation, and abandonment. The region essentially reverted to wilderness.

But that lay in the future in December of 1926 when Bud and I trudged up the trail to Kennecott. The peak years of copper production had passed, but there were no signs of stopping the stream of copper pouring from the hill. Diamond drills and prospect drifts were tapping new ore bodies in every direction. Newsmen and government officials casually referred to the lode as "limitless copper resources." There were four camps on the hill and not less than six hundred men worked for the company.

Kennecott was situated in a picturesque mountain and glacier setting, and had it not been for the purely utilitarian aspect of the town the place might have passed for one of those Swiss Alpine villages as seen on picture postcards. There was nothing picturesque, however, about the tall, barnlike mill building rising four stories high in the center of the scene, with bunkhouses, office buildings, and warehouses clustered around and a railroad track running through the middle.

One can never mistake a hard-rock mining camp for anything but what it is. They all have the same commonplace, uninspired appearance, whether it is in Alaska or Timbuktu. The town nestled at the base of a seven-thousand-foot cragged mountain with a sprinkling of spruce on the lower slopes to offset the bleakness. On the opposite side of camp, the view opened abruptly on the gleaming expanse of Kennecott Glacier. In the distance, sixteen-thousand-foot Mount Blackburn lifted its white summit into the clear air.

The surrounding landscape belonged only to God. Everything else, except the post office, belonged to Kennecott, especially the four camps, Jumbo, Bonanza, Mother Lode, and Erie.

Bud and I visited the employment office, took a physical examination, and filled out many pieces of paper, including one that absolved the company from claims rising from accidental death or injury while riding its tram. We dropped our gear in a bunkhouse and went right to work. On a nice summer's day the tram ride up the hill might have been pleasant, but on this particular winter day it was windy and cold. Bud was assigned to tramming on one level and I was assigned to mucking on another.

Jumbo was the key mine and the largest camp. The accommodations included a large recreational hall with a card room in front and a gymnasium with mats, boxing gloves, and a set of parallel bars. It was also the site of moving picture shows, offered twice a week for a nominal charge. At the end of three mucking shifts at Jumbo, I was called to the timekeeper's office and handed a transfer slip to Erie. I was shifted to contract mucking, unusual for an inexperienced hand. It turned out I had let myself in for the toughest contract job at Erie, a job no one else in camp wanted.

The next morning I rode the skip down a dozen levels to the Erie ore train for a couple-of-mile ride through a tunnel. At the Erie mine portal I stopped in open-mouthed astonishment. The mine portal opened abruptly into space, with a half-mile steep pitch downward to the glacier below. On making my way cautiously down the stair-stepped goat trail, I found that the bunkhouse, too, had little respect for the law of gravity. The large, two-story structure rested on a rock ledge which appeared to be a shoe size too small to accommodate the building. The outer side of the bunkhouse extended beyond the foundation several feet over the precipice. The place was not really dangerous, of course, unless one was addicted to sleep-walking.

I was at Erie to work a six by seven hard-rock drift on the 1,050 level, 1,050 feet below the Erie mine entrance. The problem was that the amount of copper coming out was low and the workers were not getting more than regular laborers on the contract price. My role was to work with a companion miner and we were to drill, blast, and shovel. I was to be paid like a piecework employee in a factory, according to speed of production. Contract work was done at a killing pace compared to the more evenly paced salaried work elsewhere in the mine and most workers were ready for a break after a few months. I started on the night shift.

The contract mucker had to shovel a third to one-half more tonnage than the amount handled by a salaried mucker in five hours instead of eight. Anything slower and he would be holding up the miner's work. If the contract worker couldn't stand the guff, he handed the shovel over to someone who could. One had to get toughened up, akin to a prize fighter before a title bout.

The first week, by the time a shift was over, I was a stretcher case. My back was cracked, my arms were numb, and I was dragging around stiff-legged, at any minute becoming bait for the undertaker. I took hot showers, soaked my clutched hands in hot water, and absorbed dosages of liniment. In between, I cursed myself for ever considering contract mucking. Somehow I survived the first week and after two weeks I had toughened up.

The short days of winter were passing almost unnoticed. One scarcely came into contact with the outer elements for you were either in the bunkhouse surrounded by hissing radiators or down in the mine where the temperature remained constant at a few degrees above freezing. At Erie the alternating day and night shift changes came every two weeks. On Christmas, I was on the day shift, so I made a trip over to Jumbo with other Erie miners, and visited Bud. He was in good health and spirits, but in the awkward position of trying to save his money while learning how to play poker. Bud thought the tuition was a little expensive and talked of reforming.

This was the night of the huge poker tournament. Some miners set aside most of their wages to enter. This poker marathon was hardly equaled anywhere in a mining camp. Bud and I stood in the hall watching the bloodletting for a while, but in truth it was no place for amateur poker players to hang around. There were a dozen games going at once and they had begun in the afternoon. No one was ever known to shoot himself, or given that miners were playing, blow himself up, because of a loss at this working stiff's Monte Carlo. But winners would quit their jobs, give the boys a farewell handshake, and depart for the bright lights Outside. The biggest winner might take out twenty-five thousand dollars. Then his biggest challenge was to get past McCarthy with all of its pitfalls.

There was the tale of one lucky gambler who had raked in a big kill, but got off the train in McCarthy to say goodbye to his bosom friends, the local bar owners. By some inexplicable error he missed getting back on the train. A week later he was back at his old job on the hill, minus $16,000 and $350 in IOUs.

We began January of 1927 with bitter winds painting frost patterns inside the windowpanes of the bunkhouse. There were occasions the thermometer dipped to minus-forty and it was even colder in the valley. During cold snaps the valley lying toward McCarthy was shrouded in a thick layer of fog. A wan and heatless sun peered over the mountain horizon each clear day, but it retired after a short shift of four or five hours.

On wild winter nights when a blizzard raged, the bunkhouse shuddered and groaned like a ship weathering heavy seas and the windows rattled at every furious gust. We were glad the builders had anchored the bunkhouse to the mountainside with several stout steel cables. A poker player raised his head during one blow and said, "This rat trap feels like it's slipping off the cliff. There probably won't be a man of us alive in the morning."

Professional reformers always seemed to pick on mining camps. A rough mining camp, no matter where it is situated, is not exactly a model of rectitude before a Sunday school class. But commentators, either through ignorance or malicious intent, fail to take into account certain living circumstances. There were times miners at Kennecott broke out in open revolt over the nauseating swill and starvation rations being passed off as food. There were always complaints about the women working "the line," as well.

However, the mine was in operation 365 days a year and miners had rare opportunities to let loose. It was a tough challenge to squeeze in much hell-raising in McCarthy because of a shortage of free time. All this so-called drunken brawling is supposed to take place north of Latitude 54, but the horrid truth is that the cultured, fashionable people from New York to Hollywood probably do more drinking, whoring, and general hell-raising than the Kennecott miners were able to do by applying the most ambitious effort in all their spare time. Add to them the penny-pinching miners, god bless them, who hadn't stepped foot out of Kennecott in years.

The good news for me on level 1,050 was that work was speeding along. We were on a pace to collect more than three hundred dollars monthly, half again as much as the noncontract workers. One day while I was washing up after a shift, Jimmy the bull cook collared me and said someone had taken over a bunk next to mine and moved all of my books under the bed. I realized immediately that Bud had joined me at Erie camp and when I adjourned to the bunkhouse, there he was, stretched out on his bunk.

This was part of our overall strategy. We planned to make hard-rock mining a short vocation. After that we expected to move northward to the Alaska Interior.

22

Learning Alaska History

Andy Taylor, our dog benefactor, was working the mine at Erie, too. Like Bud and me he was one of many workers from McCarthy hired on at Kennecott while planning for the future. At Erie we got to know Andy much better. At the recreational hall a wheezing old phonograph played while McCarthy dog mushers gathered in a corner and swapped stories.

Bud and I kept our mouths shut and listened and learned. We heard about the White River trail history and the Shushanna country. Andy's freighting was no simple job. He had hauled supplies for the National Geographic mountaineering expedition that made the first climb of Mount Logan, the tallest mountain in Canada. The peak is only about a hundred miles from McCarthy. Andy also carried supplies for other mountaineering groups to the Fairweather Range.

It was Andy's stories about the Shushanna mining camp that most fascinated us, however. The three major gold camps in Dawson, Nome, and Fairbanks were readily accessible to tens of thousands of prospectors. Shushanna was the roughest and toughest camp and the hardest to reach. That is little remembered except by a few gnarled old Sourdoughs who were young men when the mining began.

After two white prospectors investigated a creek later named Bonanza, a Native known as Shushanna Joe checked it out in 1909 and found a gold nugget worth $1.25. Joe bragged about his find, but people were slow to react. Finally more than a year later, a prospector named Bill James, who had worked his way over the Chilkoot Pass in '98, heard about it, but it was not until 1912 that he set out to explore the area of Joe's find. At first, using a shovel and gold pan, James discovered nothing. He moved and began panning, turning up between six and twelve cents a pan. He saw enough evidence of a larger strike and staked the land. The "official" discovery was recorded as May 3, 1913, and Andy Taylor was one of the first to the scene.

The days of the Shushanna rush were historic and brief, ending in 1927, with about six thousand to eight thousand prospectors passing through.

During my stay at Erie, a new cook was hired. He was of Japanese descent, but was stricter than his predecessor and did not seem prepared to mingle with the boys. An unnatural silence settled on the social hall. The kitchen became off-limits with everything but a machine gun or barbed wire surrounding the door. The parade-ground atmosphere did not sit well, but off-hours cups of coffee were at the discretion of the cook. Refusal to follow past precedent and make coffee available at all times grated on the men's nerves.

Worse, the quality and quantity of food declined at mealtimes. An ugly temper settled on the camp and the grousing and cursing in the washroom could be heard upstairs in the social hall. Gradually, it occurred to us that corporate management was behind this turn, experimenting to see what it could get away with before applying the policies to other camps.

A few weeks into this intolerable situation, the blowup came. It was triggered by the latest of the cook's unnecessary restrictive measures. It had been past practice to leave warming breakfast foods on the stove for the contract workers at the end of their night shifts. One day we discovered the kitchen door locked. That meant the shift had to go to bed without a meal or wait two hours to join the regular breakfast serving. The general attitude of our contract group was that it was an insult to be working for a chiseling outfit that was carrying on a systematic campaign of starvation. The foreman intervened, even though this activity did not come under his supervision, and he passed orders on to leave the kitchen door unlocked. Yet the next morning when the contract shift came in, the door was locked again.

This time my friend Mac stepped up and planted a steel-shod boot firmly against the door. In an instant the lower paneling gave way with a rending sound. In what began as a curious falsetto titter and ended in a war whoop, Mac swung his flashing boot with all of his weight behind it and caught the door at the doorknob. Bursting its lock, the door burst back on its hinges.

Despite the noise no one else appeared. The contract workers marauded into the kitchen, and then lifted the trash can and emptied its contents into the sink. A rapid survey of the shelves showed us there was plenty of food in stock even if we were being short-changed. The raiding was carried out methodically and thoroughly with the campaign patterned on the general plan of Sherman's march through Georgia. What was not of immediate use was dumped in heaps on the floor. Unknown delicacies, the likes of which we had never seen in camp, such as jars of ripe olives, cans of crab, sardines, tuna fish, pimento cheese, canned oysters, and clams.

Men began preparing their favorite foods. I looked in vain for strawberry jam. There was a shout when Mac stumbled upon packages of Roquefort and limburger cheese. The find was so stunning that we decided they must have been there since before Kennecott came into existence. In the cold room Mac and I went to work sawing off a couple of steaks for ourselves from a hind quarter of beef. We found onions to season them, too. We completed our dining, left the dishes, pots, and pans strewn everywhere, and then retreated out of the kitchen to the long bench outside the door waiting for the expected fireworks shortly after 5 A.M.

The cook went berserk when he saw the crashed-in door and the mess in his kitchen. He let loose a torrent of loud gibberish that sizzled and crackled like gunfire and was loud enough to be heard by the steward—the foreman's boss—where he was three miles away. Convulsed with anger the cook was jumping up and down stamping around in circles, beating his clenched fists madly upon his head, all the while pouring out a flood of imprecations punctuated with explosive oaths. This tantrum ceased abruptly and the cook shot out of the kitchen and dashed to the foreman's room.

A few minutes later the boss appeared in robe and slippers. The cook dogged his heels, gesticulating wildly. He was choked with such rage that his sounds were inarticulate cries rather than language. A look of disgust and annoyance passed over the foreman's face.

The dispassionate interest of the foreman completely unhinged the cook. He jumped up and down, shook his fists, danced in circles, and demanded that the entire night shift be fired at once. The foreman looked him in the eye and said, "You are fired." The cook said he couldn't do that because he was under the authority of the steward. The foreman repeated that he was fired. "Roll your blankets at once and get out of here," he informed the cook. The foreman focused on us, ordering us to clean up the mess and make sure the next work shift had its breakfast on the table.

We filed back into the kitchen and joked that it was a shame how the night shift had left things. Breakfast that morning was a sumptuous spread, including all of the unused delicacies, with a vast list of choices on the menu. The extravaganza was enough to make Kennecott Copper stock drop ten points on the New York Stock Exchange!

Down on the 1,050 level the drift was surging ahead under the incessant roar of high explosives. Mac's driving energy seemed boundless and he forced the pace for the contract workers. At the end of January we cleared $340 per man on contract. Mac called it "poker money." There were twenty-eight to thirty-one one-ton cars of copper being taken out every shift. On one shift the trammer pegged thirty-three cars on the board at shift's end. Mac was exhausted and he wasn't the only one.

One day in February, Mac and I sensed a gassy smell in the air around the drift. Some steps were taken to clear the air and we resumed working. Later, noxious fumes formed around the muck pile and I was getting the worst of the deadly stuff for I was right down in it. After three hours of shoveling I noticed a torpid feeling creeping in. I began feeling weak. My legs were rubbery. I was so weary I didn't know if I could finish the shift. I was fully aware that my dopey condition was due to the gas.

Men around the bunkhouse had been gassed and fallen unconscious and been dragged to fresh air by other miners. Contract workers had to make the call how much they could stand before the point of collapse. I heard, though, that the aftereffects of a headache and being logy could be felt for two or three months.

I was not aware of the moment when I lost consciousness and fell over backwards across the muck pile. Just how long I was knocked out I never knew. I could hear a sound of roaring wind and distant waves. I heard a sweet contralto voice singing some ageless lullaby. Voices became clearer and clearer and words became distinguishable. I heard Mac talking and I realized I was lying on a coat thrown down between me and bare rock. The trammer, returning to the 1,050 level with an empty car, had found me stretched out.

That night I ate some aspirin and went straight to bed. I had a compound hangover that jarred my teeth and there was a pounding inside my head of a thousand imps beating out an anvil chorus. Aspirin was never made strong enough to combat the violent reaction from being knocked out by power gas fumes.

At Christmas Bud and I had begun talking about moving north into the Interior of Alaska and we resumed those discussions as winter approached its end. There were several reasons for the choice. The main one was that this locality offered very limited options for making a living aside from wage work in mining. Also the Chitina Valley was isolated from other parts of the country. The economy of the valley was based entirely on mining and that offered no possibility of expansion.

Several of McCarthy's dog-team freighters were in the process of moving to the Interior and it was toward that spacious country with its broad valleys and limitless horizons that our eyes turned. We hoped to move to the middle of the Yukon basin and Fairbanks was our immediate objective. There were many placer camps in and around Fairbanks, with activity in Livengood, Circle, Woodchopper, Rampart, Manley Hot Springs, and Kantishna. We felt certain in that broad area we could rustle up a proposition.

In making a dog-team trip to the Interior, there were two routes open to us. The most logical one and by far the easiest was the route that followed the highway system. It took off at Chitina to join the Richardson Highway near Copper Center, and from there continued 275 miles to Fairbanks. The merit of the route was that it outflanked the Wrangell Mountains and the entire route presented no difficulty to winter travel. One didn't even need a dog team to follow it and indeed years later I did undertake a trip with packsack and snowshoes. There were roadhouses along the way and most of them—including Galena, Sourdough, Paxson, Rapids, and Big Delta—remained open during the winter months.

The other route outflanked nothing, stopped at nothing, and was unanimously cursed for being the toughest route to travel of any route to be found in the North. This was the route through the Wrangell Range by way of Skolai Pass. If we had listened just once to what our elders had told us about Skolai Pass we would never even have looked at a map that had Skolai Pass written on it. But we followed our own dark counsel. We chose this route. The theory behind the venture was that we needed to gain trail experience, so why not tackle the worst and have it over with rather than fritter away a lifetime trying to learn dog-teaming by practicing on boulevards made for automobiles.

The night before Bud and I left Kennecott we were thrown a little party. It was such a regular affair that there was no drinking or fighting!

23

Outfitting

March 1 was a dazzling, sunlit morning. Bud and I walked the five miles from Kennecott to McCarthy, breathing in the refreshing cold air, and opened our cabin. Frost lined the ceiling and the corners of the walls.

Walter the restaurant owner had boarded our dogs, but they were bored from loafing all winter. When they saw us coming they broke into a frenzied riot that started dogs barking all over town. The dogs sniffed out the kennels, reminding themselves about their old home. Bud and I headed back to town with a list for purchase as long as a commissary inventory. However, we soon bogged down at the bars greeting old friends and making conversation about our Kennecott experiences. The next morning we needed bromo-seltzer to get us started.

We began preparing for our long journey. We needed considerable equipment. In choice of stove and tent, we followed Andy Taylor's advice. We bought an eight-by-nine-foot tent designed like a pup tent. And we purchased a two-burner Coleman gasoline pressure stove with a folding oven attached and supplemented it with five gallons of fuel. We figured five gallons would carry us to the White River and then we would be in timber country.

Next we acquired grub for us and dog food. We were not so foolish as to believe we could live solely off the land by shooting our dinner. We had heard stories about too many self-confident nimrods who thought they could feed themselves on the trail, but got lost and barely survived without eating for a week. Alaska and Northwestern Canada game populations had been on the decline and game regulations supervised the take. We educated ourselves on the laws.

As for the dogs, in most places in central Alaska, dried dog salmon, otherwise called chum, was the standard dog food, and during the heyday of dog-teaming it was put up in the thousands of tons every season. Wrangell Range freighters, however, relied mostly on cooked food with dried fish or game chopped up and cooked with cornmeal, rice, or oatmeal. That made for a balanced and filling ration hard to surpass for keeping dogs in good condition when working hard.

Bud and I bought a hundred-pound sack of cornmeal and a fifty-pound can of beef tallow to mix in. That would serve as twenty days of rations for five dogs. We also added a forty-pound bale of dried salmon. We congratulated ourselves that we had the dog food problem licked. Until we ran into the storekeeper who told us he had a small amount of a new commercial dog food that contained proteins, carbohydrates, vitamins, calories, and more. Bud and I felt honored to be allowed to buy a fifty-pound bag of this new magical item.

As for feeding ourselves, we planned for six to eight weeks on the trail and stocked up on flour, beans, bacon, tea, coffee, salt, baking powder, sugar, lard, dried and condensed milk, rice, raisins, butter, granulated potatoes, dried yellow split peas, and dried apples. We added various seasonings, strawberry jam, and tins of syrup for flapjacks. We lost all sight of weight when we added a forty-pound sack of vegetables, including potatoes, turnips, and onions. Our grub box, modeled after other dog drivers', was built of plywood and just the right width to fit snugly into the width of the sled.

Other equipment on our checklist included a two-hundred-foot coil of rope, a coffeepot and cooking utensils, two pairs of snowshoes, four and a half feet in length, snow goggles, ice creepers with sharp spikes, a first-aid kit, a box of candles, matches, jackknives, a sewing kit, a compass, ax, a small tool kit, rolls of harness webbing, dog moccasins to protect the dogs' feet, hay wire, sleeping bags, and two rifles, a .250-300 and a .300-caliber Savage. Our clothing was the usual rough outdoor apparel of northerners, including woolen mackinaws, woolen shirts, mittens, gloves, fur caps, parkas with hoods, regular winter footwear, and rubber-bottomed shoepacs.

Years earlier, when Archdeacon Hudson Stuck, the man who led the first ascent of Mount McKinley, was on a lecture tour in the eastern United States, a matronly woman accosted him and asked, "How on earth do you people living in the North endure the terrible cold?" Stuck answered: "Madam, we have more sense than to attempt to endure the cold. We protect ourselves from it." That was to be the strategy Bud and I hoped to follow. The Archdeacon pointed to a formula simple enough on the surface, but violated more often than used. That is the difference between hardship and comfortable living in a rigorous northern climate.

Bud and I took pride in assembling a very complete outfit. It was so complete we should have had an ox team rather than a dog team to move it. My biggest mistake during our first year in the country was ordering long handed underwear. A salesman had looked at me with alarm in his eyes and I ordered a set of heavyweight, super special heavyweight woolens in red two sizes too large because I heard they shrank. The outfit was immensely large for me, but I gave it two trial runs in weather between minus-twenty and minus-thirty. But it might as well have been one hundred above in the shade. It was like living in the tropics in monsoon weather and I laid it in mothballs for a day the climate changed for the worse.

Several days after Bud and I began outfitting we learned that another party of two dog teams and three men was preparing to leave McCarthy shortly for the upper White River country. Two of them, Harry Boyden and Joe Meloy, were freighters, and the third, Fred Reynolds, was a mining man. Part of the mission was to freight in a ton and a quarter of supplies for Reynolds, who was in charge of carrying out patent work for a group of claims on the Beaver River for an eastern syndicate.

Bud and I knew of the men, but had never met them. A couple of days before our scheduled departure from McCarthy we met Boyden on the sidewalk. He was swinging along with a dog chain in one hand and paused to give us a cheerful grin. "I guess you are the fellows who are heading for Fairbanks," he said by way of introduction.

We told him we were all ready except actually loading the outfit onto the dog sled, which didn't seem large enough to handle it all. He laughed. "That's the trouble with dog-teaming," he said. "If a man can't find enough freight of the other fellow's to keep him busy, he can always work up a healthy appetite moving his own stuff around. It keeps a man guessing sometimes whether he's working for himself or working for the dogs."

We talked for a few more minutes and then Boyden said, "I'm not the sort to go around telling other people how to run their affairs—that kind of thing always gets a man in Dutch. But I was just thinking that Joe and I will be pulling out in about a week. Of course, we'll be moving slowly because we're relaying. But you fellows are welcome to join the party if you're so minded. Traveling together always makes things easier on everybody concerned. Joe and I aren't much shakes to look at, but then the dogs don't seem to mind."

Bud and I had been quietly sizing up the big dog driver. For almost a year, since we had first commenced hearing tales of the glacier trail, we had been hearing Boyden's name mentioned in connection with affairs. We were talking to a quiet, unassuming man, a man who joked easily and had a natural way of leading. At this time Boyden was about forty years old. He stood all of six feet in his moccasins and had the rangy, muscular physique and iron constitution that goes with spending years in the saddle pounding trails with a dog team. His powerful legs and thighs were especially noticeable, more so than with most dog drivers. It was a mark that we noticed even before the chuckle. Boyden had just returned from a trip Outside, his first leisurely winter in a dozen years. But the rank climate of the Pacific Northwest had failed to wash the leathery tan from his features. He looked as if he had just come off of the trail instead of being ready to start a trip.

Boyden explained the details of his party and something of its planned schedule. Their departure awaited the arrival of Fred Reynolds, who had not yet come back from a business trip to the States. The two freighters had most of their personal outfit lined up and the freight itself was being packed at O'Neill's store. At the moment, Boyden was scouting the town, trying to find a couple of more dogs for his team.

"With these stray mongrels running loose around town," he said, "a man would naturally think their owners didn't care to have them around. But the moment you step up, why these proud dog owners turn their backs on you. If you keep urging them, you are given to understand that the dog is very valuable, works good in lead and that sort of thing. If you find anyone who gives you the slightest encouragement, why the price on the dog starts at a hundred dollars."

Boyden then urged us to join him at O'Neill's where Joe was bargaining for purchases. Boyden figured his partner would stop arguing for a few minutes if he met us. Inside the store stood a ruddy, round-faced man with the stocky build of a bear in the middle of a heap of supplies blocking one aisle. Boyden met Meloy by saying, "How are you making out, Joe? Do you think we'll break even this trip, or should we just tie up the dogs and stay in town for the summer?"

A look of anguish passed over Meloy's face and a lament passed his lips. "I just can't do any dickering with Charlie at all," he said. "Every time I point to something on the shelf he slips another price tag out of his pocket and boosts the price on the article by three or four dollars."

Charlie O'Neill, the storekeeper guffawed. "It's the freight," he said. "Ha, ha. Really, it's the freight."

That was the stock alibi of all northern storekeepers. The freight charges were doing in the freighters. There was some irony in that.

Meloy agreed that Bud and I were welcome to join their party, but we felt we had none too much time to reach our destination before breakup and we could see no reason for further delay in leaving McCarthy. We were fully equipped and ready for travel. Joe interrupted conversation briefly by choking on his tobacco and coughing loudly for a spell.

When we were ready to leave, Boyden said, "Well, take 'er easy. Pick your weather before crossing the glaciers and watch for the cracks. Be careful and don't get caught out on the ice in a blow. You know a blow can come up quite sudden sometimes. It doesn't give a man much warning." Boyden paused, reflecting. He chuckled and added in a confidential tone: "People are always good at giving advice. That's one thing a man can give away without hurting himself and sometimes we give away so much we don't have any left for ourselves. But there have been times when the trail was rough and things didn't look just right. I've always found that 'easy does it' is a good rule to follow. A fellow lives longer that way. Anyway, it saves wear and tear on a man's feet, to say nothing of the dogs'."

We bid the freighters farewell and good traveling and started back to the cabin. Bud broke the silence. "Did you notice Meloy when he choked on his tobacco?" he asked. "Not especially," I said. "Why?" "Well, he didn't choke," Bud said flatly. There was a bleak look in Bud's eyes indicating he was doing some hard thinking. "I have a hunch," he said. "They think we can't make it by ourselves. Otherwise there was no reason for Boyden to suggest that we sit around and wait for them."

"Oh, rats!" I said. "Certainly it will be tough. We know that. But if they can freight a couple of tons or more over Skolai Pass, we can sure get our outfit through."

24

The Trail

The wilderness is not a place that yields to a hard and fast schedule for travel varies a great deal under different conditions of terrain, trail, and weather. A dog-team outfit meeting up with a combination of adverse circumstances may have difficulty making a few miles a day. The same outfit moving under favorable conditions on a clear trail may travel forty, fifty, or sixty miles with ease.

The conditions of travel Bud and I would face going through Skolai Pass were of paramount concern for us. It was not the distance but the weather that we were focused on. We knew in our planning that success or failure in our trip would be met within the first hundred miles beyond McCarthy. We were sure to face unpredictable weather, incomparably rough terrain, and glaciers. One might easily spend more time and effort negotiating fifty miles in this rocky, storm-blasted region of the Wrangell Range than traveling five hundred miles in valleys beyond it.

Bud and I were up an hour before the first gray light of dawn on March 10, our intended day of departure. We had only a hazy idea of how we would load everything in the outfit onto one dog sled, but an hour later when we had accomplished it we had no idea if we could do it again. The bulky load of about seven hundred pounds was securely roped down.

While we loaded, the dogs barked, bounded around on their chains, and yelped with excitement. They were ready to run. We couldn't explain that this would be no rabbit chase, but after loafing all winter the dogs were a bundle of exploding energy, ready to travel anywhere. The townspeople were still not awake when we steered the sled out of the yard and bade farewell to our cabin. Swinging into the main street, we crossed the wooden bridge at the foot of town and turned sharply to the right up a long grade which rose steeply to the plateaulike rim of Sourdough Hill. The hard pull took some of the bursting energy out of the dogs.

Despite the minus-twenty temperature Bud and I worked up a quick sweat and before we were four hundred yards from town we wondered if we had shown good sense starting out on this trip. By the time we reached the top of the grade the dog mushers and dogs were ready for a five-minute blow.

The top of the hill overlooked the snow-covered roofs of the frame structures and log cabins of McCarthy and looking beyond we could see the furrowed wastes of rock and the white ice of Kennecott Glacier. At the foot of the mountain we could see the mill and some of the buildings at Kennecott. We stood looking out at every part of the view and it seemed as if we were leaving an important part of our lives there. Less than a year earlier we had come to the valley as strangers and looking upon northern life as one would look at another planet. Now it was life Outside that looked strange. Without formally recognizing the condition, we had found in this place the essential elements of freedom.

The trail across Sourdough Hill was smooth and hard packed and the weather was ideal for sledding. The bright morning sun was warming the atmosphere and we shed our mackinaws. Only the sled was top-heavy and we had trouble managing the load. Repeatedly, the bow of the sled slipped off the trail, plunging the sled nose-first into soft snow and stalling the team. The unwieldy load turned on its side and we had to right it every four hundred yards or so.

After four miles of this on-again, off-again travel we came upon a new obstacle. A Fordson tractor with woodsaw attachment was ahead of us on the trail. The owner, Bill Berry, was sitting idly on the tractor seat. He gazed at our outsized load said, "It looks like you got everything on but the dog kennels. What was the matter? Was they froze down?"

For a while we rigged up complicated methods of trying to budge the tractor, but it didn't move. Then Bill suggested using dog power. "How's about them meat burners of yours?" he asked. "Are they any good on the tow line or just like the rest of the soup hounds? I think with a little pull this rig would walk out of here." We hooked up, the dogs pulled the tractor over a bed of logs, and the rig was free. Bill looked as pleased as if he had invented the dog team.

Calling us a couple of coyotes, Bill saw that we had not attached a gee pole to the sled. He helped us construct one and after that it helped keep the sled balanced and on the trail.

We moved on, following the summer trail. To the right was timbered country not far from Chitina. It was late afternoon when we pulled into the Nazina Roadhouse and soon Murie came out to visit us.

He asked if we had seen Bill Berry around town before we left and we told him how we had met him bogged down on the trail. Murie was surprised. Bill was on his way to the roadhouse and he wondered what held him up. Murie was more surprised when Bud and I told him we hooked up our dogs and pulled Berry's tractor out of deep snow. Bud and I washed up and Mrs. Murie had prepared supper when we heard Bill's tractor clattering into the yard.

When he cleaned up, Berry refused to corroborate our story of rescuing the tractor. "If you believe everything them two coyotes tell you, you'll set yourself back twenty years and get a dog team!" Dog mushers as a class are regarded as proverbial liars even when they tell the truth!

The smooth traveling on hard-packed trail ended at the roadhouse. Beyond there the dog-sled trail thinned to mere tracks which scattered to trap lines and a prospector's camp. The region became progressively more mountainous and rough. From here on we would relay the outfit to the White River country. It was six miles to the Dan Creek cabin and because of our late start that was all we planned to cover for the day. The sled slammed and banged over stump roots and old rotted deadfalls. There was no trail in the open part of the valley. We dodged around trying to find strips of snow.

Dan Creek cabin was a rough log structure not regularly inhabited, but which had seen much use during the years of travel to and from Shushanna. The furnishings represented something less than Spartan simplicity. The cabin contained a battered wreck of a stove, a few boxes to sit on, and a couple of bare pole bunks against the end wall. It was not the Waldorf Astoria, but at least it saved the trouble of setting up a tent. Our forward distance was only six miles, but because of relaying we had covered eighteen. Relaying meant slow and tedious progress. Some of the great explorers had used relaying to advance their objectives, including Roald Amundsen, Knut Rasmussen, and Robert Peary.

Leaving Dan's cabin we mushed ten miles before we decided a relay was in order. We ate a warmed-up lunch of beans, bannock, and jam. The dogs lay nearby and watched the proceedings hungrily. It didn't seem polite to eat without offering them something so we snacked them on dried fish. They got their regular meal once a day in the evening once the work was done. Sam had a gash on his leg, but didn't want to rest it by riding in the sled. He considered it an insult to his dignity if asked to rest extra. Finally, he just followed us for a while loose.

We advanced ten miles before choosing a pleasant camping spot in the spruce trees and we fixed up a sweet-smelling spruce bough bed for the dogs. We even had running water in a nearby river and plenty of dry wood for cooking dog food. After spending months in gaseous underground work, Bud and I reveled in the fresh, clean air. It sharpened one's senses to natural things. It also sharpened one's appetite. After supper Bud and I loafed around the campfire watching the evening shadows lengthen on the peaks.

When we woke we greeted a new weather pattern. A cold north wind was blowing down from the glaciers spitting light, flinty snow. The higher country was blanketed in lowering gray clouds and snow squalls. We shivered in the tent before downing our coffee. Sam was back in harness and we broke out our parkas and mitts for the first time because the raw wind was facing us. Snow clouds concealed the crest of the Nazina Glacier. We traveled five or six miles before we came to open water. It was our first stream crossing. We saw faint tracks where a dog sled went into the water and came out on the other side. We would never have admitted surrender, but we did reflect on all that dog mushers put up with to make progress.

The big debate was over footwear and in the interests of keeping most things dry, we sat down alongside the river, and like little boys on a Sunday picnic in June took off our boots and rolled up our breeches. We pointed the lead dog, Rex, at the water, but he balked. He had been bawled out for leading us into overflow before, or perhaps he just did not want to get his feet wet, but he refused to go. Bud grabbed him by the collar and led him across. The water was brrr cold and we hurriedly dried our feet, and put socks and moccasins back on.

We pushed the dog team into a run to help us warm our numbed feet. A couple of miles later we stumbled onto a well-defined trail and it led us to a nearly legendary large log cabin called the Homestead. It was a trapper's home and his dogs parked in the yard alerted him as to our coming.

The salient feature about the Homestead was the strategic position it occupied in this ice-locked region. It was within a half mile of the ice face of the Nazina Glacier, but was in the last dry stand of timber before entering a grim wasteland of ice and rock. The place had been the scene of several daring rescues where stormbound travelers were stuck on the glacier. Many stumbled into this port of safety exhausted. The cabin itself was a sturdy log structure, about twenty feet wide and thirty feet long inside with a low gable roof. It had served as a beacon in the wilderness during the Shushanna rush. Trappers, mushers, and other travelers always kept the cabin supplied and did any repair work necessary. It was a community shelter.

Billy Arliss was the trapper living at the Homestead. We knew him in McCarthy the previous fall. He was a sprightly chap, amicable and accommodating. Billy stepped out the door and gave us a friendly salute. "Howdy," he said with his wave. "I heard you fellows were headed this way." He ordered his dogs to pipe down so we could talk and then asked where Boyden and Meloy were. He thought we would be traveling together. Billy said he heard about us and the other mushers through "the Moccasin Telegraph." That is the nickname for word of mouth in the North.

We told him that we had decided not to wait for Boyden and Meloy and he looked thoughtful. He agreed that we could use the time gained by leaving early, but warned us about the Russell Glacier. It was getting worse to travel over all of the time. "The middle section is full of cracks," he said. Billy said that he and his trapping partner Lew Anderton might be on their way to the White River country, too, to pick up the traps in this area and set up for spring there.

The inside of the Homestead cabin was filled with reminders of its colorful past. It was steeped in a pungent atmosphere of trail and trap line. There were mingled odors of tobacco smoke, drying pelts, drying socks, and sweated dog harnesses. That might not have appealed to fastidious nostrils, but impressed one with the feeling that the place had seen life and was being lived in. The bare log walls were smoke stained to the point of old shoe leather. A Rembrandt quality of light, filtering through a window at each end of the cabin, heightened the rich, amber effect. There was a good-sized selection of fur hanging from the roof. This was most of Billy's winter catch.

Billy insisted on feeding us sheep stew rather than us using up our own grub. He said we might well need it before Fairbanks. We insisted on contributing to the dinner, though. Bud added canned corn, canned peaches, and sauerkraut, leftovers from our kitchen shelf in town, to the menu. "Lordy! Lordy!" Billy said. "You fellows shouldn't have brought that kind of stuff. You should have brought along hard grub instead."

The next morning Billy left with his team to pull in his traps. Bud and I spent the day handling a relay load, but that brought us back to the Homestead by late afternoon for another comfortable night.

25

Taming Live Glaciers

On an overcast morning in mid-March Bud and I set off across river flats to the middle face of the Nazina Glacier. We had no doubt we would find an easy route across since dog teams and horse freighters had been crossing it for decades. We were looking for places with the least moraine and the most ice. That would guide us to a trail in between the crevasses and allow us to place a load on the ice field by nightfall.

We were rank novices in glacier travel and although we had asked for advice, the veterans who informed us operated on such a higher level of knowledge we had not asked for the right details. They took it for granted that everyone was born with a rudimentary knowledge of glacier travel. The novice was simply warned to travel warily in places.

Yet routing a trail on an ice field was not as simple as all that. Behind it lay a small encyclopedia crammed full of intimate knowledge of glaciers, gained through years of experience and getting into and out of jackpots. Their Ph.D.s as glacialists were earned while prodding trails with a shovel handle through labyrinths of pressure ridges and fissures where a misplaced foot might mean sudden death.

Glaciers are impressive phenomena. The action of these great ice fields is an intriguing story written in rocks and the contours of mountain ranges and hills. One should know a few elementary facts about glaciers or he would do well not to risk his neck on an ice field. Bud and I violated this rule due to our untempered rashness, and as we later learned, gave no small concern to veterans Boyden and Meloy, who had tried to persuade us to wait for them.

The Nazina and Russell glaciers are but two of scores of similar glaciers whose origins are the great snowfields lying on the heights of the Wrangell and St. Elias ranges. One might dwell at length on the surpassing grandeur of the regions where glaciers are seen descending the heights in every direction. Glaciers, like the sea, and like the mountains that cradle them, are never seen twice exactly the same. Their appearances change with the changing light and varying atmospheric conditions and turning seasons.

We had not intended to probe the mysteries of the ice field, but we spent two days examining the area in the vicinity of the Nazina. We discovered many cracks in the ice and retreated. Also, the ice groaned and cracked with startling reports. The ghastly sounds were matched by a ghostly light. But to our delight at the largest cavern we found, everything we shouted reverberated back with an echo. We did not know that no dog musher had ever put a team through where we looked. We did decide to detour and returned the way we had come.

Several times we initiated trials, advanced a couple of hundred yards, then were faced with potholes, rough ice, and crevasses and had to turn back. The bewildering maze of fissures and pressure ridges pushed us back. By late afternoon we were dog-tired, disgusted, and hungry. The next day we began again, with the same results at first. Then we found a spot where we could advance a mile onto the face before being halted by a crevasse field. It took a lot of intricate and careful maneuvering to pass through the dangerous area. When we caught our breaths and looked around we realized that our feat of crossing through this zone would have brought on a sanity hearing had the veterans known about it.

We angled westward and higher, through deep snow, before beginning our descent. If we were correct, we should come off the glacier just ten minutes from the Homestead. When we reached the cabin Billy was back. We explained our adventures and he shook his head and admonished us for putting our lives in danger. We hadn't realized that we did so and looked at him in amazement. We asked how we could find the trail without exploring. "Lordy, man!" he exclaimed. "I didn't know you were looking for the trail. I thought you fellows were just out for some sightseeing when you talked about climbing the glacier. I could have told you where the trail was in two minutes."

As Billy poured tea I told him we thought the trail began at the face of the glacier. "No, no," he said. "The trail doesn't go anywhere near the face. It follows up alongside the moraine. The trail takes you up the outer side. There's a deep, narrow gut that guns up that way for a couple of miles or so. You can't see it from the glacier. It's wedged in between the moraine and the hillside. But you can't miss it when you're on it, either."

The landmark, something we had heard mentioned in stories many times, but dismissed because we didn't know the terrain, was a packhorse barn. Billy said it was three miles from the Homestead. For me, this was like unveiling the plot in a mystery story. The tactical approach, rather than blundering and bulling one's way through, was habit with all experienced travelers.

We drove the dogs to the now dilapidated barn which once housed a dozen horses, briefly investigated the area, and picked up the trail. It was a hard-pounded smooth depression worn into the flinty wastes by packhorse trains, dog-team outfits, and several thousand foot travelers. The trail ended on smooth ice at the end of the glacier. We discovered our own tracks a couple of hundred yards away.

We returned to the Homestead, piled the gear on the sled, said goodbye to Billy, and by midafternoon Bud and I were back at the barn. If the weather was fair on the morrow we planned to set out across the glacier and do it in one load without a relay.

Bud and I were excited. So this was the route the freighters used. This was the recalcitrant trail. We took a trial run with an empty sled. We had missed the pay streak of the gold miners, but we were missing none of the woes that plagued the gold seekers. The windowed ridges of rock lay parallel to the glacier flow and pulling across them was like weathering the storm waves that seethe over an open ocean bar. The dogs staggered and lunged. The sled pitched and rolled over boulders and shale.

We were ready to go for real. It was minus-twenty-six degrees and still going down when we stretched out in the tent. We slept fitfully, for somewhere in our subconscious minds there was unreasonable dread of the ice field trail lying before us. There were other routes, of course, but the all-glacier trail was the main one for winter freighting and mail. The blows that struck the glaciers were often veritable hurricanes rather than mere blizzards. The long crevasses had to be bridged. There were many difficult and treacherous passages, but the most notorious was the "Jump Off," an abrupt fault line on the divide in the area of the Nazina and Shushanna glaciers. The only way to negotiate this hazardous place was to climb up and down a chute which dog drivers had hewn into the ice. Getting freight down this slippery escalade was always a sweaty job.

It was minus-thirty-six as we loaded the final items on the sled and set out. Our route took an angling course up the glacier, for Skolai Pass' lower basin lay several miles farther up the opposite side of the ice field. The snow patches we saw made us wary. One never knows about these things on the first trip across. We were so focused on probing for crevasses that we were slow to recognize a weather change. There was a brassy cast to the sun and the horizon was taking on a hue of gray putty.

We were four miles out on the ice field and at least twice as far from Skolai Pass. Within an hour after first noticing the changing sky we realized we were in for a hard blow. We sought what security might be available in the lee of large rock slabs at the foot of a high ridge as the glacier head was blotted out by pellets of hard-driven snow. A moraine is only a bleak rock dump, but there are times when it ranks with Gibraltar for protection.

Still, we had to make camp. We chose a ravine nearby, though moving the sled's contents on slippery, wet ground in high winds with a storm hitting us in the face was a Herculean task. It took a full two hours. We erected the tent and the dogs burrowed into the snow. The storm had struck about noon and increased in intensity with each passing hour. In our hollow we were fine sipping tea. Fifty feet above us the wind roared.

For a brief period in late afternoon the wind slackened, but it was only a prelude. It resumed in velocity far beyond the level previously reached. The sound was a fearful drumming roar like a hard-pounding express train passing overhead. We peered from the tent to see horizontal streamers of snow pouring straight across the ridges above. Darkness came early, with no letup to the fury. Sometime after midnight I woke with a stuperous feeling, imagining I was sleeping in the bunkhouse at Erie and some callous night shifter had switched on the light. Soon I realized the soft light flooding the tent came from the moon. The storm was over. Bud snored on.

I climbed out of my sleeping robe and exited the tent. There was not a breath of wind astir. The scene was naked, hard, cold, and brilliant as a diamond, a world of ice and snow and bare rock. The mellow light flooding the frozen wastes softened the harsh contours. Pools of moonlight were splashed like buckets of freezing water across the miles of naked ice. The nearer reaches, where the ice joined the moraine, were scintillating with myriad fiery pinpoints which glittered like a jeweled tiara worn by a proud, haughty queen.

The mind finds it difficult to conceive the countless millenniums that pass during a glacier's slow creep, but the imperceptible movements are heard. Every few minutes, from widely separate places on the ice field, there came weird reports of splitting ice as the glacier shifted ever so slightly in its age-old bed. Some of the reports were so far distant they were only faintly heard. But I was startled from my reverie when the ice split directly below the ridge where I was sitting. The report, as sharp as a high-powered rifle shot, was followed by an eerie shivering sound, a long, drawn-out rending sound like silk or canvas being torn.

My teeth chattered a tattoo as I slipped back into the tent. But I was content with the venture. For a brief moment I had looked upon the naked cold grandeur of the Pleistocene ages when early man and earth were a few years younger. Such rare moments remain indelibly impressed in the mind long after the stone bruises from the trail are forgotten.

We had good traveling on wind-scoured ice the next day with clear skies. As one end of the glacier drew closer our interest centered on the lower basin. It was Skolai unfolding before us, the rugged, formidable pass which for us was as legendary as ancient Rome. We were still studying the cragged contours in the distance when an obstacle of more immediate interest claimed our attention. It was a fresh, lateral moraine, fully a half-mile wide and rougher in character than either of the two already crossed.

Stopping, we had to split the load and relay. Rock rubble overlaid a fractured portion of the ice field. The place was an inchoate hell, a chaotic mess neither wholly ice nor moraine. We struggled yard by yard. We crawled over huge slabs of rock where the dogs got hung up on the tow line and half strangled. In another place the sled had to be emptied and Bud and I had to pack the load for fifty yards over large boulders. In another place we had to lower the sled a dozen feet by rope. About halfway across the moraine we dodged some bad potholes. Bruised and battered we at last staggered into the clear.

And then we had to go back and do it all over again with another relay load. By the time we finished we had spent six hours covering a half-mile-wide moraine. We made camp by a frozen creek and because we were attracted by a lone spruce tree that made the spot feel like home. We ached in every joint, but we were encouraged in the shadow of Skolai Pass because we believed nothing could be worse than crossing the moraine. If so, the pass would never have been traveled.

26

Near Death on Skolai Pass

Skolai Pass was ice gored, glacier locked, and swept by storm clouds and blizzards. It was the cradle of tempestuous weather. The pass was cursed and maligned by travelers, but never spoken of lightly, nor with scorn. Skolai's stern character commanded the respect and resourcefulness of even the most trail-hardened veterans.

In comparison to most mountain passes on the continent, Skolai was not a high pass. But it made up the difference with its incomparably rugged character and the ferocious temperament of its weather. Moreover, nature had contrived to make the pass seemingly impregnable by flanking it on either end with massive ice fields. In all, there were about forty-five miles of trail between the head of the Nazina River where the ice field began, to the headwaters of the White River.

The Pass itself was about fifteen miles long as it scaled on the map. Within that area one encountered all the obstacles and hazards common to more reputable passes, along with numerous innovations and traps of Skolai's own sinister devising. Skolai's obstinate demeanor made it more difficult to travel the fifteen miles than two hundred miles of flat trail. Indeed, there were reported incidents of travelers going all of the way around the western extremity of the Wrangells to avoid the pass.

Our move to the pass carried special significance for me. On March 22 one year before, minus one day, I had arrived in Alaska. During that year I had transformed from Cheechako to Sourdough status.

Bud and I set up camp on the frozen creek and the next day set out to find our route through the pass. We began by dropping down to Lower Skolai Lake over a fifty-foot dropoff, a place perfect for breaking one's neck. We escaped with a few bruises. Sledding on the mirrorlike surface of the lake at the lower basin could not have been better. "If we only had sledding like this all of the way," Bud declared. "We could haul a ton and make forty miles a day." Thus do dog mushers contemplate heaven. We did stop several times to admire the surroundings. We were mostly protected from the winds and there were spruce trees, the last of them, nearby.

Soon enough the terrain began to change and we encountered rocky gulches, boulders, rougher ice on Skolai Creek, and steep slopes. There was overflow, too, and we kept our moccasins dry by riding the sled runners. The creek ice then ended in a narrow canyon that spewed forth fast-running water. Andy Taylor had warned us that here was where our troubles would begin. We camped to investigate the area for the best trail.

The dogs had been winding game and on the off chance I could spot a sheep, I grabbed a rifle. Not two hundred yards away on the canyon rim stood a big, white ram. Meat for the pot, I thought, quietly seeking position. The wind was in my favor. I eased the rifle from my shoulder, worked the bolt while muffling the sound with my mitten, and lined the sights. The ram stood broadside, a perfect target. I squeezed the trigger . . . and nothing happened! The bolt was gummed with just enough oil that in the cold weather the bolt head failed to snap. I frantically worked over the rifle, but could not fix it. Cursing myself roundly for my own inexcusable negligence, I headed back to camp to get Bud's rifle.

Bud was cooking dog food when I got back to camp and borrowed his rifle. When I returned to the site of the sheep encounter, the ram had moved on, joining a larger group, and they had departed for higher foothills in the fading daylight. Instead of mutton chops, we were having corned beef willy for supper.

The next day Bud continued his search for the right route and I set out after the ram. However, as I progressed I marveled at the harshness of the terrain, a canyon filled with moraine, boulders, jutted rock outcroppings, talus, hummocks, gulches, and ridges. I couldn't even find a place where a sledding route could be started. The sheep was never in the picture and my trek turned into a grim struggle to get back to camp alive. I picked my way down the slope not even thinking about a dog-sled route anymore.

I had been in camp a half hour when Bud appeared, shouting, "The dirty bastards!" He was frazzled and sweating and it was not until he lit a smoke and drank some tea that he started to feel better. "There were so many sheep up there and I couldn't get near them," he explained. Apparently, the sheep had spread word that we were dangerous characters with working guns and everyone should stay away from us. It worked. The sheep were just not in a sociable mood. It was corned beef for dinner again.

Frustrated, we explained what we had seen of one impassable area after another. We wished we had drawn more detail out of Andy, but without seeing what was in front of us we would not have known the questions to ask. We did recall him saying, "The Chilkoot Pass is child's play compared to Skolai!"

We investigated the north side of the canyon, thinking perhaps of linking up with the packhorse trail, if we could reach it. Brush slapped us in the face. There were tangles of deeply eroded gullies. Snowshoes were as much nuisance as use since we had to take them off every hundred yards or so. It took us two hours to move two miles above camp. I now agreed with Bud's pondering of how we would get a dog sled up there. One thing about cities is that they have elevators to go up. Better minds than ours had coped with similar problems, but then Einstein didn't find the answer to the theory of relativity in the back of the book.

I came up with the idea of following the canyon for a while and then angling over to the ridge. Bud went off to reconnoiter and I returned to camp to cook dog food. When he reappeared I asked how he made out. "I got back alive!" he said. "Then, that's the way to go," I replied. Bud amplified his analysis of the route: "Murder."

All through chores and dinner we chewed on the problem. There had to be a passable route because it had been done. And I clung to my threadbare conviction that if packhorses could make it, so could we. I was starting to think that to outsmart Skolai one had to have omniscient knowledge.

Once again the next morning I set out, this time determined to find some small hint of where mushers had traveled, whether it be a discarded tin can, some slip of paper, or other piece of trash. I did not find a clue to the sledding trail. At Frederika Basin I looked around, trying to shelter myself from a harsh wind. But the wind had blown much of the snow off of the slopes and I could see the packhorse trail. The winding ascent from the basin was not too awkward for a dog sled. After the first steep rise the trail gradually smoothed out. Most surprising, I saw the amount of work packers had put into building and maintaining the trail with crude bridges and other improvements. Yet then I came to spots that had been washed out, and an area so narrow the horses would have had to be pigeon-toed to make it through.

I intended to follow the trail longer, but I came upon a collection of sheep and once again thought of adding meat to the menu. I climbed ever higher, until I was about fifteen hundred feet above the base of the mountain, angling for a clear shot. It never came. The sheep caught wind of me and ran away. It was growing dark and I wanted to get off the mountain as quickly as possible. I found a snow slope, sat down, and began to glissade.

Things went well at first. I ruminated that people in the States paid money each weekend to slide down hills like this. After several hundred feet, however, the snow was wind-packed and as hard as cement. I picked up speed and lost all control, shooting down the mountainside with meteor-like speed. The wind whistled in my ears as I spied a rock outcropping near the bottom in direct line with my hurtling descent. I pictured my future as a mangled corpse, good only for coyote bait.

Instinct for self-preservation guided my actions. As the outcropping came rushing towards me I tensed like a coiled spring, and rising from the snowshoes I leaped into the air an instant before crashing. I sailed through the air and hit a patch of brush for several tooth-rattling seconds, ricocheted over a large area of lumpy vegetation, and ended up in a clump of willow brush with my legs wrapped around my head.

It took a moment to recognize that I was alive. Then I thought I had a broken leg and wondered how Bud could find me. Not even a rifle shot would be heard. Then I realized I had lost the rifle in my tumble. Eventually, with night coming, I tried to stand. It was an effort. All of my joints felt as if they had gone through a concrete mixer. My right leg was more useful than I thought, but the ankle provided sharp pains. Each time I stepped, I gasped. I clomped around trying to find equipment and retrieved the rifle half buried in snow at the foot of the slide. Using my jackknife, I carved and shaped a willow branch into a walking staff.

I managed to squeeze into my snowshoes and started for camp about two miles away. The travel lay across rough country where I knew several deep gulches had to be crossed. I made fifty yards at a time while studying the ground for the easiest step. Outwitting the rough terrain became an engrossing game. I promoted myself to general and assigned myself the task of out-maneuvering the enemy. The route was planned about two hundred yards in advance and every score of yards was a skirmish with obstacles. The game of avoiding barricades and traps went on a long time, but the meaning of time was lost in the physical effort of merely keeping the snowshoes moving. I stumbled on and on uncertain about how much distance remained to be covered and how much longer I could stay on my feet.

Darkness took over and boulders and rocks appeared as just vague shapes against the snow. A cold wind was at my back and light snow began slatting down. In my intense weariness I had no concern about the weather. A deadly numbness was creeping over me, a slumberous feeling which I had little strength to fight off. The pain in my ankle was overshadowed because I felt nothing from the thigh down.

Accompanying my fatigue came a strange feeling that it was not me who was floundering through the snowdrifts, but a phantom stranger whom I watched with the detached interest of a spectator at a football game. The stranger stumbled, blundered into bushes, fell down, crawled to his feet, and struggled on. With a superior smile I wondered about laying a wager on how long the stranger would last.

The snow was not cold. It was feathery and soft and light as eiderdown. It seemed that snow and willow brush would make an inviting place to recline and go to sleep, offering an escape from the torturous battle to go on. But from someplace within my torpid consciousness a warning was signaled not to go to sleep, that those who slept in the snow were doomed.

But all I wanted was a short rest. It must have been ten minutes that I lay in a half-reclining position with my back propped up against some brush. I had passed beyond the realm of sharp consciousness, but something roused me from the lethal stupor and I sat up heavy-eyed, as if coming out of a deep sleep. I was cramped and stiff with cold, chilled to the bone, and shivering. Even as I took stock of my physical condition, my mind grappled with some strange phenomenon which seemed neither reality nor illusion. It seemed I heard a rifle shot coming from a great distance. It seemed as if it came from across the glacier. Then I dismissed the thought as part of a dream.

Dreaming? The shock hit me that I had fallen asleep in the snow and that jolted me into full wakefulness. I realized the gunshot was Bud trying to locate me. With unfeeling fingers I unslung my rifle and fired a shot in reply. Climbing up from the bed of willows, I pounded warmth into my arms and fingers. I had a strong hunch that Bud fired the shot from camp, and that meant camp might be just a stone's throw from where I stood. Cautiously snowshoeing around, I had folded up in a willow patch within a hundred yards of the canyon rim and with camp directly below. The discovery that I had all but lost the bout within actual shouting distance of Bud jolted me like the kick of a mule.

The sight of the candle-lighted tent glowing in the darkness never looked so good. When I appeared, Bud was fixing a ptarmigan stew. Bud scarcely looked out of the tent flap as I set down the rifle and snowshoes. Then he asked, "How did you make out? Hell, you're late getting back. When you didn't show up after dark, I thought maybe you'd got hung up someplace. So I let go a couple of shots."

So there had been two shots. I was too exhausted to talk and all I said was, "I was on my way down." That simple statement stood until nearly a year later when one winter evening we happened to be talking about Skolai and Bud learned the whole story of my day.

Our camp was dug into the snow at the base of a rocky slope. It seemed hardly within reason to anticipate an event in which the dry, boulder-strewn gulch behind the camp might suddenly spring a bad leak and gush forth with water like the rock in Sinai's desert. But so it did, choosing the blackest hours after midnight to work the wonder. It all but set the camp afloat in minus-ten weather.

I was dreaming that I was sleeping with icy moisture creeping up all around and nothing could be done but squirm and moan in it. Finally, I roused to investigate and to my horror found the sleeping bag and the tarpaulin saturated with water. I reached out and my hand splashed in icy water. An insidious sneak attack! We thought the evil powers that ruled Skolai put a hex on us.

At dawn, we were faced with the most miserable of sights. Water was gushing down the gulch as it does for spring breakup, but this water broke out from some underground source, not from melting snow. The entire camp was flooded. We hurriedly tried to salvage all we could. We swiftly set up an alternative campsite. Our feet were numbed. We were wet and cold. Inside the freshly erected tent we warmed our freezing hands over roaring flames. We drank hot coffee and warmed ourselves by cursing Skolai.

We were learning through hard experience to eliminate errors, which were bringing down on our heads penalties at every turn. A veteran trailsman would not have pitched camp near the mouth of the gulch, no matter how deceptively dry it appeared. Nor did the veterans fall into the misadventures and traps which had been our lot since encountering the Nazina Glacier and the pass. Our apprenticeship was just beginning and we really had no right to blame Skolai for rapping our knuckles for the blunders we were making. Any stern tutor would have done the same.

27

Strategic Withdrawal

We seemed to be living a plagued existence at Skolai Pass. We were becoming allergic to the place. Flooding and the futility of route finding took a toll on us. Even passages to the foothills previously deemed impassable, anything short of suicide, was starting to look good to Bud, as long as we could put the canyon behind us.

Guiding the dogs, we set out on a spur of the packhorse trail, an extremely stiff pull that was compounded by bare ground scoured by the wind and a hard wind in our faces. We made only twenty to forty yards before stopping for a blow. Worse, my ankle gave me considerable trouble. Within a distance of a mile we climbed more than 1,200 feet and the dry, abrasive trail was growing steeper. At last, at the foot of the mountain we discovered we could go in no direction with a dog team.

This defeat needed no formal acknowledgement. We had explored every possible route. The only thing left to us was to return to our campsite and start packing everything on our backs across miles of rough terrain, across places that would be difficult even to crawl. The backbreaking job would require at least a week to reach Frederika Basin, only halfway through the pass, with another canyon beyond. Delayed and now flooded, our rations were down to ten days' worth unless were supplemented our diets with wild game.

We knew the nature of the bad gamble being made should we travel under present circumstances and it was not logical reasoning, but mulishness that we refused to consider retreat from Skolai. Bud and I got into an argument about the method and means of our future survival. I argued that we should keep pushing up the pass, even if we had to pack the entire outfit on our backs. Bud did not want to rely on shooting game since we hadn't done it yet. Boyden and Meloy, he noted, were carrying over a ton of supplies for their passenger so it might not be that easy to obtain game. He wanted to return to McCarthy for resupplying.

Skolai, really, determined our plans. If we delayed too long we might be caught in break up. If we failed to find enough food we could starve. Skolai had given us a merciless drubbing, but Bud and I came up with a compromise. While he hunted for game the next day, I would backtrack and try to find Boyden and Meloy and get more specific information about the trail.

I was mushing back as far as the Homestead and when I crossed the area of moraine that Bud and I had thought challenging I laughed sarcastically. If only I had three or four miles of "good" terrain like this ahead of me to carry us around the canyon. As we approached the Homestead the dogs added some energy to their step. And as we pulled closer to the cabin I saw two freight sleds parked there. I braked the team in a flourish of spewing snow. This was all lost on Boyden.

While waving a stick of wood he stuck his head in the doorway and shouted to Meloy, "Joe! Joe! Come on out here and have a look. It's the boys. They've been to Fairbanks already and now they're coming back!" He then turned a lively grin on me and remarked, "You're just in time. Joe's warming the beans right now. And hello, where's Bud?"

"Bud?" I said. "Oh, he's over in Skolai worrying the sheep."

We lunched on beans and they gave me the latest gossip from town. I explained my reason for the errand to the Homestead, but the freighters knew the story before I told it. They had seen such things happen and would have been surprised if it had turned out otherwise. Meloy confirmed that the north side of the canyon was "pretty badly shook up when it was invented," and agreed the other side was terrible, too. One had to go high to get around the canyon. I protested that I had gone high, but all I saw were places to break your neck.

Meloy didn't dispute me. "That's the one good thing about Skolai," he said. "You can always find a place to break your neck. Saves a man worrying too much about how he is going to spend his money in his old age."

Boyden said the right path was a gulch hard to identify because of boulders. I pulled out a map and pencil and tried to translate description to paper. "The trouble with these maps is that they're on too small a scale," Boyden said. "There's a lot more gulches and draws leading into the creek than the map shows."

When I explained about our fast-dwindling supplies, Boyden advised me against counting on obtaining emergency supplies in Shushanna. There was no recent word from there to McCarthy and he thought the only one left might have been the old man running the trading post. But even he might have left. Boyden made Shushanna sound like a ghost camp. Boyden and Meloy agreed my best course was to go back to McCarthy for more supplies, then catch up to them and have them show Bud and me the right trail for the pass.

Take 'er easy was Boyden's motto and he offered that thought again. Meloy chimed in that there ought to be a law preventing people from trying to climb Skolai Pass too swiftly.

My return to Skolai was uneventful. The day was beautiful. Boyden's casual remarks made me think. A man, so long as he remains master of himself, is never defeated even though he fails to attain his objective. It was dark when I reached camp and the candlelit tent glowed like a trail beacon. Bud whooped when I told him Boyden and Meloy were at the Homestead. We agreed to the proposition of resupplying in McCarthy, about forty-eight miles away, and joining up with the freighters.

On the way we drove right up on Boyden and Meloy. They gave us a note to present to Fred Reynolds informing him he should return with us. We pressed on and took a shortcut to save time. We paused once to survey directions and the moment we left the dogs a row began. Instantly, thanks to Chief being up to his old tricks, we had a battle royal. I piled into the melee, kicking and cuffing the dogs. But in the act of pulling one dog off another's neck the slashing fangs caught me and I was severely bitten through the left hand. Bud went after the team with the whip, silencing the uproar. I was the only casualty and of course we left the first-aid kit at our camp.

It was nearly dark when we reached the Nazina Roadhouse. I soaked my hand in hot water and Murie, who happened to be out of iodine, poured some whiskey on it, not forgetting to pour some into tumblers for a drink all around. After the drink, my hand felt better and Bud wrapped it in bandages. The last eighteen miles of hard-packed trail were the easiest of the day. We mushed right up to our old cabin.

After feeding the dogs we went right to the drugstore. Ben Jackson, the druggist, said, "Well, well. What did you forget, your snowshoes?" Bud said we had forgotten to spend all of our money so we came back to accommodate the merchants. The druggist examined my hand and gave me a stony glare. "How many times do I have to tell you two rumdums the same thing? Use the whip when they fight. Use the butt end and use it plenty." It seemed as if everyone in town knew more about how to control a team than we did.

The druggist treated my wounds with alcohol and iodine—boy did it sting—and professionally wrapped it. I promised myself not to get mixed up in another dog fight. The cure was worse than any bite.

At the restaurant the cook greeted us bemusedly. "I thought you fellows had made Fairbanks by now," he said. "You get lost? You run out of grub, huh?" We ordered steaks and told him we had been sheep hunting while waiting for Boyden and Meloy. He clucked his tongue knowingly. Just after our departure, newspapers had arrived in town proclaiming a fresh gold strike in the Yukon Territory and we read all about it. Bud and I had known too many miners to be fooled by any get-rich-quick scheming, but a fresh start in a booming place might be more worthwhile than hitting Fairbanks. We could easily change our route to Dawson to check out this Galena strike.

We woke early to take care of business. Our first stop was the blacksmith's and Mudge did not seem the least surprised at the amount of battering our sled took. He called it experience worth having, part of our education and said that it took some mushers twenty years to figure out what they were doing and some never got it straight.

Next was ordering more grub. Charlie O'Neill had already heard we were back in town. He talked up the gold strike and suggested he might like to give up his store and go. We knew it was just talk, but we invited him along in case we chose to chase it. "It certainly sounds good," O'Neill said, "but you fellows might get caught in breakup and I don't like getting my feet wet." The storekeeper's interest in the strike was based on habit and tradition. It was customary with northerners to lend impetus to the idea that stampedes, like barn raisings and cornhusker frolics, were affairs that should be attended.

At least the roadhouses, hotels, and stores benefited. There is a certain fascination in watching prospectors, their pockets bulging with worthless rocks, walking around silent and mysterious, each one keeping a sharp eye on the other fellow's movements in the hope that someone might turn up something on the basis of a rumor.

We got our grub list filled and sought out Fred Reynolds at the hotel. He was about sixty years old and his dark hair was graying at the temples. He was a sturdy-looking man and was reputed to be an extraordinarily speedy snowshoer when he was younger. He informed us he could not return with us because he still awaited the resolution of business in New York and gave us a note for Boyden and Meloy stating he was going to hire a dog driver to meet them when the time came.

Dud McKinney was at the bar and he invited us to join him for a drink. We told him of our woes at the pass and he accepted the story matter-of-factly. "You'll make it all right," he said. "You aren't the only people that have had trouble in that pass. The boys know the way through there. Stick with them. They'll see you get through."

As Bud and I made our way around town we bumped into many acquaintances. Not one discussion ended without mention of the Yukon strike. We could go to Dawson first if we chose, and then go on to Fairbanks later.

One friend talked considerably about the news from Dawson. He expressed doubts that there were any serious claims to be had. The area had been heavily prospected in past years and he didn't think it was likely large gold deposits would have been overlooked. He warned us not to throw our hearts into it, and then get all discouraged and depressed. Such prospectors, he said, "shoot themselves over little matters like that." It was a sobering talk, but Bud and I agreed that if we were going to shoot ourselves, Skolai Pass, not Dawson, was a more likely location.

We returned to the druggist to get my bandage changed and mentioned in passing that he might change our forwarding address to Dawson instead of Fairbanks.

"What's the matter with you two?" he asked. "Are you going wacky?"

I mentioned that we had been hearing about the Galena gold strike.

"Aha," the druggist said. "So that's the way the wind blows." He paused and a thoughtful look came over his face. "It's possible that stampede may be a success. Provided you two rumdums don't drown yourselves before you get there. You'll have to do some fast traveling if you want to make the Yukon River before breakup. I'll lay you five bucks to the dollar that you end this trip in a rowboat."

He might have been proven right yet, but we weren't giving up on the dogs.

28

Return to Skolai

The morning was frosty cold on March 29 as Bud and I hitched up the sled. A clear night sky was giving way to dawn and there was a trace of the aurora on the northern horizon. We wrestled the dogs into stiff harnesses and mushed out of McCarthy again. The sleeping town was as dark and silent as the surrounding wilderness.

As we left we saw sun breaking through in three directions, but a haze forming in the fourth. The team jogged along easily on the trail in the minus-fifteen-to-minus-twenty-degree weather and we wished we had such a hard-packed trail all of the way to the Yukon. Soon enough the weather changed. Two distinct storm fronts were evolving, moving toward one another from opposite directions. There was a penetrating cold wind at our backs with snow blotting out the distant hills beyond the Chitina River. In the opposite direction a blizzard was approaching from the head of the glacier and rapidly moving down on us. We watched the sky with some apprehension and the dogs sniffed uneasily as they did when they sensed a bad blow coming.

When the storms were about ten miles apart I stopped the sled. Then I asked Bud, who was digging out our parkas, what he thought. "I don't know," he said, "but whatever it is, we're going to be right in the middle of it. We'd better get off this glare ice before we get blown off." As the wind began to rise in hard gusts and visibility lessened we made for a massive pile of rocks about a quarter of a mile away. The snow began blowing in a large whirlwind so the rocks would not protect us. We turned the team and continued to travel upriver.

The wind reached its full power as the dogs pulled on bare ice. Almost at once they lost their footing and as the wind caught them broadside they were flung around in a scrambled heap to the rear of the sled. Bud tried to stop the sled and succeeded only after turning it on its side. I slipped as well and blew along the ice for a hundred yards. Upon investigation I found that every one of the pointed cleats on my creepers was bent or had broken off entirely. The contraptions were utterly worthless. The howling storm whipped sheets of snow along the ground and we had no landmarks to see where we were going.

We kept it up until late afternoon when we made a river crossing and then entered some tree sheltering. It was like a furlough from a battlefront. We were a tired and snow-plastered outfit when we pulled up to the Homestead at early dusk. Despite the challenges and dangers, we advanced thirty-five miles that day.

Bud and I were the only tenants at the Homestead and we did not plan to stay long. However, when we awoke the next morning the storm was still raging. After cutting some wood and eating a hardy breakfast, the wind's moaning died and in late morning we decided to take a chance on a glacier crossing. The glacier country never looked colder and bleaker with distant snow peaks blended into the toneless sky with scarcely any definition except for bare rock ridges showing steel blue.

We headed for the moraine and saw two sled loads of freight piled up. Boyden and Meloy had been there. We pushed on to our former route, but the lead dog aimed higher. We could see little ahead, but he sensed where we should be going. He had his tail in the air and seemed to be enjoying being on his own without the backseat drivers bossing him around. He was holding the trail unerringly it seemed, given the clues of Meloy's personal trail marker—splashes of tobacco juice. After about six miles of ice travel we came upon another cache. This route the freighters used swung an arc so high on the ice field it came down on Skolai Pass. The route was twelve miles, several more than the one we had been following, and one had to be familiar with it to locate the passage in the moraine.

Another mile and we could see Boyden and Meloy approaching with their team. When we intersected the conversation was brief because the bitter breeze nipped through parkas and they said they would see us at camp later. The route led us a mile higher than we had explored and we kicked ourselves for not finding the right path. The trail was windswept and drifted, but not so rough as to make travel difficult. After about two miles we came out at Skolai Creek and following the creek we reached Boyden and Meloy's camp.

We set up our tent about twenty paces from theirs and we were cooking dog food when the freighters returned. We sat around their ten-by-twelve tent drinking tea and talking. Boyden explained how we had missed the trail on our original foray and I came to understand these veterans attacked Skolai Pass with jujitsu tactics. If there was a weak place anywhere in the formidable landscape they found it and exploited it even if they had to travel miles around some obstacle.

The next day, as the freighters left to relay their goods, Bud and I decided to sashay up the canyon to go sheep hunting. We split up and I went only a short distance before some small rocks rattled down from the ledges above. The sheer walls obstructed my view from the receding heights, but I was certain there were sheep moving overhead. I unstrapped from my snowshoes and climbed ahead in my moccasins. The footing was precarious and sometimes I had to cut footholds in the ice with my belt knife.

I reached a ledge and more rubble tumbled down. Glancing up I saw a half- dozen ewes with a young goat in their midst making their way single file on a ledge about a hundred feet above me. They were on the verge of disappearing over the rim. I quickly unslung the rifle and took a shot at the goat, busting him in the shoulder. The instant I fired I realized the argument was only getting started.

The goat folded and began slipping from the ledge. It began falling almost in the place I was standing. The ledge was too thin to move quickly one way or the other. Instinctively, I threw myself face down hugging the rock wall. The next instant came a thudding impact so close above my head I could feel it, followed by a small avalanche of loose rocks and snow. It was a near miss. The goat almost squared the deal. My heart was pounding and my legs were weak as I crawled to my feet. The goat lay on the canyon floor a hundred feet below.

While standing there pondering the retribution of nature, I heard three quick shots, followed a minute later by another shot farther up the canyon. It sounded as if a small war was going on. I felt certain Bud and I had salvaged our honor as hunters and between us had enough meat to see us through Skolai Pass. I carefully worked my way to the goat and then looked for Bud. When I spotted him he was struggling backwards down an arroyo, dragging a large ram by the horns.

Bud summarized what happened. After I fired my shot, the sheep stampeded and although he saw them coming they were too far away when he unleashed his three shots. However, the big ram showed itself over the canyon rim and was headed Bud's way when he made the kill shot. "They must have been holding a convention or something around here today," he said.

Bud was surprised when I said I got a goat. "Goats don't travel with ewes," he said.

He looked my kill over carefully and conceded it indeed was a goat. We walked back to camp, got the dogs, and hauled the meat back by dog sled. Once we finished quartering the animals it was getting toward evening. When two dog teams approached we expected Boyden and Meloy, but we got a surprise when it was Billy Arliss and Lew Anderton mushing up to join our party. Right after, here came Boyden and Meloy.

There was considerable bustle and commotion with four outfits arriving in camp together. Altogether, with six dog mushers, about thirty dogs, five sleds, freight piled all around, and eight quarters of meat hanging on poles, Skolai took on the appearance of a busy traffic center. Boyden was attracted by the goat meat. "Now that will make some very fine eating," he said. "You can't beat young goat for tasty meat."

The next day a musher from McCarthy delivered Fred Reynolds to camp to complete the party. This was not as simple a procedure as anticipated. I set out for the Homestead to pick up Reynolds, but when I reached the cabin it was deserted. Soon after, a team of dogs burst into the clearing, but it carried no dog driver or passenger. It had broken free and abandoned its human cargo. I caught the leader and tied the tow line around a tree to park the team. Bill Lubbe from McCarthy came huffing and puffing into camp on foot just minutes later. He had already dropped Reynolds off on the glacier. I didn't understand how I didn't see them on my trip over.

If I hadn't stopped the runaway dogs they might have dashed all of the way to McCarthy. Lubbe was not happy about their escape.

"We hit a stump," he said. "Snapped the tow line. I was just hoping they would get hung up on some brush to give me time to catch them."

The sled had taken a smashing blow on one side of the bow and that knocked the whole sled bed askew. The damage was not so severe that Bill couldn't make it back to town, but he was going to need some repairs.

Reynolds accounted for the last missing member of the party. He was supposed to be an expert cook with particular expertise in making seasoned stews and we were looking forward to one of his specialties. Most importantly, he got into camp at the right time, just before the weather changed for the worse again. A blizzard swept the pass and drifts of snow piled up everywhere. The camp was sheltered from the storm by a rocky bluff. This was the one place on Skolai where the howling wind could be avoided.

We killed time eating and talking and Boyden told a long story about two old-timers, Shorty Gwin and Pink Whiskers. They had a falling out over a horse that Shorty was sure belonged to him and that Pink Whiskers thought belonged to him. Shorty went to Pink Whiskers' ranch to reclaim it and Pink Whiskers let loose a few shots that came perilously close to ending Shorty's good health.

This only made Shorty more determined to get revenge, as well as his horse. He oiled himself up really good, dressed up for the occasion, and was solidifying his will power at the McCarthy bars. Pink Whiskers felt he had routed the enemy and he came into town to celebrate. As it so happened, they ended up at the same bar in the Golden Hotel. Pink Whiskers sat at one end and Shorty sat at the other end. At first they did not notice one another, but about to chug his drink Shorty tipped his head and out of the corner of his eye he spied Pink Whiskers.

He made no verbal assault, but simply stepped away from the crowd and into the middle of the floor. He intended to quick-draw his massive pistol and shoot Pink Whiskers dead. Only after a minute or two, Shorty could not be seen. Where had he gone? A crowd closed in on him as he writhed on the floor, desperately seeking to unholster the gun caught on his pants pocket.

The spectators had previously been unaware of any feud between Shorty and Pink Whiskers, but when Shorty struggled with his gun and gave every indication he planned to use it, someone conked him with a whiskey bottle and knocked him cold.

The horse, Boyden added, returned to McCarthy on its own a few days later. Boyden said the horse just didn't like Pink Whiskers' cooking.

29

Boyden's Saga

We tried to gauge the weather and attention turned to Boyden. He rubbed his stubbly chin whiskers reflectively, eyed the patch of blue sky above, and seemed to weigh it against the massive cloud bank resting on the head of the pass. "A man never knows about Skolai," he mused. "It might hold long enough that we could make a try at it."

Boyden hitched up his team and headed in one direction to gather the last of a small cache of freight. Arliss, Anderton, and Meloy went in another direction. Bud and I stayed in camp with Reynolds. Skolai's wan smile turned out to be a smirk. A few hours later the matted layer of dark clouds boiling in the peaks at the head of the pass began settling low. Soon after, the wind began to freshen. It was between three and four o'clock when the storm really set in. Quite suddenly the air became thick with driving snow.

Boyden was somewhere out on the open ice field. The others could drop their loads and make it back to camp, if need be, but worry was etched on Reynolds' face. Visibility was shrinking quickly and we began to become concerned about everyone when we heard a shout. Meloy was leading and two other teams were right behind. We battled with them to unload their sleds and put up the dogs. The boys reached for hot tea without a word being spoken.

We were all thinking the same thing. What a fury it must be on the open ice field. Meloy spit out a tea leaf and said, "Goddamn. I just wouldn't have thought it was fixing to blow everything to hell."

"I don't think Harry thought it was going to start blowing this soon either," Anderton said.

Boyden, despite the entreaties of others, had left his eiderdown coat in camp.

"Oh, Harry will be all right," Reynolds said. "He's been in worse spots than this before, a good many times, and he's never been stuck yet."

The silence and the waiting wore on everyone. Meloy declared he was going to hitch up and go look for Boyden. Anderton said he would go with him. But Reynolds protested. "No! No! Neither one of you are going. Harry will either make it or he won't. There's no sense in the whole camp getting in a jackpot mess. If there is a man alive that can make it, Harry will make it."

Foreboding silence settled on the group in the tent. Arliss made some more tea. We had to do something. You couldn't just sit around twiddling your thumbs while a man was being mauled or possibly having his life snuffed out in a fearful storm. We sat around the tent listening to the banshee wind howling its dirge and listened to the snow swishing in drifts around us.

"Harry ought to be making it off the glacier about now," Meloy said as he stirred his tea leaves.

"Has Harry got ice creepers with him?" Anderton asked.

No one knew for sure.

Arliss talked of getting supper ready, more mulligan stew and beans. He opened the tent flap and looked out. Drifts of three feet of fresh snow had piled up in the yard. "It sure is one hellish night," Billy said.

The men put a lot of faith in Harry's lead dog, Bingle, but they worried that the dogs would get blown off their feet by such powerful winds.

Reynolds stared out the tent entrance as daylight faded. He was listening, but heard no sounds except for the wind moaning in the trees and the storm roaring in the ridges. "He's pretty cagy," Reynolds said, half to himself. These veteran dog freighters had survived as long as they did because they understood and read the conditions they were in. With Boyden there was a deep inner reserve he could call upon in adverse circumstances and emergencies. Winning against the natural odds was a matter for the mind, less of the muscle. Harry's years of freighting and carrying the mail across glaciers had been accomplished without one serious mishap.

We stirred ourselves to feed the dogs and although everyone retired, everyone was on edge. Any time there was a strange sound one of us popped a head out of the tent to peer into the darkness and the storm, hoping it was a dog team arriving. The oppressive night passed without any change in the situation. The storm raged as hard as ever.

By dawn the snow had stopped. Our sleds were buried. If still alive, Boyden had spent a fearful night in the open without even the protection of a sleeping bag. The wind was still strong and the temperature was at minus sixteen and still dropping. Anderton and Meloy were still sleeping. Reynolds made coffee and we were just passing the first cups around when we heard footsteps outside.

An unbelieving stare passed between those of us sitting in the tent. Wonder of wonders, the head and shoulders of Harry Boyden in his frost-encrusted parka were thrust through the opening. And it was no ghost. The face of the big dog driver was grimy and traced with lines of fatigue. But a broad, toothy grin began to spread over his features as he took in the openmouthed astonishment which his unexpected appearance had created.

Boyden chuckled, a deep, throaty chuckle as he always issued when amused. "This is certainly one case-hardened outfit," he said. "Here a man hurries up to make camp in time for breakfast and there's not a frying pan on the stove."

Boyden's chuckle woke Meloy and Anderton and Meloy said, "You should have sent your calling card on ahead. We didn't figure you was going to show up so prompt."

"What was keeping you?" Anderton asked. "We thought you missed camp in the blow and went all of the way through to Frederika."

Boyden pulled off his parka, took a cup of coffee, and lit a cigarette. Anderton asked where he spent the night and Harry paused before answering. "We made a little private camp of our own," he said. "The boys were a little tired after we left the glacier so we hunted up some dry spruce and camped." He said it was by the first draw after coming off the glacier.

It was just a single dead spruce tree that Boyden had seen in his travels and filed away the location in case of emergency. It was there when he needed it. So he said. There was some thought it was all a fable and Harry had had a much more difficult time of it than he let on. But he wasn't saying anything else.

We helped get the dogs bedded down and they needed little encouragement. Some wouldn't even eat, preferring immediate sleep. That told the story of the ordeal of the night better than Harry did.

Meloy and Anderton took teams out to retrieve the freight Harry had left behind. Anderton was anxious to see the spot where Boyden camped. When he found it, he read it like an open book. It had been a last-ditch stand for man and dogs. There was a big snowdrift on the lee side of where the sled had been standing, and all around were holes where the dogs had bedded down. On one side of the drift was a small, circular area, where the snow had been pounded down smooth, and was as hard-packed as concrete. Here, Boyden had spent the entire night, hour after hour, tramping round in circles, jumping and pounding himself to keep from freezing through inaction and falling asleep.

There was no question he had been as exhausted as the dogs by the struggle of coming off the glacier, but somehow he had mustered enough reserve energy to keep himself active throughout the night. When the first hint of dawn appeared he had hitched the tired dogs up and made it the rest of the way into camp.

Reynolds shook his head in astonishment after hearing Anderton's report. "But what about the spruce?" asked Reynolds. Knowing Boyden he knew his elaborate tales usually had some basis in fact. Ah, yes. There had been a spruce. Anderton grinned wryly and spit in punctuation just thinking about it.

"It was one of those little, runted, wind-warped, hand-me-down propositions," Anderton said. "Judging from the size of the stump it couldn't have been more than three ax handles tall."

Reynolds commented that it couldn't have been of much use.

"Use?" Anderton said. "Hell that spruce wouldn't have thawed out a bean pot, let alone kept a man from freezing. I had to dig around in a snowdrift to even find out where the fire had been."

That was the evidence in the case. But the essential fact was that Boyden came through the ordeal alive. Despite the blizzard, the darkness, and the exhausted condition of himself and the dogs, Boyden had known beforehand the place that he would head for and what he was going to do when he got there. That little difference makes the big difference sometimes in saving a man's own life.

Two days later it was blustery and raw, but good weather for Skolai Pass. Boyden was back in top form and we prepared to relay our supplies to the Frederika Basin. The trail led up a creek a short ways, then turned to the right up a steep, boulder-strewn gulch which was terraced with ice. It was one of the meanest places for travel to be found. Sledding the place was like crawling up the frozen rapids of a cascading creek. The dogs scrambled around and fell down, got tangled belly-up in the rigging, and we got tangled with the dogs. We banged our shins on slippery boulders and lost half as much ground as we gained.

"This is sure one bitch of a country," Bud said during one our pauses. "You know, if I really wanted to do somebody dirty, I'd turn the sonofabitch loose in the middle of Skolai Pass and let him find his way out."

High above us we could make out the two leading teams, Boyden and Meloy, angling to the left and going still higher. At least there was some satisfaction in knowing we were getting someplace. It astonished us the places these freighters would put a dog team in the course of an ordinary day's work. My early conception of dog-teaming had passed through so many stages of disillusionment I was coming to think bitterly of all prose and poetry related to the subject. The sweating, groveling, crawling, backbreaking stuff had somehow escaped the eye of the dog-mushing intelligentsia.

The four men ahead of us were standing around talking and spitting tobacco juice when we joined them on the edge of the famous Glory Hole, spoken of in awe in all of the mining camps. It was impossible to traverse on packhorses, but dog teams could make it across by plunging down the two-thousand-foot canyon and back up the other side. It was the frozen ninth circle of hell. The only choice was either to go through the place or turn around and go back home.

Next day we were trapped in camp because of Skolai's winds. That meant the discussions became windy. One topic was the value of Siberians. Billy was the strongest defender. Reynolds said, "They're just like women to handle. If you cuss them out, they make you apologize right now."

A long story followed about a deaf mute in Valdez who communicated with dogs by sign language. After the team dumped him in the snow once and he had to be rescued, Meloy said, he cursed the dogs so hard and long "he busted three fingers and two thumbs just spelling out cuss words."

In the afternoon I grabbed the rifle and went sheep hunting. Just above the rim of a ledge I almost stumbled into a ram so close I could throw a stick at him. We were equally surprised at the sight of one another. In another instant came a rumbling and sharp rattling of hooves. About forty sheep suddenly sprang to their feet in startled flurries of snow. I had walked right into the middle of an area where they were bedded down and drifted over with snow.

The sheep were panicked and standing right in the middle of them while they rushed around in circles I was startled to the point of forgetting what I was there for. Pandemonium had been going on for several seconds when I, in a fever of excitement, began shooting. When the magazine was empty there were five dead rams down within fifty yards of me.

Then I realized my task. It was late afternoon and I had to clean five sheep and haul the meat back to camp. The boys were still sitting around drinking tea and talking when I asked for someone to bring up a second sled. They weren't as grateful for the meat as I thought they would be. There was too much of it and it would have to be hauled. Several teams joined me, but Boyden took me aside as we were about to climb to the rams' resting spot and lectured me about only killing what was needed for the camp without bringing on extra work. He said this all with a cold stare. The matter was settled in his mind, the lesson learned in mine.

When we stripped the camp and began moving ahead it was a surprisingly warm day on Skolai. On one of his freight passes, Meloy stopped, looked my packing job over, and nodded. He brought out his snoose packet and made an elaborate gesture to offer me some, although he knew I didn't chew. To be contrary, this time I pinched a chunk and put it behind my lower lip as we mushed on.

As we bounced along the trail I swallowed more chew than I chewed. Finally, feeling a little bit queasy I spat out the rest. A minute or two later I began to feel strangely light-headed. I developed the peculiar feeling of floating through space. I wondered why the law of gravity had suddenly been repealed. Then my stomach began palpitating and I knew I was going to be sick. Stopping the team I flung a desperate glance at Bud and jumped for the side of the trail where I proceeded to heave up everything down to my moccasin innersoles.

Bud was unaware of my flirtation with the tobacco and blamed breakfast, which he had cooked. "From now on," he said, "you'd better do your own cooking. I can eat anything I cook without throwing it up."

This segment brought us to the edge of the Glory Hole with all of the supplies. It was sunny and no one could guess how long that would last. The walls of the craterlike pothole were almost perpendicular, with giant boulders and huge slabs of rock embedded in ice and glacial silt. The ice and snow made treacherous footing. One had to watch every step. Of all the homicidal traps on Skolai, this one was the worst. There was never a place more perfectly designed for breaking arms, legs, or one's neck than this diabolical pothole. We spent hours ferrying supplies by hand and lowering the biggest, bulkiest items of one hundred pounds with ropes. At the bottom of the Glory Hole the cargo and equipment looked like salvage from a shipwreck.

Even the dogs sat around in mixed groups, wearing bored expressions as though this affair was conclusive proof of the mental incapacities of their drivers. Not even a prideful snarl emanated. Apparently, the dogs had reached an agreement that this dastardly hole was no place for an argument. Then the goods were transported a third of a mile to the other side of the hole.

Harry scouted and chose the place for the ascent. One shudders to even recall the ascent because nothing like it was ever invented for killing off a man ahead of his time. Packing over three-and-a-quarter tons of equipment was an inconceivable job. By the time the job was finished eight hours later, without a stop for lunch or a cup of tea, there was nothing left of us except a sack full of aching bones.

Even then we kept moving, encountering another major obstacle down the trail. We had to cross a deep pool where the ice was thinning. Harry scouted it and determined it could be done. We lightened the loads and got the dogs running at a sprint to cross the ice. Rex, leader for me and Bud, seemed to be aware that this was a lead dog's show, and was pluming his tail proudly when I stepped to the runner of our sled. But I took no chance on his dallying in this place and I cut loose with a shout that would have scared the team into a run if they had been tied to a tree stump. They hit the crossing full tilt, but even with the throttle wide open I could feel the ice settling slightly as the load shot across.

It was evening when the outfits reached Frederika Basin. The sun had set behind the mountains and the peaks stood in bold relief against a glowing amber horizon. Our target was a relief cabin built by the government at the height of Shushanna freighting. Homely and weather-beaten, made of rough boards, tar paper, and nails, it marked the end of a strenuous long day's journey on the trail.

The small shack was a storm-battered derelict. Fierce winds had torn most of the tarpaper from the roof and outside walls. But something else caught the attention of the boys. A conscienceless villain had been there ahead of us. The door hung loosely on one hinge and the window was broken. Inside, the cabin was a shambles. The stovepipe had been knocked down and trampled flat and the old stove was overturned and ashes, soot, and broken glass were strewn all over the floor.

There was no mystery surrounding this dastardly deed. Huge claw marks on the splintered door, the door frame, and on the window sill all showed plainly that the grandpappy of marauding grizzly bears had entered by the door and after paying his respects had taken his departure by way of the window. Despite this compound felony, the boys commented on the bear's tactfulness in leaving the walls and roof standing.

Camp was pitched. Some repairs were made on the cabin and otherwise we set up as we had been. Some went into the surrounding area to seek willow to burn as sheep meat was cooked for dinner. The next day, when it was sunny and calm, teams hustled to the Glory Hole to relay the two tons of supplies left. It was so bright we needed snow goggles. We worried about the water crossing and the trail getting mushy since the temperature climbed well above freezing.

As he wiped sweat from his goggles, Meloy said there was always something affecting mushers whatever the season, from heat to mosquitoes, blizzards, and bears. Boyden listened to the grousing and told Meloy maybe he should retire to get married. Meloy said, "I was just speaking of the small troubles in life. I wasn't aiming to go in for the big ones."

On my last run the ice sagged like rubber and cracked as the load sped across. On the last run of the day, taking out the final bit of cargo, the ice sagged and cracked under Arliss' sled. Billy had thrown himself from the runner and hanging to the rear of his sled had been dragged out by the team led by Skooky. Billy arrived in camp soaked up to the thighs and up one side to the shoulder.

Bud and I thought about how we still had 350 miles to go before breakup.

30

Over the Pass

The wind was pounding the shack with a fury that made the walls tremble. The place yawed, creaked, and banged as though it was on the verge of being blown to pieces. A spray of fine snow was driving in through the cracks and knotholes and on the lee side of the building it was swirling in through the open window, forming a drift on the floor.

We had been ready to tackle Skolai Pass, but the blizzard attacking us showed the pass was not in the mood to welcome us. A day like this was useless. You just crossed it off the calendar and hoped for a better one on the morrow.

"She blows and snows," said Meloy. "In summer time she blows and rains."

Lew and Harry hitched up their teams and went in search of willow brush because we were running low on fuel. A long time passed and when they hadn't returned there was concern about how they were faring in the blizzard. Those in camp debated the merits of the mushers' lead dogs. It was noticeable that talk always turned to lead dogs whenever it came to pinches. The length of a man's life sometimes depended on the length of his lead dog's nose.

Faint shouts were heard above the storm. The two teams pulled into the lee of the cabin. The snow-blasted outfits could not have been recognized one from the other except that Anderton's team had two more dogs. The men were plastered white from head to foot with fine snow driven into the fabric of their clothing and the fur on their drawn parka hoods sheeted in snow and ice. Both the boys had a sort of dazed expression on their faces, something like a swimmer who has taken a hard bump on the bottom of the pool when diving.

Boyden said he was trying to keep Lew in sight the whole way, but couldn't. "The bastards were trying to play down on me," Anderton said. "I don't know what was the matter with them. They never tried that before."

The next day, April 12, the weather improved and Harry said it was worth making an attempt to get over the pass. The steep hillside made a hard pull. We were carrying our complete outfit on the sled. We took the hill in short stages, fifty yards at a time. When at last an easier grade had been reached we were puffing and sweating and our quivering legs felt as if they would fall off.

As we angled higher we came to the edge of a deep, canyonlike gulch. The place was tricky to travel. The gulch ended in a sheer precipice. Should a man slip and roll down the gulch he was good for a free fall of a thousand feet. As we worked, shoveling paths and relaying supplies, the clouds mounted up. There was no doubt we were in for another storm. We worked so steadily that we got two days' worth of work done in one. The outfit moved slowly, carefully, keeping the loads balanced on the inside of our passage.

There was enough traffic coming and going that the hilltop resembled a busy rail yard. Under gathering storm clouds we made haste. Our outfits were spread all over the hillside, like gunshot geese. Then we were enveloped by a fresh blizzard. One minute we could see teams a half a mile ahead of us and then they were gone. Thick granules of snow pummeled us like sand. The snow was blinding.

I realized the lead dog was no longer following a trail, but weaving back and forth. We were moving up the basin like a blind man trying to locate a doorpost while following the middle of the street. Visibility was reduced to fifty or sixty yards. I had no idea we were pulling across a small ledge. Only when the team stopped short did I recognize that something was wrong. Glancing up, I saw the lead dog backing into the swing dog with a snow ledge crumbling under the team. There was no time to do anything. All I could see in the blinding storm was space over a bottomless gulch. In a frantic effort to hold the outfit, I flung my weight backward against the load, shouting to Bud to hold the brake.

No good. The entire snow ledge was crumbling for twenty yards in each direction. In the midst of the collapse of an ocean wave of snow, the dogs, myself, and the sled with Bud hanging on went plunging downward in an avalanche. The gulch was about twenty feet deep. The outfit piled up in loose snow at the bottom as more snow fell on top. In the middle of this adventure I had managed to get my snowshoes fouled in the rigging and had landed at the bottom of the heap with my legs pinned by the overturned sled.

The mishap unnerved the dogs and put them on edge and they immediately began a free-for-all dog fight. Head down in the snow, my rear end being trampled by fighting dogs, it was a toss-up whether I would die from apoplexy or from my butt being scalped by a snarling wolf pack.

Getting ahold of the whip, Bud knocked a sense of decorum into the team. Another century or two passed before he got around to boosting the sled from my person and dragging me feet first into daylight. We righted everything, but the gulch was too steep to drive the dogs up, so we mushed downhill and around. Pushing against the blizzard, our travel was infinitely slow since both the dogs and the mushers were terribly tired from the day's work. The good news was that we were only about a hundred yards from the relief cabin.

Inside, Boyden was trying to work the stove to get a fire going to warm up all of us. In the end, that night the dogs ate most of the remaining sheep meat.

Rather amazingly, the next morning it was apparent that the latest storm had increased in intensity to stronger than anything we had yet seen. The cabin was shuddering under the impact of furious, sustained blasts of wind. We didn't have to look outside to realize how severe the weather was. A fine snow was driving into the cabin through the loose door so that we had a small snowdrift there. And the stove was out, so there was no heat.

Meloy suggested that maybe if the wind changed direction it would simply blow our tons of supplies upward and save the trouble of freighting. He was making a joke, but it was no joke wondering if the cabin would blow away. Tremendous blasts of wind shook it to its foundation. The walls vibrated. Sometimes it sounded like a ship at sea in a gale. At least we still had a roof over our heads. That was something to be grateful for. The wind slackened a bit by the time we went out to feed the dog. As soon as we could see them, that is. They were fur balls hunkered down in snowdrifts. I whistled up Rex, Spike, and Sam and they burst through the snow.

Twenty-four hours after the winds converged on us, it was still blowing. We were running low on fuel and at one point we realized Harry was not among us. There was speculation he had gone out to take a leak, but when he was gone much longer than was necessary for such a task, concern mounted. Then he reappeared with a large block of wood in his arms.

"When did you pack that up here?" Lew asked.

"Last summer," Boyden replied.

He had cached it in case of emergency on another trip. There was, he said, another block of wood parked outside the door. Talk about foresight. Harry had envisioned the possibility of an emergency down the line even when he didn't know if he would be back in the area.

Another day passed without the storm weakening. On and on it went. Much of the time we lay around in our sleeping bags listening to the monotonous racket of the wind whipping against the cabin. "I've seen these blows go for a week at a time," Anderton said, proving less-than-cheery news.

Still, the boredom doing nothing lost out to the intrepid energy of the dog drivers. Boyden and Meloy left in the storm to load supplies on their sled. Anderton went in search of more willows for firewood. And Billy walked out carrying his rifle, going hunting. "They're crazy," Reynolds said.

Stir crazy, for sure. Boyden and Meloy returned completely snow plastered, half frozen, and half dazed. Harry looked like an apparition. It took a long time for them to warm up. Harry couldn't even open his hood at first. Meloy pulled pieces of ice from his whiskers. "You're sure a tough-looking case," Harry told him. "You know, you look just like Santy Claus."

"Yeah," Meloy said in a weak voice, "but I ain't got nothin' to give away. Has anybody around here got a chew?"

Joe Meloy's immediate indulgence showed that chewing tobacco can be life-saving. Fred Reynolds, however, carried snoose with special properties. It was a souped-up mixture that added certain foreign ingredients to the original product. They were something of a mystery because he never divulged the complete formula. The boys claimed it was cayenne pepper and nitroglycerine, with a dash of strychnine.

The fact was known that Reynolds saturated the mixture with 151-proof rum as it aged in a humidor for months. Reynolds' snoose gained a reputation. Packers asserted that merely uncorking a box was enough to knock the legs from under a horse. Dog drivers, despite their iron constitutions and immunity to all usual hazards, could not be persuaded to touch it. Such a recommendation is properly taken as a warning rather than an endorsement.

Later, Meloy was discussing with Boyden the troubles he had had on the trail with his lead dog Rusty. He wasn't certain what was wrong with him, but he knew he had some worms. Boyden suggested that perhaps Meloy try a treatment that included Reynolds' snoose. "Oh, hell," Meloy responded in horror, throwing his arms up high as if to ward off a blow. "I don't mean to kill the poor dog. All I'm aiming to do is cure him."

Four days passed and we were still prisoners of the storm and somehow the cabin held together. We had enough provisions for a prolonged siege without skimping on rations. We even had a choice between flapjacks and cooked rice and raisins for breakfast. But Bud and I were losing time that might wreck our trip later on if breakup came too soon.

The wind subsided just enough for a party to mush out to gather willow for fuel, but we were still in a blizzard. By dinnertime the sky had at last cleared and the mood in camp was jubilant. We were being released from our long confinement and we moved quickly to make progress.

After two more days of packing and relaying in sunny minus-twenty-degree weather, the loads had been transferred to Russell Glacier. The freighting through Skolai Pass was complete.

Bud and I tended to regard it as a significant moment insofar as our experience was concerned. The redoubtable trail through Skolai was no longer a visionary trail seen through the eyes of others, a trail which had flaunted its challenges to us for about a year. Our experience, brief as it was, was now joined with the experiences of hundreds of stampeders, and it was joined with the scores of freighters who had been traveling this rugged country for years.

Most importantly, in coming to grips with Skolai, we had broadened our knowledge of dog-teaming and begun learning the essentials necessary for living and traveling independently in a wilderness country. Skolai was a hard schoolmaster and dealt out stern lessons. But they were lessons in survival that were lasting.

There were more lessons to come, too, as we traversed the Russell Glacier, filled with crevasses and cracks, each one of them probed by the veteran dog teamers. They used a shovel handle to test the ground ahead of us and to tell the difference between true, thick snow cover and potholes that could swallow us up. Travel was painfully slow.

We reached a point at the altitude of the divide where it passed through the moraine at around five thousand feet. Standing astride the divide I mused over the ruling order which this ridge played in the disorderly landscape all around. Bud scrambled over to join me and hugged himself against the cold. He took a disinterested squint at the surroundings. This was our first glimpse of the White River Valley.

I was more intrigued by where we were standing. "Look!" I said to Bud. "If my right leg followed the water down on this side it would end up in the Gulf of Alaska. If my left leg followed the water down this side, it would be standing in the Bering Sea!"

Bud turned an uncomprehending look at me. My great revelation aside, he didn't care what I was saying. He was freezing.

The terminal moraine, leading off the glacier, had a reputation for breaking the backs of men and demolishing their sleds. The glacier had worked for centuries depositing miles and miles of rock debris on the lower point and a musher had to struggle for four miles before freeing himself on the White River flats.

The day was ending as we walked off into some nearby spruce and made camp for the night. Timber! Our reaction to the sight and pungent smell of spruce was like home cooking for sailors after a stormy voyage. As much as the site meant to all of the dog drivers, it meant more to me and Bud. We had a feeling of accomplishment for here on Flood Creek the difficult drudgery of travel was ended. Sledding from now on would be comparatively easy.

Bud and I scanned the distant broad sweep of the valley as we walked along the flats. This valley and river would lead us to the Yukon Territory. Already one seemed to sense the drier, lighter atmosphere that is noticeable when passing from the coastal regions to the Interior. There was a different appearance and feel to the country, too. Here one found the spaciousness of rolling hills and the sweep of broad, open horizons. The Interior country we were entering was a peaceful, changeless, tranquil land, untroubled by ceaselessly grinding glaciers.

The freighters organized their sleds and relay plans. It was time for us to split up with Meloy, Boyden, Arliss, Anderton, and Reynolds. They were going ahead with their own mission. Bud and I were headed down the White River to the Yukon, moving ahead with our adventure. We owed much to these men who had educated us about the North and its glaciers and dangers.

On our last morning together, we shared a cup of coffee. We paused for a farewell salute to the boys standing in front of the headquarters tent. The dog drivers wished us good luck and fair traveling. Then Bud and I broke camp to mush on to Shushanna.

The lead dog swung to the channel leading to the frozen river and we started on our way down the winding valley to the Yukon country farther north.

Epilogue

Ted Lambert and Bud Guiler continued on the trail, mushing 125 miles through the White River country before spring breakup caught up to them and interrupted their trip. Giving up dog-team travel, they had to switch to other means of transportation after all. Eventually, they reached the Yukon Territory, and the local newspaper wrote a story about their journey.

> When the duo finally finished the four-hundred-mile trip from McCarthy, Bud and Ted occasioned much local comment and a *Dawson News* description: Conspicuous in their battered "glad rags" of the forest, garish toques and faded sweaters, bronzed as a couple of young Pontiacs from the effects of their long hours out under the blazing sun, adorned with a crop of Robinson Crusoe whiskers, but otherwise looking as rugged as a couple of Alpine mountain climbers, two young miners, Ted R. Lambert and George W. Guiler, of Montana . . . pulled up their boat on the Dawson waterfront Monday morning.

One gets the feeling that the two young bucks probably didn't stop smiling for days after completing their trip and given their recent past they probably also celebrated with some powerful liquid refreshment. They had been challenged and they succeeded. They did what they set out to do, but the friends never undertook such a serious journey again together.

The journey across Skolai Pass and on to Canada was the greatest dog mushing adventure of Ted Lambert's life. Neither gave up on dogs, either, after acquiring all the useful experience. For a time Lambert and Guiler became freighters in Canada and then they took over a mail route between Dawson and Kirkman Creek that covered 140 miles in each direction. They also trapped, sometimes splitting up, sometimes working together. Guiler was attracted to gold mining in the Yukon and Lambert roamed Alaska's backcountry, trapping in Eagle and Forty Mile. He even returned to Kennecott as a contract mucker again in 1930. Also that year, Lambert snowshoed the Richardson Highway.

After a year or so of this peripatetic lifestyle, Lambert moved to Fairbanks and began developing the artistic skill that would become his true life's work. He first drew sketches and made etchings. After saving some money, Lambert returned to Chicago in 1932 to study at the American Academy of Art. Finally, he realized his destiny lay with the talent he had uncovered as a youth and he dove energetically into watercolor and oil painting.

After moving back to Fairbanks, Lambert, who also spent considerable time in Copper Center, was a more accomplished artist. His oils garnered him acclaim and although he admired Sydney Laurence as the greatest Alaskan landscape painter, he sought to learn from Eustace Ziegler in Seattle. Lambert passed a winter studying with Ziegler and the men became close friends. During his stay in Seattle, Lambert had a rendezvous with Bud, later described as a three-day celebration. This could easily be defined as a three-day drinking bout. Guiler left Alaska for good, but Lambert always returned. The last known contact between Lambert and Guiler was in 1946.

As the 1930s advanced, Lambert became a more thoughtful painter with more depth in his work. In 1936, Lambert and Ziegler took a much-heralded boat trip along the Chena, Tanana, Yukon, and Kuskokwim rivers through many remote Alaska villages. What they saw was recorded first in sketches, then oils, and provided material for both men for the rest of their lives.

When he was penning his manuscript, Lambert made a brief detour away from his Sourdough lifestyle description to comment on the relationship between Alaska artists and their subjects and what he felt was the unique relationship between Alaskan artists and their customers. There is little beyond this statement recorded in his book that testifies to Lambert's opinions about Alaskan art, its artists, and the marketplace. It is clear that he identifies with this brotherhood/sisterhood and would like others to see him the same way, but he does not brag about his inclusion in the ranks of these artists.

"Alaska's artists have shown a capacity for dealing with the essentials of their environment, painting the landscapes of great beauty around the territory, the Native life of the people who lived in Alaska before Sourdoughs made the trek north, and the animals that populate the land," Lambert wrote.

Canvasses which depict northern action are strong and pulsating with life. The landscapes in all their various themes of wind-blown summer skies and silent winter, of sunlit valleys, mountains and tundra, interpret the moods of nature in all its pristine freshness. There is nothing either sentimental or decadent about northern painting. It is as vibrant and free-flowing as life itself.

Northern art has retained its own identity and integrity of character in the face of the landslide into the eccentricities of modern art. The Sourdough artists have not felt it necessary to reflect the spirit of modern art. Alaska has been proud of her artists. There is no place in the continent, possibly no place in the world, where people have shown such boundless enthusiasm for paintings and pride in ownership.

To northerners a painting is not simply a wall hanging or a financial investment. To them an Alaska painting is a living creature in itself, a creation that interpreted familiar surroundings and gave expression to their own experience and their own feeling in a country which they knew intimately. Such paintings are a constant source of enjoyment, something to be lived with, something that becomes an inseparable part of their lives. Many Alaskans buy paintings rather than buying a needed piece of furniture.

Old Sourdoughs living in weathered log cabins often had one, two, or several Laurence paintings on their walls. Businessmen have collections in their offices. So many artworks were purchased directly from the artists, sales initiated with down payments of one dollar or ten dollars. This condition of purchasing the artists' work was of such phenomenal proportion that it appears to have been unequaled anyplace else the world around.

Even during the following decades, Alaskans did seem to maintain a track record of buying what they liked and wanted to look at on the walls every day rather than buying paintings simply for investment. That was most certainly true in Lambert's prime because few Alaskans' works sold for very much. One aspect of this common-man buyer that Lambert did not address, but is certainly true, is that the purchase of these paintings was also related to the fact that the artists were accessible, lived in the community, and might be bumped into at the grocery store or drugstore when they were not wedded to their easels. So the customers could identify with both the subject matter and the artist.

When he was in Bethel, traveling with Ziegler, Lambert met a schoolteacher named Lovetta Gusky, who helped shape the rest of his life. She was a government-paid teacher from California and when Ziegler left the community to go home, Ted stayed and nurtured a budding romance. In 1937, the couple married in Copper Center and settled in an old log cabin, on loan from a Ted friend, that had no heat. In 1944, the Lamberts had a daughter and she was officially named Patricia, although usually called "Pats." Ted was seen as a doting dad, and he saved baby pictures at his remote cabin until his disappearance. But tension arose between Ted and Loretta.

Loretta complained to friends that she thought Lambert was becoming para-
noid and having psychological issues that needed to be treated. Loretta did not enjoy
Alaska as much as she had as a teacher. In 1945, complaining of arthritis, she said
she had to go to California for the winter. Baby Pats went with her. Lambert got
word that his wife might be seeing another man in San Diego and he was furious.

In December of that year after returning to Alaska, Loretta filed for divorce.
She obtained a restraining order prohibiting Lambert from seeing her or Pats.
The divorce was finalized in February of 1946, and after Loretta went back to
California, neither she nor Pats ever saw Ted again.

During this troubled time in his personal life, Lambert's reputation as one of
Alaska's preeminent artists was solidified. He painted pictures of villages seen during
his rivers journey with Ziegler. He painted pictures of cabins and caches, symbols of
the North he was intimately familiar with from his own pioneer days. And he painted
many popular and admired pictures that featured dog teams, certainly an example of
an artist reaching into the personal memory bank to depict scenes.

In his diary, clearly from a vantage point of many years after he came to Alaska
and became an artist, Lambert mentioned other Alaskan painters whom he knew
personally whose work he admired. In the half-century-plus since then, the reputations of these men and women have only been enhanced. It is intriguing that he
singled them out with unerring accuracy as major influences in the local art world.

Lambert wrote,

> There are few places in Alaska and the Yukon Territory where the north-
> ern artists have not set up their easels, ranging from Ketchikan to Point
> Barrow one way and from Whitehorse to Nome the other. Yet it is though
> the existence of northern artists was a state secret. The work of northern
> artists has been of such high caliber that they coldly turned down the
> pandering WPA [Works Progress Administration] during Depression
> years, even though living on some pretty thin soup at the time.
>
> Already making names for themselves were Sydney Laurence and
> Eustace Ziegler. They were independent of the WPA in the tradition of
> the Sourdough.

Lambert would portray his personal political beliefs as extremely leftist and he
had disdain for the government, so that might be one reason he wrote harshly of
the WPA.

The man who pioneered Alaska painting was an artist of international
reputation. He is Sydney Laurence, a beloved Sourdough who spent the
first dozen of his forty years in Alaska prospecting in various localities.

He knew the pioneering life intimately and he knew the North as only one can that has lived in it and become a vital part of it.

In his youthful years Laurence studied in New York, Paris and Rome. He exhibited at the National Academy of Design in 1882 and later exhibited with honors in London and Paris. He was a member of the Royal Society of British Artists. His paintings have hung in various galleries, including the National Art Gallery in Washington, D.C. His reputation as a marine painter was established before his arrival in Alaska at the beginning of the twentieth century.

During his years of prospecting and working at rough labor, he never completely forsook his palette. When at last he turned back to his painting, the sum of his broad and intimate experience began to unfold in the colorful, glowing canvasses that bore the stamp of genius. His talent was versatile and there was sureness and broadness of statement in his facile brush. He is famed for his many paintings of majestic Denali, or Mount McKinley, but his marines possibly even surpass the magic poetry of his landscapes and express profound feeling for the ever-changing moods of sky and sea.

Another of Alaska's foremost artists is Eustace P. Ziegler, whose home and studio for many years was in Cordova. Ziegler studied at the Yale School of Fine Arts before coming north during the construction days of the Copper River and Northwestern Railroad. His paintings have shown a great versatility in the fields of portraiture, figure painting, and landscape. His work has a quality of virility and rugged strength expressive of the North. He has worked in oils, watercolors, and done a great many etchings and drawings. In all, his work captures the colorful interplay of northern life in action. His strong, masterful canvases have won top honors several times in both jury and popular prize awards at the Northwest Artists' Annual in Seattle.

Ziegler left Alaska in 1923 to make his home in Seattle, where he has maintained a downtown studio through the years. He has tutored many students and several of the foremost painters in the Pacific Northwest studied under him. Still, he has always considered the North his painting locale." [Lambert did not report that he was one of those Ziegler students and that the men had a deep friendship and shared mutual respect].

The Crumrine team, Nina and daughter Josephine, are two more highly accomplished artists whose works are prominent in Alaska and the Pacific Coast states. Nina has devoted most of her life to colorful landscape, although her character studies of Sourdoughs and early-day Indians are equally well known. Josephine, who studied in Colorado Springs, as well as under her mother's tutelage, is famed for her portraiture of northern sled dogs. The huskies and malamutes are always on their good behavior when Josephine is around, and never tire of modeling like some professional models do. At least not as long as they are getting choice snacks of beef or hamburger every few minutes. Josephine's work has been reproduced extensively. The works of both of these excellent artists are in hundreds of homes and may be seen in the lobbies of leading hotels in Anchorage, Fairbanks and Juneau.

Fred Machetanz is another top-flight artist. He has devoted himself largely to portraying Eskimo life. He too is versatile in his work, having written and illustrated his own books and done illustrations for others. His brilliant paintings in bold form and pattern convey all the clarity of color and crisp line that is an outstanding quality in northern latitudes. Occasionally, in winter months, Fred and his authoress wife Sara take a turn around the States on a lecture tour in connection with his work. In spite of his busy career he has found time to build his own charming studio-home of peeled logs near the town of Palmer.

The noted Eskimo artist George Ahgupuk is nationally known and his work is seen throughout Alaska and in several metropolitan centers in the States. His vivid drawings portray every aspect of Eskimo life. They are done in expressive line with tonal touches and often on vellum prepared from reindeer hide. Ahgupuk, whose home was in Shishmaref on the Bering Sea Coast, is a gifted natural artist, entirely self-taught. Early in his career he was given a kindly boost by Rockwell Kent, who himself spent a year on Fox Island in Alaska near Seward where he painted and wrote a book.

Jules Dahlager is a life-long Alaska painter, with a residence studio in Ketchikan. His strong, vivid portrayals of southeastern Alaska are seen in colorful canvasses in many northern homes and with many proud owners of his work scattered throughout the States.

C. R. "Rusty" Heurlin of Fairbanks, longtime painter and illustrator, has devoted much of his work to portraying Eskimo life and has spent several years at Point Barrow. He is an excellent artist and much of his work has gone to purchasers in the States as well as Alaska.

The husband and wife team of Harvey Goodale and Ellen Henne, with a studio in Anchorage, are both artists of outstanding caliber. Their oils and watercolors have been purchased by many people in the States, as well as Alaskans.

Anyone possessing a serious Alaskan art collection would likely have pieces painted by most, if not all, of those artists, plus Lambert, of course, if they could afford such expenditures. In his writing, Lambert expressed admiration for some of the same things in artists that others see in him—their lived-it authenticity.

"He painted what he knew," Len Braarud, a La Conner, Washington–based art dealer who is an expert on Alaskan art, said of Lambert. "He worked. He did those things. He was a wonderful artist. If there was a blizzard in a picture, he lived those conditions. He ran dog teams and people just love Lambert dog teams. He was a tough guy. I have a feeling more Alaskans bought his stuff than bought Laurence and Ziegler."

Laurence and Ziegler, said Braarud, painted for the tourist trade and painted similarly composed scenes again and again. Their paintings number well into the thousands. Depending on who is doing the estimating, Lambert might barely have painted a thousand pictures, or less.

"Oh no, no, he wasn't nearly as prolific," Braarud said of the body of Lambert's work compared to Laurence's and Ziegler's. "And you don't find that many identical Lamberts."

In Braarud's mind Lambert is indisputably one of the most important of Alaska artists and he deserves a ranking among the so-called "Big Four" of Alaska historical artists, a list that in his mind would include Laurence and Ziegler, as well as Jules Dahlager.

Another big fan of Lambert, Anchorage art dealer Joe Crusey, puts Lambert on his "Big Three" list with Laurence and Ziegler.

"My hat goes off to Ted Lambert," said Crusey, "because he really did live the pioneer life, [and for] his ruggedness, determination, and great ability."

Crusey counts fifteen Lambert copper engravings in his personal collection.

"I always liked engravings," Crusey said. "There can be no mistakes."

Lambert established a brand name with his constituency—Alaskans. It is Alaskans, more than other American collectors, who most appreciate Lambert's work. Alaskans who have fine taste and long memories, as well as deep bank accounts that can afford the Lambert paintings that now might fetch $10,000 to $20,000 in many cases.

"He is near and dear to a lot of Alaskans," Crusey said.

Lambert was an amiable man who got along well with people, as evidenced by his experiences in the mining camps where being irascible could land a man in hot water and make enemies quickly because of close quarters.

Lambert maintained many friendships with Sourdoughs in the Fairbanks area, but after his divorce he grew more reclusive. In 1950, Lambert took a major step to change his circumstances. He moved to remote Levelock at Bristol Bay, a place sparsely inhabited and reachable only by small plane. Friends worried about his mental health and that concern only grew over the following years.

There he lived in a cabin, with the nearest neighbors a few hundred yards away through the trees. There, too, is where Lambert wrote out his "Tide North" early-life Alaska story in longhand. As the years passed between 1950 and 1960, Lambert penned his opus, painted somewhat erratically, and closed off his circle of contacts to the world. The late Kay Kennedy, an Alaska journalist whom Lambert first met in 1937, visited his homestead. Babe Alsworth, a Bush pilot, popped in for visits and to drop off mail and supplies as Lambert needed them.

Living on the other side of the trees were the Meggitts, John and Eilene, a married couple, and their teenage sons, Ron and Chuck. They kept watch on Lambert, and were friendly, though they did think his behavior somewhat unpredictable. Sometimes they had him over to dinner, as occurred on the night of July 27, 1960. The mail had come in and Lambert read letters from his brother Ronald in Illinois, ate dinner with the Meggitts, and seemed distracted as he rolled and smoked his own cigarettes.

Lambert returned to his cabin in midevening. Sometime that night or the next day, Ted Lambert disappeared and was never seen by anyone again.

The next day, the Meggitt parents left on a medical emergency. Two days after the dinner, the teenage boys went to check on Lambert. They found no sign of him, only his dog, which surprised them because he was very solicitous of the animal and they did not believe he would leave it to fend for itself. The boys reported Lambert missing.

No sign of Lambert, or his body, was ever found. People do not know if he walked away into the wilderness to commit suicide or if he had an accident. They do not know if he was murdered or eaten by a bear. For some time there were rumors that Lambert had been spirited out of Bristol Bay and lived under an assumed name in another location. But there was never a shred of evidence that this was true.

Babe Alsworth, Lambert's pilot friend, was the one who was supposed to be at the root of this theory. Alsworth, who later settled in Hawaii, was eighty-four in 1993 when asked about Lambert's last days. He denied flying Lambert off over the horizon. "Some people thought I had him over here somewhere," Alsworth said. "They want to believe everything but the truth."

The truth is unknown, however. The Meggitts were sure that Lambert committed suicide. They said his actions had become increasingly erratic and troubled. Alsworth said Lambert told him to stop flying in to see him. Almost all of his contemporaries and friends have died, so if there was a secret surrounding Lambert's disappearance, it probably died with them.

Some of Lambert's friends flew to his cabin after he vanished and retrieved his belongings. There were some poorly cared for art pieces that were unfinished and showing none of Lambert's old skill. He had scribbled thousands of additional words of a virtually unreadable political diatribe on the back of "Tide North's" pages. Odds-and-ends items were salvaged and most of them were deposited in the University of Alaska Fairbanks archives, where they have reposed in storage boxes for half a century.

Pat Lambert also obtained some things. She never knew her father, but she does possess some of his artworks. She, like everyone who knew Lambert and appreciated his artistic talent, wonders what became of him.

Josephine Crumrine, another well-known Alaskan artist who has since passed away, once said she liked to believe that Lambert had engineered his own disappearance and made a fresh life for himself in his golden years under a new identity.

There is no evidence that Ted Lambert pulled off such a scheme, however. If he did, no one would like to know about it more than Pat Lambert. In the mid-1960s, when she attained adulthood, she traveled to Alaska and tried to find her missing father. She worked in the state for a couple of years, but didn't stay. She picked up no useful clues about whom he knew personally last days or hours in Levelock beyond what was tucked away in the library.

More than fifty years have passed and Pat Lambert has no more idea what happened to her father than anyone else. But for years, she has had possession of his "Tide North" manuscript. In the absence of the man in the flesh, she has relished the stories the great painter told about a life unfolding in the North when he was young and anything seemed possible.

—Lew Freedman